THE BOOK OF SHEEN

THE BOOK OF SHEEN

A Memoir

Charlie Sheen

GALLERY BOOKS

New York   Amsterdam/Antwerp   London
Toronto   Sydney/Melbourne   New Delhi

Gallery Books
An Imprint of Simon & Schuster, LLC
1230 Avenue of the Americas
New York, NY 10020

For more than 100 years, Simon & Schuster has championed authors and the stories they create. By respecting the copyright of an author's intellectual property, you enable Simon & Schuster and the author to continue publishing exceptional books for years to come. We thank you for supporting the author's copyright by purchasing an authorized edition of this book.

No amount of this book may be reproduced or stored in any format, nor may it be uploaded to any website, database, language-learning model, or other repository, retrieval, or artificial intelligence system without express permission. All rights reserved. Inquiries may be directed to Simon & Schuster, 1230 Avenue of the Americas, New York, NY 10020 or permissions@simonandschuster.com.

Copyright © 2025 by Charlie Sheen

Note to readers: Certain names and identifying details of people portrayed in this book have been changed.

All rights reserved, including the right to reproduce this book or portions thereof in any form whatsoever. For information, address Gallery Books Subsidiary Rights Department,
1230 Avenue of the Americas, New York, NY 10020.

First Gallery Books hardcover edition September 2025

GALLERY BOOKS and colophon are registered trademarks of Simon & Schuster, LLC

Simon & Schuster strongly believes in freedom of expression and stands against censorship in all its forms. For more information, visit BooksBelong.com.

For information about special discounts for bulk purchases, please contact Simon & Schuster Special Sales at 1-866-506-1949 or business@simonandschuster.com.

The Simon & Schuster Speakers Bureau can bring authors to your live event. For more information or to book an event, contact the Simon & Schuster Speakers Bureau at 1-866-248-3049 or visit our website at www.simonspeakers.com.

Interior design by Jaime Putorti

Manufactured in the United States of America

10 9 8 7 6 5 4 3 2 1

The Library of Congress Cataloging-in-Publication Data has been applied for.

ISBN 978-1-6680-7528-9
ISBN 978-1-6680-7530-2 (ebook)

For Mom and Dad
and for every gangster-poet out there still chasing the dawn

"Courage is grace under pressure."
—ERNEST HEMINGWAY

"Dave's not here."
—CHEECH & CHONG

CHAPTER 1

On September 3, 1965, in New York City, at 10:58 p.m., I was born dead.

We're talking toe-tag, meat-wagon fukken dead. The delivering doctor had already sprung into code blue-baby, umbilical-strangulation 1960s ass-whoop action.

My poor mom Janet had to watch the thrashing while mired somewhere between "Don't stop!" and "He's had enough!"

My father Martin Sheen, a career Catholic—or Cathaholic, as I like to say—was rosary-wringing, eulogy-crafting (a short one, no doubt), and already demanding they wrangle a nearby priest to read the baby his last rites.

Primed for his first close-up in the scene, Irwin Shaybone, OB-GYN, dramatically spun toward my Dad. Like a flaming arrow from his Hippocratic bow sizzling through wafts of incense and dread, his words claimed the room: "You do *your* job and I'll do *mine*!"

And did he ever.

The man beat on me like I owed him money. My parents silently watched and waited, hoping beyond hope to finally detect the initial *sputtercoughcry* that has signaled new life since the dawn of time.

And *sputtercoughcry* I finally did. (Sort of.) The way my parents describe my awakening bore no resemblance to the straining warm-up of a car engine on a frigid morning. It was more like a bucket of water to the face of a vagrant in a drunk tank.

As a direct result of the doctor's heroics, my parents proudly bestowed upon me the middle name of Irwin. Carlos Irwin Estevez. Gotta admit, I'm a fan of letting a child grow up a bit and, once they're able to flush the toilet, be granted a vote in the middle-name department. Never has there been a more obvious candidate than mine. *"Irwin?"* Are you kidding me? Hey Mom, Dad, you had two choices, not fifty. Because even as Carlos evolved into Charlie, and Estevez made way for Sheen, it's the undeniable clunk factor of *Irwin* that you can smell all the way down the hall. (*Charles Shaybone* is about as PB&J as it gets.)

Fuck it: Irwin saved my life. Or at least kick-started it. Literally.

The whole born-dead event has had its hooks in me for a very long time. Insomuch as being fascinated by my odd arrival, I'm equally tormented by its shadow. Okay, *tormented* is a bit dramatic. *Bewildered* more foots the bill, tip included.

The umbilical cord is a lifeline. A time-tested conduit for delicately adjusted three-squares-a-day mom-chow. It's been difficult coming to terms with that lifeline morphing into a hangman's noose in *minute one*. The very same tube that kept my body perfectly alive for roughly nine months was viciously restricting the switcheroo moment where air, food, and speech need to be quickly rerouted.

This many years later, I remain convinced that my childhood stutter—the one that still haunts the adult me—is inextricably linked to that New York hospital accidental crime scene, otherwise referred to as *my birthday*.

Is this merely a folktale I insist on embracing, at times even *worshipping*? The facts are the facts—how I choose to interpret or deconstruct them falls squarely on me. At some point we're all victims of our childhoods. How often we choose to go back there and lend an ear to those whispers is some serious wheat/chaff fuckery.

CHAPTER 2

Memories are tricky. To clarify: One's recollection and the actual event never seem to wind up on the same road trip.

Early life memories can be the thickest fog to cut through. I can never decide if an image came from the moment itself or from a badly creased photograph I glanced in a grainy album from the '80s. As I said, tricky.

I was two years old, still living in New York, and headed to my first surgery. As a colorful distraction, my parents decked me out head to toe in a very stylish Roy Rogers cowboy ensemble. Mini Stetson, boots, spurs, and two chrome Colt .45 cap guns. Surgery be damned, those cattle rustlers and horse thieves were no match for this gunslinger.

Gotta back up the covered wagon a bit.

Six months earlier, I had developed a dramatic reaction to people staring at me. If I noticed someone so much as glancing in my direction, at the top of my lungs, no location spared, I would bloody-murder scream, "STOP STARING AT MEEEEE!!!"

Bummer for all of us, because I was a pretty handsome child.

It's prophetic that I had such disdain for those ocular invasions and ultimately became one of the most stared-at people of all time.

My parents' attempts to uncover the cause of this sudden distemper produced zero results. Some shit just shows up one day and decides to stick around. (Kinda like people.)

A couple months into my chronic outbursts, a new twist crashed the pathology party: My hand would shoot down into my pants, grab my balls, and wrangle that part of my crotch. The louder I yelled, the tighter my grip. (Yeah, I still scream, I still grab my balls, just not both at the same time and never in public. Progress.)

It was a therapist friend of Mom's who witnessed the performance one night and after putting two and two together; she recommended that I be checked for a hernia. The strain and force of the screams had apparently torn a gap somewhere below the gun belt. A few days later I was dressed to the nines for my gunfight at the O.K. Corral. The surgery was a success—and somehow the staring tantrums pulled up stakes and moseyed on out of town.

I have no recollection of the story I just shared. It's a piecemeal arrangement of dinner chatter and parental reminisce. The kind of nights you didn't want to end, sandwiched by the days you always knew would.

My "memory" comes from a single photograph that I am convinced I glanced at in a grainy album back in the '80s. In my mind, it's me in the cowboy costume, staring perfectly and evenly into the eyes of the camera. I'm still searching for the actual photo, but right now I'm content with the memory of it.

CHAPTER 3

My Dad left Dayton, Ohio, in 1959, on a Greyhound bus with fifty dollars in his pocket and a one-way ticket to New York City. He won a statewide speech contest and used that dough to pursue his dream of becoming an actor. He didn't just idolize James Dean, he was determined to pick up where he left off.

To activate this mission, prior to skipping town Dad intentionally failed an entrance exam to a local junior college. A broken promise by design to his father, where apparently they "shook" on some deal that involved higher education. Pop still wears the crown for the worst score in the history of that institution. His father, Francisco Estevez, whom he adored and whom I never had the pleasure of truly knowing, worked at the NCR (National Cash Register) factory for nearly fifty years. He was a Spanish immigrant and spoke very little English (if any). He met Dad's mom, Mary-Ann Phelan, at a local dance for the newly naturalized. She'd arrived on a ship from Ireland searching for a better anything. The two of them hit it off, got married, and then proceeded to have *ten* children, nine boys and a girl. In what was an Uncle Circus growing up, my sturdy Aunt Carmen was the lion tamer.

Dad's mom died when he was eleven and his pop never remarried. A measure of sorrow for a child I cannot begin to envision or pretend to grasp.

I think as a result, Dad has been on lifelong expeditions to the dual homelands of his parents to unearth who they were and what they stood for, either through living relatives or the stories and memories they both left behind. His quest is beautiful and heroic and ongoing. Some may call it chasing phantoms; I choose to call it becoming whole.

Around the same time that Dad was planning his great escape, my Mom was drawing up similar plans to flee that state as well. Not *with* him, mind you, as their paths were still yet to cross. Can't really say what was up with Ohio at the time, but a trend seemed afoot.

Janet Templeton had her bags packed and her sights set on anywhere but Cleveland. With a food-service job awaiting her in Provincetown, Mass., for the summer of 1960, and a scholarship to the Art Institute of Boston in her pocket, Mom was a few bus transfers away from her calling as an artist. Yet on the morning of enrollment day at the prestigious institute, Mom did an about-face, declined the scholarship, and hopped on another bus, this time to the Big Apple. The allure of New York's burgeoning, eclectic art scene was all too exciting for her to ignore.

Before long she was working as a dental assistant by day and moonlighting at an art gallery in SoHo by night. The first friend she made at the gallery was a nice chap named Jim.

Just across town, months earlier, Dad was holding down the position of usher at a movie theater, with Al Pacino as his wingman. Yes, *that* Al Pacino. Imagine those two leading you through the dark picture house with red-cone flashlights and bad matching coats?

Dad was fortunate enough to land a few plays during this time but not fortunate enough to afford his own apartment. A gracious stagehand on one of those plays offered him his couch until Dad could pony up for his own dwelling. His name was Jim—he worked at the art gallery, with Mom.

My parents had left Ohio in search of a better life. In a constellation of chance and fate, they wound up in a city of 7.7 million people and, separate from each other, befriended the same man, their unwitting Cupid.

Thank you, Jim: you did a lot of good.

Following a few klutzy first dates where Dad's small talk at the diner was getting smaller, he sensed he was on borrowed time with Mom's affection. He was mid-run in an off-Broadway production, *The Connection*, and yearned to get Janet away from the gallery to see him in action on show night.

The tense one-act drama, bringing him his first taste of critical praise, had his confidence exactly where it needed to be. Dad devoted his entire performance to Mom's front-row seat. When he saw her face in the standing ovation at closing curtain, Dad knew in that moment he'd no longer be alone in this life.

Years later he'd describe her reaction that night as truly mesmerized, hypnotized even. Mom's retelling, perhaps not quite as fantastical. *(Downplay it all you want, Mom, here we all are sixty-four years later.)* In a matter of a few months, they were playfully carving up the streets of Manhattan together, Mom already pregnant with my eldest sibling, Emilio. The relationship wasn't without its challenges. Mom had to hit pause on her dream of becoming a legitimate artist, while selflessly going all in so Dad could remain one.

Many sacrifices on both sides, money scarce, jobs infrequent.

It's the reason Dad has a focus and a drive that can't be taught. I have to believe that his unspoken credo of "no matter what" was established during those lean times. He has that true moxie you can't quite pin down or put words to—but it's there, and it's real. Mom has it, too—she just fixes everything when no one's watching.

My parents were married on December 23, 1961, at St. Stephen's Catholic church on East 28th Street in Manhattan. Mom gave birth to Emilio at the New York Lying-In Hospital on May 12, 1962. The math is pretty simple: Emilio attended his first wedding before he attended his first birth.

My folks were doing their trial-and-error best. The learning-as-they-went approach, constantly adding to a list of the things they didn't want the next child to endure. I guess hospitals made that list, as my brother Ramon was born at home in August of 1963—more specifically, in an apartment on Staten Island. The midwife called in sick that night and it came down to Dad and four members of New York's "Bravest" to safely welcome Ramon. (Man, to have been a fly on that lath-and-plaster wall.)

The origin of *Ramon* stemmed from Pop's real name, Ramon Antonio Gerard Estevez. (Those Spanish Catholics went full word salad in the names department.) Amazing initials and a monogram party waiting to erupt, with R.A.G.E. begging to find its way onto every cuff and briefcase within reach—items that Pop never reached for.

When Dad arrived in New York in 1959, he was quietly and awkwardly informed around the campus that he'd have a better shot at his goals with a less Hispanic-sounding name. He'd recently met a casting director named Martin and as a kid was a fan of the televangelist Bishop Fulton J. Sheen. Mashup complete—the name Martin Sheen was here to stay.

Not being entirely comfortable with his *nom de fake*, and not wanting to purge his heritage, Pop decided his children needed to carry the Spanish flag instead.

Good luck making your way through Malibu in the early '70s as Emilio, Ramon, and Carlos. *Oh kool, you're here to fix the fence.* Our sister Renée slid past that checkpoint, as her name leans in many different directions.

Maybe it's true that we don't choose our family. Maybe it's also true that we do choose (most of the time) the *size* of our family. With everything going on in their lives back then, it made perfect sense for them to call it quits as a four-pack. I'm really glad that they didn't.

1964 was going to be a pivotal one for Dad. His final year of folly, before he had to deal with his biggest creative challenge yet: me.

CHAPTER 4

The Subject Was Roses is a Pulitzer Prize–winning play written by Frank D. Gilroy in 1964. Okay, that's as *Wiki* as I'm going. It turned into a really big deal for Pop. The play had three cast members in total: Dad was flanked by Jack Albertson and Irene Dailey—their energies in perfect harmony as they took Broadway hostage and sallied forth as the toasts of the town. Sold-out performances night after night, awards on the horizon. Well, awards for Jack and Frank, not Pop. No big deal—Dad always claimed that he was never acting with awards in mind or to earn a "prize." (Much further down the road when he did start racking them up, I know deep down it had to feel pretty snazzy.)

The only sour note in the *Roses* bouquet took place on a cool summer eve in 1967, when Dad's father Francisco attended a performance. It would mark the first time that his pop would experience his work as an actor. Fighting through a whirlwind of nerves and self-doubt, Dad brought the goods, leaving all in attendance awestruck. All except one—*the* most important audience member of the night. Before Dad had a chance to speak to his pop after the show, Francisco spotted a poster in the lobby with Dad's fancy new American name. He left the theater without saying a word. Dad was crushed. The weight of an entire country's heritage poured over Ramon Antonio Gerard Estevez like the liquid fire of La Palma. When it comes to their kids, leave it to parents to fuck things up in a way no other being in the galaxy can eclipse. I can only hope they had a chance to put some of that lava back in the volcano before Francisco's very sad and sudden death in 1974.

Roses had a solid run for a few years and occupied five different theaters during that span. It also propelled Dad into a much broader conversation, one that involved television and film. The auditions became frequent, and the jobs started to pop. Over the next year or two, Dad worked on a lineup of classic TV shows that included *Flipper*, *Mission: Impossible*, *Hawaii Five-0*, *Mannix*, *Ironside*, *Columbo*, and a show called *Mongo's Back in Town*. (I wasn't aware he left.)

That was also when the travel began, not just for Dad but for the entire gang as well. That entire gang now included my sister Renée, who finally joined our ranks in 1967. Important to note: She was also delivered by Dr. Shaybone, and just like me, was denied awesome-middle-name status. No idea how she wound up with *Pilar*. I'll make sure to raise it at the next family mixer.

The Estevez-Sheen six-pack was on the move, making our way through bus and train stations and airports galore. Our dear pal Gary Morgan would always say we were the most civilized group of gypsies he'd ever known. (And that dood joined the circus when he was twelve, so his was an expert observation for sure.)

* * *

On January 12, 1969, the Estevez-Sheen troupe was on the *big* move. Dad's next film, *Catch-22*, was gearing up, and—win, lose, or draw—very soon it was Mexico or bust.

His tradition of taking the whole family with him for the entire duration of a shoot began in Guaymas, Mexico. From the very beginning, Dad was insistent to the various studios that this provision was *not* negotiable. It became the marrow my family relied on for stability during those exotic globe-trotting years. If the extra travel costs were ever nicked from Dad's salary, I'm sure he didn't care. Dad grew up so poor, matching socks as an adult felt like the High Life. Woven in and around the TV jobs, this was his second film in two years—very soon he'd need a bigger sock drawer.

The production set us up in a humble dwelling near the beach on the Sonoran coast. My *only* memory from Guaymas took place in one room and involved three questions.

Each morning I'd make my entrance into the room—a kitchen-dining-breakfast catchall—with thumb in mouth and trusty blue blanket dragged behind me. I'd approach Mom as she was prepping the various a.m. needs and wants.

The Three Questions:

1. "What day is it?"

"It's Thursday, Carlos." Her reply always the correct one.

2. "Where *ARE* we?"

"We're in Mexico, sweetie."

3. *"When are we GOING HOME?!"*

The *O* part of *home*, drawn out like a saxophone player's final blow to close a raucous night. It woke the whole house, it woke the dead, this was a four-month shoot. At face value, those three questions had reasonable and truthful answers. To the asker, any response brought nothing but terror and tears.

My parents were deeply concerned. The same kid that had just put them through hell with the stare-scare phase, and now this? Mom had three other children to care for, and Dad had a job to finish. From my own experience as a father of five, it's a solid truth that a bustling life doesn't always afford the needed pauses to satisfy every child's wishes at the exact moment they arise.

Even if somehow I could sit down with my four-year-old self and offer some insights or advice, what would those even *be*? How would they sound or feel, how would they land, if at all?

Those three pressing salient questions, artlessly posed in that Sonoran kitchen, still reverberate and pry to this day. A cat to my door, left in the rain.

When are we going home? Turns out we weren't.

The only "home" I had known to that point was a walk-up on 86th and Columbus—the scattered details that begin to shape the idea of home, long before a child has all the puzzle pieces to define it: shared bedrooms, borrowed furniture, tough but fair love.

My next concept of home sat mysteriously on the other side of a train's whistle screaming us to a grinding halt from Mexico. Our Gypsy Express had arrived in the City of Angels.

CHAPTER 5

The house my parents rented on South Castello Avenue in West LA sat a birdie putt from Pico Boulevard. A modest single-story with a couple of lawns, front and back. One street over was Roxbury Drive, the first hint you were well within range of the gaudy opulence of Beverly Hills. To travel east past Roxbury meant traveling south into your pocketbook. No accident that our humble cottage sat just inside that border town, discretely apart from the well-heeled denizens.

Dad never favored the overt or the obvious. He was much more at home in just that—a home. Trying to picture him in a mansion would be like trying to picture Bob Dylan singing metal—some shit just doesn't fit. I get that. I've come to believe the more glitz and doubloonery you rely on for identity, the more *un*identified one remains. (Took me a while, and the lesson was *really* pricey.)

Getting acclimated to Los Angeles following New York was a lot easier for us than if it had been the other way around. As a kid, the best way to gather a feel for your surroundings is to gauge how your parents respond to them. Mine seemed a lot more relaxed as soon as we got there. The decision to relocate was a great call. Soon as Mom learned to drive, it would be even better.

*   *   *

The City That Never Sleeps also never drives. Having traded subways for highways, Mom took it upon herself to *Yellow Pages* that shit and courageously slide behind the wheel. Pop was in Italy with my two brothers shooting the final scenes of *Catch-22*, leaving Mom to deal with me and Renée by herself. With no extra dough for a sitter, Mom had to plop the two of us in the back seat of the driving lessons.

With LA's four thousand square miles spread out before her (think Delaware and Rhode Island combined), Mom took to those streets. She did her best to tune out the nonstop rabid fights between her two children just over her shoulder. The driving instructor chain-smoked his way through every lesson. No idea how she pulled it off—six weeks later she aced her road test and was the proud recipient of her California driver's license. At the age of thirty.

Her newfound freedom now an ignition-twist away, she decided to brave the late-summer heat and follow a real estate lead she plucked from the *LA Times* Homes section. My parents were on the hunt for a more affordable rental. Mom noticed in that same section, the farther away from the city and up the coast you went, the less expensive the properties became. Impossible to imagine now that traveling north on the Pacific Coast Highway could lead to anything cheaper.

Mom's first stop was in the Pacific Palisades and the landlord seemed pleasant enough. Yet upon hearing it would be a family of six living there, she 86'd the deal, citing fears that the septic system couldn't keep up with a brood that size. Essentially telling Mom that our family was showing up with too much *actual* shit to live there. Crazy to think how this trajectory-bending moment in our lives came down to an underground waste-pot praying for less Charmin.

Mom had circled another listing much farther up the highway, one that had a ton of land and sat toward the northern end of Malibu. More importantly, it fell within our budget. The rent was four hundred dollars. (That's what I used to spend as an adult on cigarettes every month—*when I was trying to cut down*.)

She toured the second rental courtesy of its owner, Dr. Marwah, a dentist known for working on Liz Taylor and Muhammad Ali. The house was much bigger than the Castello digs, ranch-style and surrounded by rolling acres of unkempt land with very little attention to curb appeal. (Didn't matter, I suppose, as there wasn't any curb nearby to appeal *to*.) Mom thanked the good doctor and told him he'd have an answer shortly. She rushed back to West LA to share the exciting news about the Malibu house with Pop. He wasn't as excited—their current mid-city location and its proximity to all the studios was a convenience he didn't want to give up.

A week later Charles Manson sent his crew of brainwashed demons up to Cielo Drive to viciously murder six people. The very next night they struck again, at the wrong address. My parents took these tragic events as a serious sign to pack up the gang and head north. Shortly after my fourth birthday, we did just that.

The Chumash referred to it as "the surf sounds loudly." Other native tribes claim *mali* and *wu* as "where the mountains meet the sea." We just went with what the fukken Beach Boys called it: Malibu. That wonderful place became my home for a very long time.

Finally.

CHAPTER 6

Birthdays for me growing up signaled two things: the end of summer and the beginning of a school year. A double gut-punch I could never curry any favor from. Summer felt like a fifteen-minute montage, whereas school dragged out like front row at the opera. I turned six at our Malibu rental, a place we nicknamed the Marwah Ranch. I was finally on the doorstep of mandatory attendance at an *actual* school for the first time in my life. (Some tutoring on Dad's sets here and there that mostly amounted to crayons and glue.)

First grade is when my sentence was officially set to commence. I'd be doing a twelve-year stretch. None of it shaved off for good behavior. The crime I was found guilty of? Being a kid with intent to grow up.

My Uncle Mike, one of Dad's fifty brothers, was helping him deliver me as promised to Juan Cabrillo Elementary to begin my term. It sat just minutes up the road, tucked in a few hundred yards from the PCH. Dad walked me out to the car, secured me in the rear seat, and went back inside to check on Uncle Mike.

The car was running, and I was alone. They were taking their time for some reason. Maybe the final touches on a brown-bag lunch, or a to-go cup of that week's organic coffee. Whatever the delay, it gave me enough time to rummage through my favorite invisible accessory, the scheme-pouch.

Dad and Mike finally emerged from the house and must have thought I was ducked down in the back seat as a prank or stealing a quick nap before the big day. They peered deeper into the vehicle. No sign of me. Dad went back into the house while Mike checked the garage. No child to be found. He and Dad drifted back to the idling station wagon to call a play in the huddle:

"You go around the left side of the house, I'll take the right, and we'll see if we can flush him out," Dad told him.

"He can't have gone too far," Mike replied as he ambled off in search of me. Mike had a fake leg, so his amble was a bit more involved than your average uncle. It was 1971 and prosthetics were still bulbous and creaky. Mike's looked like he fleeced it from a mannequin graveyard. Truth be told, it was an anchor with toes, but it was Uncle Mike's anchor and, more times than not, he was ours.

Dad hadn't quite completed his half of the perimeter when Mike called out from unseen yonder, "Any luck, brother?" A Dad voice from not near Mike calling back, "I got shit."

I was in the dark, the *actual* dark—on the floor of a makeshift woodshed, at the exact rear of the house. Dusty spiderwebs and pill bugs, my hands wrapped tightly around a cold, dense object. I could hear them. Some words an inch away, others from the moon. Could they hear *me*?

Mike's heavy leg gravel-scraped to a stop just outside my bunker.

Dad's youthful strides galloped in to join him.

"How the hell did we miss *this*?" Mike asked.

They each pulled open the swinging wooden doors, suicide-style like Kennedy's Lincoln.

The blinding sunlight flooded the tight space, disrobing my conceal. Shovels and old brooms, a dead forest behind and around me. Knees gathered to my chest, shaky hands clutching a pitted red brick, tears painting dirt canals down to my chin.

I can remember the two of them staring at me, trying to piece it all together. The hiding I'm sure made sense, but a *brick*? Knowing full well who my pursuers would be, why on earth did I feel the desperate need for a crude weapon? Was my big move gonna involve braining Pop and my favorite uncle? And then what—head for the hills and live off the land?

They disarmed me, dusted me off, and led me back to the waiting car.

As Mike buckled me in, he shared a story about his first day of school as a kid—since they couldn't afford bricks he told me he was clutching a can of beans instead. True or not, it lightened the mood and put the school-fear back in the tube.

Dad and Mike handed me off at the classroom to a nice lady with large hair. Many introductions to faceless kids, various workstations pointed out. The adults were satisfied, at ease even. Goodbyes traded, the day had a shot.

When I discovered neither Dad nor Mike would be stickin' around, I proceeded to lose my bricklaying mind. The only way to restore order was for Dad to stay behind while Mike drove around the block once or twice. (They assumed a few minutes would put out the fire.) Mike could have driven to San Francisco and back and it wouldn't have made a difference. Dad was stuck.

This played out in similar forms for the next couple of years. Not every day, usually strewn across the first few weeks at that year's new school.

Change for me was a toe-dip into the unknown. Gators, eels, strangers. This was gonna take some time and patience, the two areas my parents had to be running low on (or out of). They had their hands full with me on this front much in the same way *mine* were full with that brick. In hindsight, I've come to realize that brick wasn't a weapon—it was a symbol.

One year after moving into the Marwah Ranch, we were handed our walking papers. The celebrity dentist must have raised the rent or insisted my parents go halfsies with him on a new septic tank. Whatever the beef, our welcome had timed out and it was clear to all we needed to locate a new spot. We moved across the highway to another rental house. This one on Birdview Avenue, a quiet street on the northern stretch of a community called Point Dume. Before it was fashionable to memorize your address in case you got lost or kidnapped, I had the new one down pat:

"Seven-Two

One-Two

Bird-View

Avenue

Mal-ih-Bu."

My first poem.

It was a single-story, not so many bedrooms, fewer baths, very far from beyond. The house didn't come with any furniture. We didn't come with any furniture either. Pretty lean times over there on Birdshit Avenue. Emilio recently reminded me that all four of us slept in sleeping bags on the floor in the same room—for a year.

When I wasn't "camping" at the new house, I was attending a new school: Carden Elementary, a franchise chain with its roots in the 1930s. They set one up in Malibu and parked it out of sight near the top of a canyon.

The architect of the school's maverick approach to learning was Mae Carden, and phonics was her game. A dressed-up concept based on the introduction of images, connected to sounds, to then form words inspired by perception. (Hey Mae, we have that already; it's called *television*.)

I had only been there a week when my parents were already being summoned to have a sit-down with the top dog. (Not Mae, she was long retired by then and counting her war bonds.)

The issue at hand was my refusal to stand for the Pledge of Allegiance. My chief complaint was the God part. Didn't seem fair that I wasn't given a choice. (Maybe He and I spend a little time before I'm forced to go all in.)

Always the brilliant mediator, Dad showed up to douse the flames. They reached a compromise where I didn't have to stand, and if I did, I didn't need to recite the pledge. Problem solved, the waters calm again for me to continue a peaceful tread in the stillwater pond of phonics.

I do remember actually enjoying a few things about Carden, but I also remember suddenly *not* being there anymore. My time at Phonics Tech was cut short when Dad took the whole gang to Colorado; the primary location for his career-turning film *Badlands*. The shoot covered nearly three months and after his character went on a crispy date with the electric chair—Dad wrapped the future *classic* and the Gypsy Express rumbled its way back to Malibu.

The timing of *Badlands* overlapped in such a way with the school year—I wasn't able to pick back up where I left off and resume my curriculum. Scholastic consistency was *always* a moving target.

In an effort to prevent the disjointed prospect of me repeating second grade, Mom found an alternative "home school" just across the highway and not far from the Marwah ranch. When she dropped me off for day one at the *newest* new school, she was less than impressed but didn't wanna judge the book by its cover. Years later, and in *her* own words; Mom has no problem titling that book: *Patchouli Hippies with Dirty Feet*.

I stuck it out for two weeks, but after school on that fourteenth day, Mom had caught a vibe that *something* had me firmly in its grip. She kept trying to pull it out of me and I couldn't get from feelings to words.

Someone on their staff (or *with* staph) had set up an 8mm projector. I was expecting to see some boring nature-themed flick with whales or lions. It was anything but. When Mom asked me to describe the film they played for us, I carefully eked out, "It was a giant bulldozer pushing hundreds of naked skinny dead people into a huge hole in the ground." (Half a century later, I can still see it in high-def.)

Mom knew instantly what this was. She was horrified. Dad was brought up to speed, and in a flash the car keys were ripped from countertop—those dolts had bought themselves a livid Martin Sheen. All sales final. A room with no doors.

Why on earth was an elementary school (alternative or not) showing a classroom full of seven-year-olds vintage stock news footage of the Holocaust? (*The pledge* at Carden was an issue, but *this* isn't?) A well-thought-out lecture with context would have been too much at that age, and these thoughtless clods chose silent film to deliver the lesson. It was as if the *clickety* drone of the cheap projector was spitting out the missing audio from the treads on the bulldozer.

A line had been crossed. My Pop let 'em know what was what.

The dippy hippy school of morons was a wrap.

The child was on the move. Again.

CHAPTER 7

Right before my eighth birthday, my folks were finally able to purchase their first home. I was thrilled for them, I was thrilled for us. The day the lease expired, we loaded up the station wagon with the scant belongings from Birdview, setting sail for a home we could finally claim as *ours*. No more power-hungry landlords or wimpy plumbing anxious to see us go. This joyful domestic chapter was unfolding beautifully, a mere two streets away. We could have walked our stuff to the new place.

It was a modest four-bedroom single-story, offset and complemented by a mammoth wide-open backyard. Ahead of those grounds being overrun with forts or play sets (and a host of many other family hobbies), it was the sacred space where I discovered my love for baseball. Long before I joined a team, I'd spend the entire day throwing that perfect sphere hard and far. When I wasn't using my arm, I was using my glove, tracking the endless fly balls Dad or Uncle Mike would hit to me from just outside the kitchen door. There was as much time to play as there was to dream, and that's really what baseball is all about: the dreams it inspires. I was hooked. My first drug.

* * *

My parents knew it was time for the traditional approach at the public school a few blocks away from the new house, Point Dume Elementary. It lived on the corner of Grayfox and Fernhill, two streets that sat mid-loaf in the geographic breadbox of Point Dume. "The Point," as it's known, is a rural promontory between the PCH and the Pacific Ocean, with a mile-long cliffside ridge surrounding its beach side. If you lived on the Point, you could walk to the school.

With a month lost into the tie-dye sewer, I showed up late to the Point Dume academic party. I had to assimilate much quicker than the day-one kids in my class. I wanted to fit in but not stand out.

I needed to make a friend or two who would show me the ropes and have my back. I spotted that hope almost immediately in a small group I could tell had a history together. They wound up being the foursome of Chris Penn, Miles C., and the Heath twins (names you'll come to know, as their stories peppered my road to adulthood). They took me under their collective wing and dulled the edge of my biggest fear: *anything* new. It was a huge box to check in this fresh arena.

Now I just had to do my part.

A few weeks after my arrival, I was confident the hardest challenge of the transition was behind me. Turning that fantastic four into the fantastic *five* was a big reason for the relief I was feeling. I had a solid crew, and they had me.

The class had just returned from a forty-minute lunch break. Our third-grade teacher, Mrs. Haynes, gradually reclaiming order. Her pleasant voice the shiny spoon to a wineglass pre-toast at a banquet.

She was a kind and patient lady somewhere in her early thirties. We weren't necessarily a rowdy flock, we just knew the stuff outside those walls had a much better chance of capturing and holding our attention. Some of that stuff being the girls, three in particular: Anne, Debbie, and Quintana. Removed from a sterile classroom, I could behold that trio from various perspectives and in much more flattering light. For all of us.

With ten minutes left before the final bell, Mrs. Haynes posed a question to the entire class. I knew the answer right away. Silence. No one taking a stab at it. I waited. No hands. Really? Anyone? Mine finally shot up. Mrs. H smiled and pointed to me. Most of the class swung their attention my way.

I opened my mouth to say the answer; no words came out.

Okay, minor hitch, let's regroup, reload, breathe, we can do this.

Second attempt: no dice.

Beads of sweat where they'd never gathered.

The taste of panic in a mouth too dry.

The word was stuck in my throat and in my *mind* simultaneously.

The air or vibrations needed across the vocal cords to kick-start a letter, or the syllable of its initial sound, were *detained*. Adding to the confusion, I could still *see the word*. Like it was floating, levitating near my eyes. (*Phonics, anyone?*)

I faked a cough, fidget-tussled my hair, and tried a *third* time. Nothing. Fuck.

I was locked up with a double-pulse, spreading a shame-fire.

How can this be? During kickball, I could speak, yell, and laugh.

Why *now* can't I wrap speech around a basic word, a simple sound?

Was I dying? Is this the first sign? When the laughter and catcalls erupted, I wished I *was* dying. What about the girls? How would I ever face them again, good lighting or not?

Saved by the bell took on an entirely different meaning for me.

The class filed out, averting any eye contact, my crew included.

Mrs. Haynes tried to tell me I was going to be okay and not to focus on it too much—reassuring me that a temporary stutter was very common in children coming to a new school, and not to overthink it. If that were true, how come I'd never seen it before with anyone else? Terrific gal but her pep talk was pepless.

I made it to the side exit on Grayfox. The Heaths were there and so was Chris. I could tell they didn't really want to ask, and even if I was willing to volunteer something, I had *no* idea what the hell to say about it or even if I'd be able to.

The following morning, barely picking at a slice of seven-grain, I tried to make sense of the senseless. Knowing what I knew about the details of my original birthday, I began to build my flimsy case. The words were cut off in the exact spot where I was cut off from life. So, *why now*, after all these years? The two had to be intermingled in some form of biopsychology (a label I'd learn much later on in life). At the time all I had to go on was, "throat-bone's connected to the *wh-wh-wh-wut the fuck bone.*"

When I spoke of gators, eels, and strangers, I had no way of knowing that list was incomplete. That "toe-dip" moving forward would now include a nasty fucker I came to know as the Stutter-Ghoul.

CHAPTER 8

The very first Super 8 film camera I got my hands on was a silent Movexoom 2000 during our time in Ireland in the spring of 1972. It was a surprise gift from our folks right when we got there. Pop was filming a TV movie called *The Catholics* (I know, I know) in County Cork, home of the Blarney Stone. We were gonna be there for a spell, two months if not longer, and they saw the camera as a creative tool for us kids to capture the lush countryside of the sister bookend to Dad's ancestry. I'm sure they were also praying it would become a useful distraction so Dad could work in peace, and Mom could claw back a stitch of *her* day, here and there. That camera was a dingy silver box with three buttons and half-a-knob to go along with a shitty fixed lens—and we *loved it*.

The first press of my eye to the viewfinder was startling; I couldn't believe how *dark* the magic box made the world appear. Emilio reached over and pulled off the lens cap. Good start, Carlos. I didn't hear the end of that one for a while.

Filming nature assignments or touristy crap was nixed right off the bat. This wasn't gonna be some plotless documentary-style nonsense to screen later for a room full of yawning relatives. We went straight to the meat and potatoes: the dramatic, violent fiction our Dad was portraying. After seeing it firsthand on so many of his sets, we wrapped our cinematic arms and hearts around that specific theme.

Emilio elbowed his way to the front of the line as our director and cinematographer. Without any sound to ruin, he'd give us the basic shape of a scene, then talk or yell us through the rest of it as it came to him while rolling. The bullish takeover didn't speak as much to an early filmic prowess as it did to Emilio's habit of seizing instant control with anything new. Ramon and I fell in line and followed his lead—one minute, in front of the camera as his actors; the next, behind it as the crew, documenting Emilio's earliest theatrical stylings as well.

By the end of the first day, the camera was being passed around and handed off like a baton. The only way to wind up on camera was to give up control of it, which created an opportunity to learn from both sides of the lens all at once.

Our prop department consisted of anything that was handy on the day. Whatever we lacked in fancy accessories we more than made up for with invention and passion. If we had a mop and a diaper, our baddie would become the murderous, incontinent janitor. We were trying our best to mimic Dad's profession: making the fake stuff seem real, while doing so fearlessly.

Eight weeks later, *The Catholics* was a wrap and we were headed back Stateside.

We couldn't wait. *Our* films had only just begun.

Back on the home front, our pilot light became a blowtorch. The Super 8 passion from the Emerald Isle turned our Malibu home into a beehive of ambitious fictional pursuits. What began with me and Emilio filming each other crashing bikes in slow motion soon blossomed into a neighborhood gathering spot for our friends to join the magic Bactine party. The films commandeered both yards, front and back. Emilio's older friends set the bar for intimidating stunts that my younger group had to live up to. When not testing the limits of our bikes, we were filming each other jumping off the roof into cardboard boxes, trying our best to live up to the heroics of a Six Million Dollar Man. It was scary as hell but the filmed pain was worth it.

Chris Penn became a central figure around this time.

We were a unique medley. Yin and yang with no room in the overhead bins. It's almost impossible to entwine two *more* divergent personalities. I'm a Virgo. Fastidious, linear in preparation and execution. Chris was a Slobittarius. You knew what he'd eaten the night before by just looking at his hair the following morning.

The stuff we did share was a galvanic love of film, a mischievous curiosity for the ladies, and a deep-seated hatred of the three schools we attended together for nine years. We knew right away that we were brothers from a different sire. From the beginning of our friendship in third grade and all the way through high school, my second dwelling became Casa Penn (a fifteen-minute walk, or a bike ride in half that time, from my house).

They lived in a ruggedly elegant layout that overlooked the Pacific Ocean from a hilltop perch on the southern branch of Point Dume. His folks were vivid and loving and pugnaciously artistic. Eileen, the Momma Penn, an actress, fairytale-devoted to her life's love Leo, the Poppa Penn, a film and TV director.

Both of his folks drank a bit and made no bones about it. I remember being curious and a tad jealous at how regal and appointed they made it look. As though the setting was lifted from a *Life* magazine old-Hollywood sepia spread, the twinkling crystal tumblers, the sipped and savored high-dollar scotch. I wanted so badly to join in, extend my pinkie, and *wow* the room. I could see clearly, even then, the astute confidence it brought about the *instant* that special sauce made contact. I was trapped in a belief that they were free and I was not.

Easy child, your time with all of that will come.

Our Super 8 filmic foursome was lean and dedicated. Chris, Steve and Kim Heath, and myself. The Heaths, sturdy and identical twin brothers, lived on the inland side of the PCH, about seven minutes from Point Dume. They would man the grip and electric side of the production. As reliable as a sunrise, those two.

The ideas for our movies weren't cut from the traditional cloth of page to screen or hatched during a scheduled time in our secret think tank in an unknown cave near Zuma Beach. Our think tanks lived atop our shoulders and were as agile as we were.

The size of our productions relied heavily on how Dad was doing work-wise. The dough we needed for our basic creative ingredients (film, guns, and fake blood) played out as an easier request when he was employed and distracted. Between jobs? It was whatever he could afford, and if a ten-spot or a Jackson was all he could fork over, we were grateful.

We couldn't wait for the weekends, and when the summer finally arrived, that became our golden window. It was three months of weekends on standby to explore the backlot of the endless Point Dume Studios.

It was during the summer of 1978 when my folks upgraded the

battle-tested MX 2000 to a brand-new Elmo Super 8 *with sound*. The transition was a revelation. We now had our own version of Howard Hughes peeking in on Al Jolson's *Jazz Singer*, hearing a theater filled with the actors' dialogue for the very first time.

We had to learn the basics of cinematography: lighting and editing. We didn't have the resources to invest in a film-friendly lighting package and lived at the mercy of whatever indoor lights our houses came with.

Exterior filming was just as unforgiving. In a constant losing race with the sun, we took whatever she gave us. Shadows become a problem when assembling outdoor sequences in postproduction. Unless you can disappear them, they never match. Chris would always say, "If my performance is good enough, no one's gonna care about any of that crap." He was more than good enough, he was *great*. And he was right: No one ever said a damn thing about the shadows his talent made disappear.

We tried to keep the camera off the tripod as much as possible, shooting a ton of film in our preferred style of handheld. Not thrilled with how shaky a lot of it was, I tried to build a Steadicam with surgical tubing and a Hula-Hoop—in theory, allowing the camera to "float" in the middle of the plastic ring. Helluva try, but that thing didn't make it through rehearsal.

So much of the process was very much like a lab. If science is, as they say, "a constantly updated history of corrected mistakes," so too was the work we were doing from one film experiment to the next.

The postproduction work fell squarely on me and Chris. We wound up deep into many nights in his cramped, junk-filled bedroom, holding tiny strips of film to bare lightbulbs, searching for a crucial edit-point the X-Acto knives and Scotch tape dared to merge.

It was an early form of literal cut and paste, where I had to work around the fast food that Chris glopped all over the edit station.

Easily the most exciting and satisfying part of the entire process was when we were finally able to show the finished film to friends and family. Our earliest presentations were projected onto a white sheet taped to the wall in my parents' bedroom. Mom felt bad for us and showed up one day with a standard sixty-inch retractable screen. That screen would travel between the Penn den and the Sheen family room, unfurled in whatever room was darkest. We never offered anyone popcorn; the films were too short to enjoy it.

After a screening one night in my folks' living room of a film called *Rooftop Killer*, my Mom asked why a certain actor had to die so early, and why we didn't spend more time developing their character. Chris and I lied and said we had in fact filmed those scenes, but the sound was so problematic they had to be cut. Then quickly added, "But how 'bout that head shot, when the white wall got *Jackson Pollock'd* with his final thoughts? How frikkin' kool was *that*?!"

The *ooohs* and *ahhhs* from any audience that saw this scene were so consistent, we'd be high-fiving in the back of the dark room and thinking about just *where* our parents could cram their character development.

PennStevez Films at your service.

Long before Sean Penn dazzled the world with his seismic talent, he was one of our earliest supporters with the Super 8s. Five years our senior, he continuously dared us to stretch our vision, to never settle, to *"feel the burn* in the muscle on the top floor."

Sean frequently brought that same passion to our sets, recommending better camera positions and spot-on dialogue changes. Sean was an inspiration, and let's face it: when he spoke you fukken listened.

To round out this embarrassment of imaginative riches was Michael, the eldest Penn sibling. Michael would go on to become a world-class musician, composer, and platinum-selling performer. When music was needed or missing from one of our projects, a short walk to his door brought forth something that landed between the two Johns: Lennon and Williams.

There was such an abundance of unique talent at both houses, it felt like the perfect blend of late-'60s Laurel Canyon and mid-'70s Stella Adler. It became a "proving ground" that proved every dream is worth chasing.

Chris did Chris in ways never to be retraced. He made us insane; he made us howl with laughter; he made us better. In due season his foibles became weightless. He was a mud-caked diamond. The gem inside *always* well worth the cleanup.

I'm proud of the work we created and left behind. If Chris were still with us on the journey, I guarantee (after a few cheeseburgers) he'd second that emotion.

CHAPTER 9

I'm not sure how old we were when we started packing our own suitcases. I gotta believe the turning point was when we stopped trying to cram the family dog into Dad's Samsonite. Our foursome used to make packing lists of all the junk we were convinced we'd need in a place we had never been to before. My lists looked a lot like my fantasy demands at Christmas, which to my parents were more for practicing my penmanship. (Just because I knew how to write "Shrinky Dinks" didn't mean Santa put 'em in my stocking.)

One item that never needed to be on the register was the Movexoom 2000: That magic box was a given—and went with us everywhere. When Dad announced we'd all be going to Italy for a spell, you can bet within five minutes the MX2K was being carefully wrapped in several of my softest T-shirts (that Mom had picked out for me).

The timing of the trip was incredible; we had just watched a slideshow in Mrs. Jones's class from her summer in Rome, and the imagery was stunning. As each colorful still *kachunked* into place through the whir of the Kodak fan, I mighta been looking through her lens, but it felt like I was filming it through mine. When Dad broke the news about the trip, I wasn't thinking about bringing the dog—I wanted to smuggle Chris and the fukken Heaths instead.

We arrived and got settled in at the nice apartment they'd arranged for us. Dad's workload on *The Cassandra Crossing* was a heavy one right off the bat. He'd leave early and come home late, and the only way we could spend any time with him was at the iconic Cinecittà Studios on the outskirts of Rome.

It was fine at first, but after a while we'd get antsy and need to stretch our legs and minds. One of the disadvantages was that we couldn't film while they were filming. The MX was so goddam loud it could be heard all the way across the massive soundstage. Sucked for me and Emilio because once the deadly virus makes it onto the train, there's machine-gun fire every other scene and hazmat doods getting ripped to shreds. (It'll all make sense after you look it up.)

The star of Mrs. Jones's Roman slideshow was the Coliseum, and by the end of the first week in the ancient city, Mom took all four kids to see it in person. They offered guided tours that held my interest for all of seven minutes, and I could tell that E was just as bored and seeing the place in the same way I was: *as a giant amazing set*. We hatched a plan that night and were back at the Coliseum the following morning to begin filming.

Our plot concept was pretty basic. Emilio was the American exchange student/photographer who has a chance encounter with a homeless kid (me) in his new "home"—the Coliseum, all the way down to the spooky catacombs. The working title was *Rubble Child*, a bit on the nose but c'mon, we're the same outfit that called an assassin film *Rooftop Killer* and a card-cheating drama *Deadly Aces*. Why stray from a proven formula? (And no, you can't look up any of 'em.)

The shoot lasted a few days, and our camera was as loud as it wanted to be. After E's character finally earned my trust, the plot hit a snag—we couldn't figure out what to do with a rubble child away from all the rubble. We were running low on ideas and film, at which point the action taking place on Dad's set was about to get a lot more interesting.

Dad was on Stage Five working with a star-studded cast. Among those stars: Orenthal James Simpson, "O.J." to friends and family (and mistresses). During a lengthy break between production setups, I got into a heated and surreal game of ping-pong with that same man by his other nickname, The Juice.

The volleys were furious, we were tied at 21-all, it was many hours past my bedtime. O.J. was extremely competitive and clearly didn't give a fuck that his opponent was a shy ten-year-old child. We had a superstar audience of Dad's other costars: Ava Gardner, Richard Harris, Sophia Loren, Burt Lancaster, and a *very Method* Lee Strasberg. Most of the Italian crew had drifted in as well to see what all the *commozione* was about.

O.J.'s view of me had to have been a tad comical. The table was tall, and I was short. He was playing against a floating head with long hair and a paddle. O.J. was exceptionally vocal, as vainglorious as he was congenial—a brand of "friendly" you'd find on a soap opera. His endless running commentary gave us an early taste of his post-football work in the broadcast booth. Whatever his strategy, the game could not have been more exciting. I was in the match of my life with the greatest athlete on planet earth, and I was two points away from pocketing *the* most improbable victory ever.

That's when his paddle changed hands.

The sneaky move was so smooth and subtle, I'm positive it went completely unnoticed by everyone. (They were shooting nights, and most of the stage was pretty sauced by that point, principal cast included.) O.J. saw that I clocked it. He was staring right through me when he made the swap. It was a silent signal telling me in no uncertain terms: *Not tonight, kid.* He'd given me the underdog-deluxe show I'd unleashed, but the *win*? Not a chance.

The game ended in unspectacular fashion, those final two points a blur.

His winning shot was a missile that ricocheted off a wardrobe cart twenty feet behind me. Please understand that I'm *still* describing his ping-pong skills when I say: His right hand was fukken lethal.

The postgame congrats from the actors and crew buoyed my spirits enough to calm my bitter disappointment. A kiss on the cheek from Sophia Loren didn't hurt either.

O.J. and I shared a secret that night. He knew that I knew, and for whatever reason it stayed right there, between the two of us. The more I thought about it, the more I felt like I was set up. Lured in with the off hand, only to be crushed like a bug when it mattered most. What a tool. Last I checked, Sophia Loren didn't kiss *him* that night.

A week later, the film's producer, Carlo Ponti, and his wife, Sophia Loren, invited the entire cast to their opulent villa for a beautifully prepared shindig. The house was incredible, the food was world-class, the day was amazing. Our hosts were fully engaged and generous with their time to everyone in attendance. Well, actually, all of their chauffeurs who'd delivered the guests were stuck outside in the rain under a shitty catering tent. Dad caught wind of it and made sure the staff brought them coffee and food—per usual, Saint Martin to the fukken rescue.

Toward the end of the party, we were herded into their home theater to watch an American movie that had just been released in the States. A whispered game of *telefono* spread through the crowd, as many tried to guess what the film might be. Pretty sure I heard Anna Strasberg side-mouth to her husband Lee, "*I really hope it's not one of Carlo's.*"

The screening room, with priceless art on every wall, seated close to thirty people. Carlo introduced the film with three words I'll never forget: *Dog Day Afternoon.*

"Oh kool," I thought, "I love dogs."

Al Pacino's performance absolutely floored me. It was as elegant as the masterworks we sat beneath. Not since Dad in *Badlands*, two years prior, had an actor transported me so completely. The Ponti-Loren movie night was a key moment where I began to muse over what it really took to become an actor.

Dad and Al.

Not too bad for a couple of former ushers who never gave up on the dream.

Shortly after our glorious dog-day at the villa, Dad received a 3 a.m. overseas call from his agent. Dad was being asked to fly from Rome to Los Angeles for a meeting with the brilliant director Francis Ford Coppola. Fresh off of a multi-Oscar takeover at the Academy Awards for *Godfather II*, Francis was the most celebrated and valued director in the known universe.

The meeting would have to take place at the airport. Francis had a two-hour layover before he needed to board another flight. (They'd met a few years earlier when Dad auditioned for *The Godfather*. After the difficult screen test, Dad told Francis that Pacino was better for the role. Francis listened.)

Two days later Pop was on a flight to LA. Frustrating delays in customs left them with only fifteen minutes together in the first-class lounge. Francis handed Dad a script, explaining that his lead actor, Harvey Keitel, needed to be replaced. Following whatever could be gleaned in 900 seconds, they thanked each other and said their farewells. Dad headed back to Malibu to read the script that night and stay on the Roman time zone.

He returned to Italy to finish his last week on the film and wait for an answer from Francis.

The call finally came. It was on.

As soon as he wrapped, Dad had to throw a bag together and board a flight to the Philippines. When it landed, he barely had time for a wardrobe fitting and a snack. In the next instant he was sitting in a Huey gunship, documenting the very first frames as Captain Benjamin Willard in the greatest motion picture ever made: *Apocalypse Now*.

To steal a line from the film, "Get your people back, this is gonna be a big one."

CHAPTER 10

Mom and us four kids departed Rome for Los Angeles the day after Pop headed to the Philippines. It was great to be home. Mom would join Dad on location in a place called Baler A week later. They made arrangements with Uncle Mike to come live with us and hold down the fort. He was our favorite uncle, and I think secretly Dad's favorite brother. It was a *lot* to oversee with so many moving parts and variables. With Mike's military background, they assumed his authority would prevail. We would do our best to make sure Point Dume was more challenging than Korea.

My folks had voted to put the *Gypsy Express* on hold for a minute to get the lay of the third world land before they brought us over. As seasoned as we were by then with the *no child left behind* family doctrine, this new set of unique challenges had *measure twice, cut once* written all over it. The political climate in the Philippines was pretty dicey, the actual climate even more so.

My parents would look like frikkin' soothsayers a month later, when the deadliest typhoon in decades ravaged most of Luzon. Given the name *Olga* (*Didang* locally), it tore through a place called Iba, reducing many of the elaborate sets to soggy toothpicks. The storm killed close to 400 people and left another 1.3 million homeless. A good portion of the *Apocalypse* crew had to seek shelter in local homes and hope for the best. It was a humanitarian disaster for the region and a major setback for the production.

Francis had to make the difficult call to relocate, rebuild, and suspend the filming until those enormous hurdles were cleared. It was during that downtime when my folks decided to return Stateside. We were thrilled to have them back at home safe and sound, yet probably not *nearly* as thrilled as Uncle Mike. That man must have been dancing a one-legged Charleston in his mind, knowing his guardian duties were no longer required. It had been a long month for him with the four of us.

In July of '76, Dad got the word it was time to head back to the Philippines. He and Mom made the decision that we'd travel as a complete unit for round two. The plan was that we'd stay there until the end of summer and make it home in time for the beginning of the new school year. Plans work better for architects. Not so much for a family of six going on location halfway around the world.

Apocalypse Now is one of the most intensely researched and documented films of all time. I got there as a ten-year-old, and saw things most adults never experience. The chronology of these events isn't perfect, nor is that my goal. I'll leave all of that to the legit journalists and desperate wannabes.

These are my stories.

The American doctors packed inoculations into our bloodstreams, I packed *The Giving Tree* into a carry-on, Filipino stewardesses packed *us* into a PAL DC-10 wide-body. The 7,000-mile trek was the longest any of us kids had ever been faced with. We could have watched all five *Planet of the Apes* films during the flight (much like Emilio and I had recently done at Grauman's Chinese Theatre).

We weren't just going on location with Pop, we were headed to a culture entirely unexampled for us. During takeoff Emilio reminded me to enjoy one last good look at LA and kiss it goodbye. Thanks bro, think I'll go sit with Ramon.

My first impressions when I arrived were very specific. As soon as I stepped off the bird, it was the smells—constant overwhelming plumes and whiffs of burning rubber mixed acridly with indigenous street food and sliceable humidity. If *down on one's luck* and *oppression* had a signature scent, that was it.

Driving from the airport through the impossibly congested streets of Manila, our soft-spoken driver named Reno was pointing out a variety of landmarks. I wasn't looking at the buildings as much as I was the people. At first glance I could see and feel the hope, the hustle, the next mouth to feed. Almost existing in unison as one giant over-caffeinated organism. There was an energy I couldn't recall feeling anywhere back home, especially in Malibu.

I spotted an ancient man shout-singing a word I'd never heard before at the top of his lungs. "*Ba-looooot!*" was the cry echoing through diesel fumes, the zealous street-carny pressing skyward an object that looked like an ivory pear. None of it made sense. Reno explained it was a traditional street snack known as *balut*. A developing duck embryo boiled alive and eaten from the shell, feathers and all. No chewing—it was an oyster wearing a fur coat. Welcome to the Philippines, kid.

* * *

It was a three-hour drive from the airport to a remote hideaway called Lake Caliraya, the place we'd call home for a good stretch. Overlooking the ten-square-kilometer, midnight-dark body of water, the lush hillside was dotted with bungalows situated equidistantly from one another. We checked into one of the nicer options—a three-bedroom with mosquito-netted bunk beds, a small kitchen, ceiling fan, and a large deck that surrounded the entire abode. No confusion how the place got its name, we could see the lake from every room.

The heat in the Philippines was unlike anything I'd experienced previously. By 8:00 a.m. it was 115 degrees, and that shit *stuck* to you, drenching clothes and scrambling thoughts. It was gonna require some getting used to. Even when it rained, the heat didn't let up, and the rain itself was merely a quick moisture exchange for the sweat. It brought the value of a morning shower into serious question.

Another distraction: the amount of bugs we dealt with every day.

The mosquitoes didn't just fly in swarms, those bastards rolled in like a *cloud*.

There was also the crawling type—we had to bang out our shoes in the morning and check under the pillows before bed. On day two I found a praying mantis on my toothbrush, and, if that wasn't enough, the goddam roaches could fly. During an outdoor dinner with my family and a lady with complicated hair, one of those hell-hatched fuckers dive-bombed into her French twist. It sounded like a supersonic, epileptic dart. She had to pry that thing out with help from a busboy. Pretty sure no one ordered dessert.

For the first four months, I divided my time between three essential outposts: Lake Caliraya, the Pagsanjan Rapids Hotel, and Kurtz's Compound. (In the interest of carpal tunnel, we'll know them as Cali, PRH, and KurCom.) I viewed these three localities as separate venues or campuses, each one being wildly unique in the experiences and memories they helped create. Over the course of my time on location, an incredible amount of life was lived inside this treasure of a film.

It would take years to sort through what I brought home from the experience, and perhaps even longer to figure out what I left behind.

Mom and Dad weren't the only parents who showed up knee-deep in kids. Francis and his wife, Eleanor, had drafted their brood into the journey as well, uprooting sons Roman and Gian-Carlo (Gio), and daughter Sofia. Roman was my age, and Gio a year or so younger than fourteen-year-old Emilio. Sofia was five and with her mom most of the time.

Emilio and Gio became fast friends. Roman and I did as well, then bonded even deeper when the two of us saved a local kid from drowning in the pool at Cali. It was intense and we were treated like heroes after that. When I saw that Roman was just as uncomfortable with the hero label as I was, I knew we had a lot in common. Humility tends to seek itself, and the sons of *Apocalypse* had each other's backs from that point forward.

One of my first few times at the PRH, we were told that Francis was throwing together a makeshift screening in the room where he'd been watching the dailies. They were showing a movie one of his actors had starred in and directed.

The actor was Dennis Hopper, the film *Easy Rider*. Although it had debuted in the States six years earlier, Dennis thought it'd be a fun experience to introduce the movie and field questions afterward.

I was relieved to have a lengthy break from the heat, and with the word *easy* in the title, I was confident I could settle in and let this calming film relax my mind. When I'm wrong about something, it's *never* halfway.

While it was nothing like I had anticipated, I did love the film. Performances, direction, storytelling, all of it. Another takeaway from Hopper's opus was the constant references to something they called "grass." It had a presence in nearly every scene, and I was so curious how they hand-rolled it into wrinkled, cigarette-style tubes and smoked it. Grass was given so much screen time, it became its own character in the movie. (I was too shy to bother Hopper about it when the screening ended; he was probably too hammered to explain.)

On the drive back to Cali that night, I was asking my parents what the big deal was about grass, and why it was handled with such secrecy between the characters. I wouldn't shut up. I told them, "Look, there's grass everywhere, even right now on both sides of the road." I reminded them of the huge amount we had in our backyard at home and wondered how would that work if I decided to roll some up and smoke it. I heard Pop mumble-whisper to Mom, "You wanna tell him or should I?" Mom filled me in and I felt really stupid. Much more stupidity would follow when grass and I became better acquainted in the coming months. For the time being, I had to be content just walking through it, hoping my feet didn't get so high they turned into mayonnaise banjos.

The following day, Marlon Brando, one of our Cali neighbors on the lake, stopped by our bungalow for lunch. Brando and Mom had formed a special bond a few weeks earlier when they put their own spin on *lemons to lemonade.* Having survived the typhoon, she made a list of everything she coulda used during the disaster, and central to that inventory was bottled water. When she and Dad came home for that month of shutdown, she organized a twenty-box shipment of essential supplies along with a pallet of drinking water. When we all returned to the Philippines as one, Mom's box-village was waiting for us.

A week after he arrived in the Philippines, Brando came down with a hideous case of dysentery. Mom caught wind of his condition and came to his aid by delivering case after case of the water she masterminded. Knowing full well Mom's imported water led to his swift recovery, Marlon was beyond grateful. In no time he was back on his feet and shipshape to begin filming. There's great wisdom in the adage *When in doubt, overprepare.* Overpreparing is something we should have done with the food ahead of that lunch with Brando. More specifically, the amount of it.

Before any food was served, the Estevez kid quartet had a few minutes alone with Brando on the deck where we'd be eating. He was thoughtful, funny, charming, and brilliant. Being one, I could tell right away how much he loved children. I got the feeling that he knew kids understood him in a way that adults could not. He gave the four of us equal time, no favorite chosen.

In addition to his supernatural presence, his brain seemed to be wired differently. With the midday sun glowing off his perfectly shaved dome, he proved it with an impossible display of coordination and dexterity. Marlon dared us to follow along as he drew a circle in the air with his right index finger, while simultaneously drawing a square on his chest with his left. He did so perfectly while maintaining a conversation that had nothing to do with circles or squares. He then said "change" and effortlessly switched hands with the shapes—square in the air and circle on chest. It was fascinating to watch, it was impossible to duplicate. (I've tried for nearly five decades and it still frustrates the hell outta me.)

During the month of downtime back home, my parents had taken us to see a film Brando had in theaters, *The Missouri Breaks*, where he played a vicious bounty hunter with an impressive body count. I was mesmerized by the special effects from that era, and I asked Marlon how they created the fantastic exploding wounds that filled all those pine boxes with his foes. Without missing a beat, he cocked his head in my direction and unblinkingly said, "I killed them." I quicked a look with Emilio—*did we hear that right?* Brando continued: "It was their last day, no one really liked those folks, so we went ahead and used real bullets and I killed them."

I was in shock and felt instant regret from my dumb question. Were we about to have lunch with a killer? Dad came out to set the table, heard the tail end of it, and started to laugh. That broke Marlon's spell—he finally gave in and let out a bellow that echoed across the lake. I'd never witnessed an adult get such a kick from humor too morbid for a child's ears. My mind was blown open like those bullet wounds. I was also really flattered that Marlon Brando somehow knew I could take it.

Mom finally joined us, placing a huge bowl of spaghetti smothered in butter and parmesan at the center of the table. That meal could have fed most of Brando's rebel force at his compound. Keep in mind: we all had plates in front of us, we all had napkins in our laps. Marlon was in a back-and-forth with Dad (something poignant, I'm sure) when he nonchalantly reached out, curled his thick forefinger over the lip of the spaghetti bowl, and in one slow-motion, fluid maneuver, pulled that vat to a stop directly in front of him.

Okay, he's gonna serve himself and then pass it to the left. Good on him, I thought, maybe he's a fellow Virgo and doesn't want to mess the table. Nothing close to that etiquette happened next as he picked up his fork and dug in like Kurtz. The first *stab and lift* reminded me of a giant raiding a farm, eating hay bales with a pitchfork. Our mouths more agape with his second bite, a move that made it law—the bowl was his. There's a great line in the film where Kurtz talks about the means by which the war is fought: "Cow after cow, village after village, army after army." We all sat stone-faced, watching in awkward amazement as we experienced our own version of it: *bite after bite, meal after meal, hungry child after hungry child.* Sometimes the show is worth the sacrifice.

The Spaghetti Western lakeside lunch was the only quality time I shared with Brando during his time in the Philippines. I'd spot him occasionally on the grounds at Cali, drifting between bungalows in a robe or some type of ceremonial wrap. I don't like to bother people on their days off; if he needed me he knew where to look.

I'd be the kid on the patio deck screaming *Fuuuuuck!* to the heavens, trying to draw an imaginary square on my chest.

All of Brando's scenes took place at the stronghold named for his character, Kurtz's Compound. The interior sections of the massive temple set were designed in a way that didn't afford any extra room for spectators. I used to joke with Mom that if she camouflaged me in twigs and mud, I could sneak in there and blend into the wall. *("Cut! What's with the blinking rock?")* The other factor with KurCom, when it came to watching Dad work there, was its massive scope. With the money and muscle that went into it, Francis wanted to capture and convey his unique achievement in every artistic manner conceivable.

All of the larger, more complex scenes that involved scores of extras incorporated a host of additional cameras as well. So much of the filmable real estate of KurCom was constantly being documented. Finding a vantage point to observe from really amounted to just locating a safe place to hide. You didn't want to accidentally walk into the shot of an F.F. Coppola film. I saw it happen once and I *still* feel bad for that guy.

The great misconception about my time on *Apocalypse* is that I had a front-row seat to its most iconic moments and groundbreaking spectacle. Hate to disappoint, it didn't really go down like that. I missed all of Dad, Brando, Hopper, Larry Fishburne, and Robert Duvall's greatest hits. Those hits were either too dangerous, too cramped, or too late at night.

One of those late nights, I was dialed in to watch them blow up the Do Lung Bridge.

Finally, some real action to write home about. The effects rigging was taking forever, so I decided to grab a few winks and come back when they were good and ready. Most kids don't take successful naps at three in the morning. The final blast was so strong it blew open the door of the room where I was sleeping.

Hardly the koolest story to share that I *felt them* blow that famous bridge to pieces. And on it went. The closest I came to seeing a performance from Duvall was when he barged into our bungalow one night in his underwear while Renée and I were watching TV. He was playfully drunk and doing a bad impression of a Comanche war cry. He saw that it was two kids on the couch and realized he was in the wrong unit. Duvall sheepishly apologized and left as quickly as he showed up.

Not exactly *smell of napalm in the morning*, but if that's all I was gonna get, I'll take it.

The main arena of congregation at KurCom was the basecamp,

a dedicated area for the equipment trucks and the various trailers. It was close to the compound and sat between the jungle and the river (a geographic description for 90 percent of the sets on *Apocalypse*). The two trucks I spent the most time exploring were the prop truck and the armorer's rig. The prop truck is where I'd go for American candy. After weeks of pineapple and lychees, it was amazing how quickly a Snickers bar could restore my sanity.

Prop truck's neighbor was the armorer, and they let me fire a machine gun for the first time in my life. (I think it was a Schmeisser.) There was nothing more exciting. Within a week I could break down an AK and fieldstrip an M16. When I wasn't in a sugar blackout with automatic weapons, I was in Fred Blau's special effects makeup trailer to study his wizardry as much as Fred would allow. I watched for three hours one night as he applied the prosthetic neckpiece to Fred Forrest for his Kurtz decapitation. Since then, gore in movies for me has always been technical and rarely emotional. The highlight of Blau's shop was when I helped cover a hundred Kurtz followers in blood and crud for a scene at the temple. Not sure it made the final cut, but it certainly made mine.

A scene where I *was* front row had me wishing I was still asleep at the Do Lung Bridge. In a night scene at KurCom, I watched as a water buffalo got its head chopped off. The bovine was sacrificed by the group portraying Kurtz's Montagnard army. In reality they were Ifugao, an ancient tribe known for the Banaue rice terraces. The offering is a ritual they've performed for centuries, and Francis decided to symbolically weave the graphic images into the termination of Kurtz's command.

It was brutal. This wasn't a Brando joke, or a fake body hanging from a palm tree—it was a real kill that required nothing from Mr. Blau to enhance the impact. Later that same night, the Ifugao did wind up eating that buffalo at a grand feast. (I guess that's one way to process it.)

During the time I spent at KurCom, I never felt that I was excluded from anything. The adults were there to do a job, an impossibly difficult one. Maybe us kids were there to remind those adults *why* the job had value—lend our unintentional insight as it related to matters of the make-believe. As kids, that's what we do all day. In many ways, that compound was a playground for the darkness of imagination. I gotta believe our kidtribe was able to brighten some of it.

The only thing we killed was time.

CHAPTER 11

In total, my first tour of the Philippines covered the entire second half of 1976, from June to December. The plan to make it back to Malibu for the beginning of the school year was gradually inhaled by the jungle, as collateral scraps of Dad's sanity were pulled in with it.

During a family set visit to celebrate his thirty-sixth birthday on his lunch break, I could tell those scraps were missing. I had no idea what was taking place behind the walls of that hotel room set. We were just there to cut some cake and leave. Those details wouldn't be revealed until years later in the Eleanor Coppola documentary *Hearts of Darkness*.

Her film let loose a visual record of Dad's devastating pain for the world to consume. It was so difficult to watch, I wanted to reach into the celluloid to give him a hug and let him know it was gonna be okay.

As we waited for him to join us at an outdoor table to light the candles, rumor had it he was walking naked through the streets. We weren't offered many details, only that it had been a very trying series of events that morning.

By the time he did join us, they'd wrapped him up in a couple towels, his right hand covered in a mass of thick gauze that used to be white. There was so much blood, I thought for sure he had lost a finger. Shortly after he sat down, he turned to face me with the blade of a military-issue KA-BAR knife chomped between his teeth. My first instinct was to laugh, my second—run. His body may have been with us; the guy we called Dad was not.

There was nothing any of us could have done at that stage to help, causing Mom to pull the plug on the birthday celebration attempt. We watched sadly as other-Dad was escorted away from us, until he disappeared like a ghost around the corner of a building.

Ramon's twelfth birthday was in four days, which prompted tasteless jokes by me and Emilio about keeping Monie away from the vodka and mirrors. Humor always got us through the rough stuff.

The next day Dad was back at work bright and early to finish the sequence. He'd brought "no matter what" to the jungle.

The Pagsanjan Rapids Hotel in many ways represented the practical heartbeat of *Apocalypse*. The hotel sat at the mouth of its namesake river—most of the cast and crew lived there, and the only entertainment for many miles could be found in its bar and restaurant. Traditionally themed, the booze and chow hall presented itself as an oasis to soothe the day's bone-deep grief and exhaustion. The fictional Nung River in *Apocalypse* is described as "a main circuit cable plugged straight into Kurtz." As the film continued to blur the lines and test the paper-thin veil between art and life, the same can be said for the Pagsanjan River. KurCom, Do Lung, Cambodia—all outposts either marooned on her banks or seduced by her undertow. That mysterious snake of water, a circuit cable by its own right, plugged straight into Francis. A mad genius—his lab the jungle, his control group out of control.

For years I've wondered which character Francis best related to, and if not one specifically, then maybe a shred of each that he held in praise or scorn. Kurtz's vision, Willard's resolve, Hopper's insanity—quite a variety he had at his daily disposal. The film never really chooses a side, and I can say with confidence, neither did Francis. A moral dilemma more responsibly left in the hands and hearts of the audience. My interactions with Francis were few and far between during my time there. To approach him at any point always felt like asking a guy carrying a piano if he had the time. I learned to read the room at a very young age in high-pressure environments. No better place to develop those skills than the Heart of Darkness.

Dad was usually a master of disrobing from the character before he walked back through that bungalow door after work each day. I still can't fathom how he had anything left to offer his family by way of Dad-duties or emotional engagement. I gotta believe we were a relief most of the time, a grounding post of sorts. Other days it must have been quite the opposite. I was trapped in what I can only describe as an age vortex. Too young to fully grasp the weight and consequence of his lashings, while just old enough to recognize which mask I was greeting. Whatever the score, we never judged and we never pried. *Reading the room* held its powder dry on the home front as well.

The days ran their way into months. Emilio flew back to the States in mid-September to reclaim his educational status and celebrated campus activities. I, on the other hand, didn't pose *any* resistance to missing school. They're starting without me? Please, go do that. The longer I stayed in the Philippines, the better the chance that they'd completely forget I was ever enrolled. To my dismay, Mom sought the help of Larry Fishburne's mother Hattie James, a veteran New York City public school teacher. She and Mom spearheaded a homespun tutoring setup for us. After one week in our thatched-roof classroom, we all realized that traditional education during *Apocalypse* was manifestly futile.

The filming schedule had caved in on itself. It became a perfect storm of many imperfect actual storms. With an uncooperative sky, Francis knew nothing would match from one day to the next when it came time to assemble it. Since Christmas was fast approaching, the production would hit pause for a month, allowing everyone a much-needed break from what Kurtz described as "the horror."

There was a large celebration at the PRH to properly send everyone off in style. All in attendance by then were so eager to leave, they would have welcomed evac on a military transport plane. With the pillars shaking deep into the night, the festivities culminated with a crowded, hotly competitive ping-pong tournament. The universe does play fair at times—I was the last person standing and won the whole damn thing. It was a hugely satisfying bookend to the O.J. grudge I'd been carrying across a few continents. I knew somewhere out in the world, the Juice felt a *tremor in the force* as my "winning shot" dropped a trophy taller than me into my calloused hands. *Touché, Orenthal.*

The common hub to clear customs from the Philippines was Hawaii. The sleigh bells would catch us there as we made it back onto US soil. We spent a week at the Hana-Maui hotel, and even though it was another tropical setting with a healthy amount of rain and swelter, Dad was temporarily released from the clutches of the jungle and the sorrows of Willard. It was a treat to see him smile again authentically, instead of the grimace he often hoped we bought.

After the new year, Dad had a measly twenty-one days before he had to report back and continue his journey. Mom would be the only one going with him. I'm grateful to everything I hold dear that she did. Many things changed forever on that final leg.

The person taking care of us during the time Mom and Pop were gone was a young lady named Mary Arnold. She was the longtime girlfriend of Marc Coppola, Francis's nephew and Nicolas Cage's brother. She was very pretty, capable, and friendly. Mary took shit from no one, our foursome included.

Around five weeks into her stay—which she had been told would be six weeks, tops—I was in a gully on Point Dume at sundown with Chris Penn and Miles C. We had scrounged up enough dough to afford what Chris was selling us. Three eleven-year-olds, a ten-dollar bill, an expertly rolled joint. Transaction completed, Bic lighter flicked, the moment had arrived when I'd find out just how *Easy* the *Ride* was gonna be.

In a flash Chris was gone, calling back to us that his mom would beat him like a drum if he was a second late for dinner. That left me and Miles to maiden voyage the experience together. He was a reformed bully who'd taken a shine to me, and we'd been tight since the third grade. The first few puffs went down pretty smooth and tasted amazing. The change it poleaxed into both of us was instant. Miles was suddenly the funniest person alive, and to him, so was I. *Dear Dennis Hopper, I fukken get it now. PS—I shall pray at night to you.*

As a new world was taking shape around us, we levitated from the gully right into the blinding headlights of a loud car pulling to a stop. The window was already down; we could see clearly it was Miles's ill-tempered father. A giant of a man, his style of parenting disproved as healthy a century earlier. The reeking weed stink all over us, we got in; we had no choice. As a total psyop, he dropped Miles at home first. Mr. C and I didn't say a word the entire drive to my place. Trying to hold my breath to contain the odor, I was nervously visualizing what was in store for Miles when the giant mean parent returned home. The punishment *never* fit the crime in that household.

I came through the front door and Mary called out that they were all seated and I was late for dinner. I yelled back that I had to hit the bathroom and would be right there. I shut the door to see how I looked, and it was messy. My eyes were as red as fire-engine cherries.

I'd recently made the cut for a Little League team, and the only hope to conceal my blazing eyes was the baseball hat sitting on top of the dresser. I put that thing on and pulled it so low the brim was touching my nose. I had to stare at the floor to see where I was going as I *felt* my way into the dining room to join them. I sat down. I'm pretty sure my siblings were there. Blinded by that stupid hat, I couldn't see them—I could only feel them staring at me.

I was so high I felt like I was in a movie where hats were illegal because they were filled with chocolate potato salad. None of it made sense, and I was starting to panic. Mary knew exactly what was up. Her words dipped in sarcasm, she asked what the deal was with the hat. "Big game this week" was all I could muster. She insisted that I lift it up and show her my eyes. "Jesus, Charlie, you're high as hell," she stated. (All I heard was *Jesus* and *hell*. It freaked me the fuck out.)

Mary sent me to bed with no food and a threat that she was going to call my parents in the morning. I said she was pretty, capable, and friendly; I never said she was fukken *kool*.

The bed-with-no-food thing was fine at first, until about three hours later when the munchies hit me like a city bus. Mary had gone to bed early. That night, the pantry was mine. Take *that*, hunger-cop.

Mary didn't have to call them the next morning. Mom would be calling *her*, with some news from the Philippines that was deeply worrisome.

The initial reports about Dad's health were fragmented. Some were saying heat exhaustion, others speaking to matters more serious. It grabbed everyone by the throat. Those 7,000 miles between us and Dad suddenly felt like light-years.

When we finally spoke to Mom, she calmly expressed that it would be in Dad's best interest if we all came back to support him in any way we knew how. That was all we needed to hear. We dropped very little, gathered even less, and boarded another PAL flight. We were handed our own mission for a different part of the river: to go uncover the truth about what happened to our Dad.

Fire up the in-flight *Apes* films, help is on the way.

When the plane landed, we went straight to Mom and Dad's hotel in Manila. We wouldn't be *Going Back to Cali* just yet; our return to the lake would come later.

When we arrived, Pop was outside the lobby, framed by an amazing pool—walking very slowly toward us, tears streaming down his face, gripping a cane that guided each four-inch step.

He still had color, he still had a gleam. Very carefully we all embraced, wanting to hug him while not wanting to break him. He looked older. Not in a withered way, more in a way that befitted the survivor of a tragic crash. It was still Dad and we were still us: a family.

An hour later up in the room, my parents sat us down and explained that Dad had suffered a mild heart attack. As disturbing as that was, it did render some satisfaction to finally learn the truth. All we cared about was that he was still alive. We were there to support him by providing whatever he needed or didn't need from us, joining him in his rehab activities or giving him some space—the kind of space where a quiet can exist and the artifacts of the crisis can be explored in privacy and prayer.

I've always said, when in doubt, stick to what you know. What I knew was baseball. At the last minute before leaving LA, I'd packed two baseball gloves and a new ball into my luggage. I was the only ballplayer in my family, and since I'd just made the team back home, I was hoping to find some local kid to either toss with or teach how. The *last* person in the galaxy I envisioned as my throwing partner was my health-maligned Dad. He saw it as an opportunity to be outdoors in the sun and fresh air, while getting reacquainted with his hand-eye skills and overall physical awareness.

We did this together every day for about two weeks.

In no rush to overachieve, we began day one with us about ten feet apart, throwing very softly maybe fifteen or twenty tosses, for a short five minutes. Subsequently the distance between us lengthened, the toss-count grew, the time we spent stretched. I could feel in real time his *spirit* becoming revitalized. He was smiling, he was a bad-joke factory, he was my Dad again. To share this with him, and have such a central role, connected us in ways moving forward neither of us could have predicted. This had to be the closest I'd get to the celebration Dad experienced watching me take my first steps in this life. A touchstone moment shared.

Dad and I are proud of our place in the Friendly Game of Catch annals, rewriting a page or two of this time-tested tradition. If you ever come across that box-score, you'll find that we threw a combined perfect game.

Day by day, while Dad was making terrific progress for a heroic return, Francis was exploring all options to find a way to keep shooting in his absence. He finally landed on a sibling-swap, to keep the boat on the river. It was decided that Dad's younger brother Joe Estevez, looking *just* enough like Pop at a distance, would fly in and suit up to film a series of long shots on the river in the iconic patrol boat. (*Willard-light* was the nickname Emilio and I pinned on him.)

There's a line in the film when Willard says, "The bullshit piled up so fast in Vietnam, you needed wings to stay above it." *Apocalypse* had a way of speaking to itself, of narrating its own reality. No wings for Francis. Dad was coming back to work.

Answering the call with love and patience for our Dad cemented who we are as a family. We came away from his health odyssey knowing if we could do that, there wouldn't be much the future showed up with that we couldn't solve.

We did finally make it back to Cali. Nothing had changed. The people we'd come to know previously were genuinely happy to see us again. It was mutual.

Dad was fit as a fiddle by then and seemed much more at ease.

What was still left for him to shoot was a monster, but this time around Dad was no longer its servant. After staring down that tunnel on the night he collapsed, into whatever the next realm offers, no one was gonna tell him what really mattered anymore.

I never had to count the days in the Philippines. The jungle and the rain did that for me. The month of June sat just over the next ridge, signaling a full year since my initial arrival. The running joke on the set was the new title: *Apocalypse Never*.

Francis throwing a party to celebrate one million feet of film being shot didn't help. I missed the bash, along with Mom and Renée, the three of us opting instead to go explore Hong Kong for a weekend. A week before we left I told Mom I wanted all the days leading up to Saturday to disappear, so we could get to Hong Kong faster. Her response is one that never left me: "Don't wish your days away, sweetheart. They'll vanish on their own, quicker than you can imagine."

With every passing minute, truer words never spoken.

Our time in the Philippines was drawing to a close. Though Pop still had two weeks of work to finish, a decision was made to send me, Ramon, and Emilio home together. We were making good on the space we had promised him. Renée would hang back with the folks, leaving whenever they did.

I was having severe anxiety about going home without my parents. The last time we were separated, the ground beneath our feet vanished. Mom assured me over and over that Dad was in great hands and there was no chance of that same lightning striking twice.

I believed her. Mom never lied.

I made it home safely, and over time, added back some of the missing pieces—my scraps—to feel okay again. All of my friends couldn't wait to hear my stories, of which I had many. More importantly, now I felt that I had the courage to share them in a way I was never able to before. Even if a few words got stuck, screw it: Whatever struggled out next would be worth the wait.

The majority of Dad's work in the final week was handled with a keen eye on his well-being. It helped that Francis was corpse-fatigued by then and didn't have the energy to push *anyone*, himself included. It wasn't baby steps Dad was taking, while at the same time it wasn't running from a "*fucking tiger*" either.

Whatever exists between those two extremes is the line he walked. Marching for some of it, tiptoeing in other parts when needed. As badly as all of *us* wanted to taste the home front, Dad's thirst for Malibu had to be as deep as its ocean.

I guarantee that was one week Mom was just fine with him *wishing away*.

On time and as promised, Saint Mom completed *her* mission, by delivering Pop back to us in the same condition as listed on the manifest: whole.

If you were watching our reunion from across the street, you'd be convinced that group over there had just won the lottery.

In so many ways, we did.

CHAPTER 12

It was the summer of '77 and Zuma Beach was packed. The famous quote "Charlie don't surf" was not yet a celebrated catchphrase in the cinematic lexicon. (I'd have to wait a couple years until my resistance to the popular sport had Colonel Kilgore to back me up.) I'd been home from the Philippines for a month, trying to squeeze as much as I could into the last window of freedom before I made the move to Malibu Park Junior High School: home of the Dolphins.

"Annnnnd, action!"

The hand, clinging to a rusted chain-link fence that zigzagged along the summit edge of a 200-foot cliff. The knife, carving through the back of that hand just below the knuckles. The owner of that hand, hoarsely pleading with his tormentors, begging mercy from the three-man gang. The savagery gaining momentum as they chant in unison, "Cut it off! Cut it off! Cut it off!" His cries for help, blending into the macabre rhythm of their depraved mantra. The knife's promise keeping its word, two or three slices from fence guy free-falling into the outcropping of jagged boulders far below.

The next spoken "cut" doesn't include "it off"—it's yelled by Emilio, our esteemed director crouched behind the camera. He knew the scene had reached a place where a reset was necessary for the final shot of the day: a life-size stuffed dummy (with half a hand) taking the brutal plunge to the bottom of splatsville. Sean was there too with Chris, the Heaths, Miles, and Tony Barrera. (Barrera was a dear pal who became a chef and died way too young. He and I fell out after high school—it had nothing to do with his cooking.)

I was in my element with another violent Super 8, its plot once again being reverse engineered. I'd managed to cart a few tokens home from the Philippines—Balisong knives, Ifugao tribal jewelry, and the star prop that inspired the madness atop that cliff. Consisting of four fingers with the knuckles still intact, it was the upper part of an effects-makeup severed human hand. The bone nubs and tendons visible on the underside left nothing to the imagination. The gory souvenir had been a parting gift from Fred Blau, and I couldn't wait to show it off. Chris was mesmerized by the KurCom foam facsimile, a scattered detail the ravages of war leave behind. More importantly, it stole the entire show when we saw it on film.

There was a lot of stuff I brought home from *Apocalypse*, and not all of it as useful as that FX hand. Some of it by choice, other things that chose me. Kids never really know what they need—they're too busy hounding the adults for what they want. What I wanted was the freedom I had in the Philippines, while enjoying the comforts of Malibu. What I needed was someone to remind me that those two were never gonna coexist.

Junior high was complicated and crowded—a good portion of every day spent wondering if anyone else felt as unprepared as I did. The crew I relied on so heavily, spread out and missing from most of my classes. Updates at lunch and scattered after-school plans didn't satisfy what we'd left behind at Point Dume Elementary. There was an innocence that evaporated as quickly as that first morning bus ride. I felt lost and late the entire day trying to adapt to the size of the new campus, and the number of teachers I'd have to eventually outfox. I also took special note of how puberty collided with the sudden exposure to that many girls. It was either a giant cruel joke *or* the grooviest situation ever. (Only time and skin-clarity would tell.)

The challenges of the new landscape would test me in ways the Philippine jungle couldn't. Back here not much had changed.

On that side of the world, it didn't matter if my shirt had an alligator or how my hair looked. My fear of judgment at the new school wasn't just about the ladies, I had to stay *en garde* with the guys as well. I wanted to tell 'em all to back off, that right before I came there I had prepped 100 warriors for battle in a Cambodian temple, then helped my Dad recover from a heart attack so he could go kill the evil poet who ran the place. But I never did. Reading the room still had tremendous value, I just had to get used to *that* many fukken rooms.

The junior high was right next door to the schoolhouse where I'd attended first grade. Our bus had to drive past it twice a day, and what really stood out was how tiny it looked from the outside. When I was six years old, the place felt cavernous from the inside, which gave me hope that a similar shift in perspective was in the cards. Stuff like that can't be forced; it functions on its own timeline. What I came to discover was that it had nothing to do with the size of the structures but rather how safe I felt walking through their doors. A sense of security made possible by the friends I already had and the new ones I made. As our friendships grew those buildings shrunk, eventually not a single edifice was left unconquered.

One of my new pals was David Anderson, aka Dave the Rave, aka Brown Dave, who would become a friend for life in a life that really needed him. Dave had enrolled at Point Dume while I was still in the Philippines, and when I finally returned, the Heaths and Chris were describing the new guy as being so kool—he reminded them of *me*. Flattered and threatened at the same time, I walked right up to Dave the new me-guy and introduced myself. He couldn't have been nicer—within five minutes we were both laughing like two old chums.

A unique sense of humor, especially at that age, lets a person know almost instantly there's a connection that can't be manufactured. It's there, or it isn't. I asked him where he was from, and when he told me he was half Filipino, I couldn't believe it. I had just spent more time in his homeland than he had. It was a fascinating way to form a friendship—sharing stories about a faraway place he'd only ever heard about from his mom and grandma. He joined our crew that day and we were beyond thrilled to have him. Forty-nine crazy years later, Rave and I still "get it."

When I wasn't making a Super 8 or hoping that one of the cute girls thought I was *rad*, I was playing as much baseball as possible. The school didn't have its own program but they did have a field, which felt like the equivalent of a nice pool with no water. Really begs the obvious question, and believe me, it's one that I asked about 20,000 times. That didn't stop me or the Heaths from playing all three years in the various PONY and Colt leagues within our region. Outside of a few fields just across Malibu Canyon, we still wound up playing most of our games at the junior high. Go Dolphins!

Whatever I lacked in offense, I made up for with my arm. Every time I let one rip, the other kids on the team wondered why my throws *sounded* so much different than theirs—like a lit fuse versus a dying bird. The more I tried and failed to explain it, the more I realized how special that skill truly was. The two positions that require a great arm are shortstop and pitcher—I fell into both spots and never looked back.

I loved striking out my classmates and making them look feeble, especially when the girl I had a crush on was rooting for them and not me. That lit fuse of mine wasn't just a weapon *on* the field, it did check a psych-warfare box now and again. I had control problems from the mound off and on, and would occasionally bean someone into a collapsed crying heap at home plate. I would feel so bad afterward, that shit would stay with me for days, asking my parents to call Welty's mom to check in on him. (Coulda been one of the reasons I never went pro—not to mention all that dope.)

It's impossible to know at that age what's gonna stick and which lessons will fade away. When I look back on the whole experience, I can remember most of the things we learned and very little about what we were taught. I wasn't taught about teamwork in a classroom, or how to ask a girl to the dance; I learned one through baseball and the other from an *Archie* comic book. I learned more Spanish on location with Dad in Durango than I ever did from Mrs. Escalante. Mr. Poole may have shown me how to work the band saw to cut wood, but what he couldn't offer was how to preserve that pen holder and caretake it for forty-seven years. He gave me a B-minus, and right before he died ten years ago, upgraded it over the phone (with help from his son Bryn) to an A (minus).

Had I known junior high was gonna be the last school I'd ever enjoy, I'd have spent less time in the gully with Miles and a lot more time just laughing with Brown Dave. Good news I suppose is that I finally understand after all these years why they changed the name from junior high to middle school: it's the *midpoint* between elementary-silly and those last three years of hell. High school would pack a much meaner punch.

CHAPTER 13

Malibu didn't have a high school back then. It was either Santa Monica High School or the bad *home* version, and there was no chance my folks were giving up those eight cherished hours. Samohi's campus was enormous. Eighteen miles south of Malibu, it occupied twenty-six acres on Santa Monica's west side, with a population of over 2,000 kids. It was daunting. It had zero charm. Concrete, steel, murky glass. A few scenes from *Rebel Without a Cause* were filmed three decades earlier in the quad. Outside of that, pretty grim pickens.

During my first month, I wore a bulletproof vest to school. An early model from the Second Chance company that was bulky as hell and hard to conceal. It was on loan to me from a Native American Vietnam vet friend of Dad's named Two Blue Jays living in a trailer in our backyard (I'll not explain later). He was paranoid about the state of the world, and his dystopian overspray often drifted my way. I became the moron in class sweatin' balls and out of excuses as to why I couldn't take off my jacket. Knives were the only weapons we dealt with back then, so I finally ditched it. (In light of what those knives were replaced with over time, Two Jays's existential paranoia was not so outlandish after all.)

Hoping to live up to the spirit of our mascot, the Vikings, I made the sophomore baseball team as a pitcher and shortstop. I still struggled at the plate, so the only action I saw was from the mound. The key to my success was a pitch I threw that the school hadn't seen in ten years: the knuckleball. Thrown properly, it dips, jukes, and flutters with zero rotation. When thrown improperly, it's a meatball that usually gets clobbered. The metaphoric intersections were blatant—to survive the next three years, I'd have to emulate this unique weapon in my baseball arsenal.

Not a lot of practice with the flutter. *Juke* and *dip*? I'm your guy.

My sophomore year (the tenth year of my bid) was redundantly hobbling along with all the energy of a sick dog. I was desperate for a sign of any kind. Shortly before spring break, a weekend trip to Las Vegas with Dad and cousin Joey showed up like the face of Jesus on a burnt piece of toast.

I had a hunch the nickname of that famous town wasn't earned from gambling alone. On the short bumpy flight there, a wily plan bubbled to the surface. The percolating combo of teenage hormones, along with my secret stash of nudie mags, turned the port of call into a rite of passage. Joey and I both lost our virginity to a gorgeous redheaded Vegas escort named Candy.

I snuck into Dad's connecting hotel room and into his wallet to "borrow" his credit card while he was asleep. We explained our situation to Candy, and she responded with a level of physical generosity neither of us knew existed. She was Ann-Margret in her prime with a

Mastercard swiper. (I didn't care that the swipe took longer than the sex.)

It was everything I'd hoped for, it was *never*ything I could have imagined.

When she saw the name on the credit card, she asked if I could wake Dad for an autograph. I told her that would be impossible. As I hugged her good night, I whispered that if I could ask him, he'd be very flattered. *Viva Las Vegas, Candy-Ann.* (For the record, I went first.)

As soon as we returned to LA, Joey flew home to Ohio. Not having Joey around to quietly celebrate the perfect memories of Candy created a void. I had to tell someone, so naturally I turned to Chris. *Huge* mistake.

Another mistake: using Dad's credit card. During Dad's two-hour lecture to me about sex versus love, I kept stressing how gorgeous Candy was and what a great deal Dad and I *both* got for the price. The look on his face told me we were done. That was my cue to leave and walk all the way to the Penn house.

Chris was so jealous, he insisted that a common ground between us on that front had to exist. That dood would've robbed a bank to find *his* Candy and even the score. Thankfully, it never came to that. We robbed our parents instead.

In 1980, Santa Monica was a hotbed for illegal massage parlors, many of them within walking distance from Samohi. Post-Vegas, Chris and I were no longer searching for food during lunch. The same hour once spent lamenting our female failures through Taco Bell burps now saw us prowling into that sketchy neon landscape.

Chris got his mitts on a sordid weekly publication called *L.A. Xpress*. You could nab one at a street-side news rack on Pico Blvd.

The cheap smut-guide had an idiot-proof rundown of the good, the bad, and the *yikes* Santa Monica had on its menu. We were fine with anything between the three. Venturing into the not-so-hidden alcoves of the city's seedier side, we were encountering more rejection at the massage parlors than we were customer care. This was unacceptable. We needed to get creative.

In 1980, Amazon was still a river and a rainforest no one could point to on a map. Chris had the key pieces to build a fake ID mail-ordered to his parents' front door. A basic stamp kit with various ink colors and laminating supplies. The local market had a photo booth for passports.

We applied the same skills we'd been using to edit our Super 8s: cut and paste and spit-shine the rest. Displayed quickly in the shit lighting of those hovels, the IDs didn't need to be perfect. Passable or not, bogus credentials were only half the battle. Without any moolah, we'd be staring down the barrel of a shutout.

Bad cover stories to fleece our parents for the funds were wearing thin. (There's a limit to how many Ticonderoga No. 2s or three-ring binders a student needs.) We concluded that "nighttime activities" justified a bigger ask—dinner and a movie for fifty bucks wouldn't raise too many eyebrows. (The two of us wound up going to a lot of frikkin' "movies.")

Once inside, parting the beaded curtain that separated waiting area from private massage rooms was like crossing into a section of the abyss you never hear much about: the fun part. Our pilgrimage of bliss was the groovy side of dangerous—dirty, edgy, and sexy.

As fabulous and enticing as that world seemed, it was easy enough to lose sight of the fact that we *were* still in school. The only way to keep it below the radar was to pick our spots and not get greedy. On a few occasions, we did *actually* have dinner (usually at the Hamburger Hamlet) and go to the movies (usually a slasher film). We didn't broadcast our adventures; we never gave away our locations. The fewer in the know the better.

Early mornings in class following those late-night runs—the two of us telepathically basking together in that clandestine part of our lives. Day after day, staring at the same blackboard as the other students yet seeing the *absolute values* they forced us to care about in the manner *we* chose.

We were certain in those moments that not a single soul in that room had completed a homework assignment remotely close to ours. It was a powerful feeling to know what we did and the lengths it took to accomplish. They may have had PennStevez's bodies on that campus, they sure as fuck didn't have our minds.

It's been overstated that "What happens in Vegas, stays in Vegas." I'm here to call bullshit on that one. Vegas followed me home, and changed its name to Santa Monica.

During my junior year at Samo, there was no such thing as the slow lane on the Pacific Coast Highway. Pat K (my primary passenger on most of these commutes) was a best bud and fellow weed enthusiast. We had originally met in the second grade at Carden. I didn't see Pat again until junior high, and we stayed tight all the way through high school. The only things more dense than the traffic on those mornings were the pot clouds above the car as we inched along at three feet per minute.

We'd always track the California Highway Patrol sedan several car lengths in front of us, timing our bong hits and massive exhales to the precise moment we fell into the cop's blind spot. (Hand-crank sunroof the preferred exit port.)

We also had to stay alert for other Chippies creeping up from behind in the middle lane. When that happened, we were forced to hold in the massively drawn hits until they passed by (those plumes not as visible above the car, as our brains swallowed most of it).

The car was a silver BMW 320i. I talked Mom into buying it for me while Dad was on location in Canada filming *The Dead Zone*. (Told her it would do wonders for my self-esteem. It didn't.) Prior to the Beemer, I was driving a Ford Escort. (I've heard every joke you're thinking.)

The only music on those mornings: Led Zeppelin's double album soundtrack *The Song Remains the Same*. Hands down the greatest rock concert in the history of music. Pat and I had been going to the midnight showing of the album's movie version on Friday nights at a theater in Westwood, a city between Bev Hills and Santa Monica.

The helium in our dirigible for those midnight runs was bountiful amounts of magic shrooms. We tried to synchronize how long they took to kick in, hoping that first wave coincided with the opening credits of the movie. Plenty a time those fuckers went off way too early. We'd be trippin' at the concession stand, ordering things that didn't exist or trying to drink the Red Vines. At one showing, Pat was convinced that two audience members were actually John Bonham and Robert Plant, sent there to secretly watch us watching them. We'd spend the following week recovering from the muscles we pulled laughing.

Pat was a much better driver when coming down from psilocybin. I'd get us there; he'd get us home. One post-Zep evening, we parked in the middle of a short bridge near Pat's house for a sativa nightcap.

The weed was so strong, we both passed out like two hobos on free-beer night. I woke up to no Pat and many happy birds.

The community he lived in right near the PCH was beautiful in the morning. The sun's rays had transformed the tree leaves around me into a pulsing orange cocoon. I'd been out for almost five hours. Those same rays were glinting magically off the golden hunk of metal banging against my driver's-side window. Shiniest badge I'd ever seen. The cop it belonged to, much less so.

I told him a lie about the car breaking down, and me being too tired to push it to the side of the road. He didn't care and demanded the standard documents. I opened the glove box to retrieve them; that cubby was a mobile head shop. Eyeing the travel bong, he sternly asked me, "Like to smoke a little pot, do we?" To my credit I flatly stated, "I do." (My *least* expensive outcome ever involving those same two words.)

Cuffs, Miranda, and a quick trip to city hall in central Malibu. It was my first arrest. Very few sounds come close to a slammed and locked cell door to punctuate a situation.

Having my rights harshly yanked from me was a sobering kick in the teeth. I sat in the holding tank for two hours, replaying the avoidable mistakes that had landed me there. Mistakes number one and two: the sativa nightcap and the place we parked to do it. Number three was a toss-up between not walking to Pat's with him and not hiding the contraband under a nearby rock.

My parents showed up an hour later to bail me out. I played the contrite card to perfection on the drive home and well into the following week. Extra chores on my plate to go along with being grounded for a month. (On day three I negotiated that down to two weeks.) It was a time to process and reflect—to take inventory and begin to see the impact my poor choices could have on others.

In reality, I was focused on how long the unfortunate speed bump would prevent me and Pat from a return trip to Westwood on a Friday night. We both knew precisely what had to change—ingest half the normal amount of shrooms; no nightcaps, bridges, or Cheech & Chong naps.

Three weeks after the arrest, we were headed back to the launching pad. Familiar rock blasting in the car, egging on the first tinge of brain-wobble. We'd already forgotten where we parked when the melty-faced ticket taker ripped our stubs in half with cartoon dog paws. *Woof.* I remember settling into my seat with one very clear observation: Led Zep wasn't lying—the song *does* remain the same.

Senior Year. I had just completed my third summer at a place called the Mickey Owen Baseball School in Miller, Missouri. Each stay had been for the entire month of July. My final trip there I was offered a scholarship at a community college in Kansas called Pratt, a feeder school for the University of Kansas.

My grades were awful, and the community college stressed that if I could bring them up significantly, it would activate the deal. A hell of a lot was riding on whatever happened next.

I was failing biology. The frogs we carved up had a better chance of passing the class. At worst, a B-minus on the final would keep me within striking distance of the minimum credits needed to graduate. The margin for error was razor-thin. One point on either side meant the difference between a skyward mortarboard or summer school hell. I made it clear to my parents that I'd sooner live in a tent on Zuma Beach before I gave up my summer. No graduation obviously meant no scholarship.

Despite all the truancies and academic distress, I was still thriving on the mound. For the time being at least, a piece of the fake dream was still alive. (Life support *is* technically considered alive.) The Heaths informed me that a fellow student was offering the answers to the biology final for a hundred bucks. Perfect timing. I scrounged up the dough and made the purchase.

Just when a guy thinks he can't possibly fuck shit up *any* more thoroughly, that same guy surprises even himself. All the answers to that complicated test were hidden on a tiny paper beneath my hand. Having no idea what a believable completion time might be, I finished the test and walked it to the teacher's desk at the front of the class. I assumed many others would be falling in behind me to do the same. No one did.

I was the first person to finish, forty minutes ahead of everyone else. Ms. Teach (I've forgotten her name) gave me a look as I walked up, like I'd just floated in from the clouds.

I sat back down and watched as Ms. Teach began to grade my paper. Whatever plan I walked in with was suddenly and uncontrollably splat-ploding into the dungarees of regret. She waved me back up to her desk, ice-cold whisper-daggers as she leaned in too close, our noses almost touching.

"Your score is *one hundred percent*. How is this possible when you maintained an *eff* the whole year??" Spittle from the extra *F* tickled my cheek. I leaned back into her, eye contact *en fuego*.

"Sometimes a guy just gets lucky" was all I had for her.

All she had for me was a fail.

Following a few valiant attempts from Mom to find a loophole or a hint of compassion from Teach, the principal handed down his edict: A week before the playoffs began for the state championship,

I was kicked off the baseball team. The rug was yanked, and I was forced to hang up my cleats.

I remember having a bittersweet laugh with my dear pal Tony T when I asked him, "You wanna call the coach at Kansas, or should I?" His response was poetry: "Fuck Kansas. You got the whole world, C."

In that moment, I felt like I barely had that tiny patch on Zuma.

I had a girlfriend by this time. Her name is Paula. I use *is* because she's the mother of my first child in this life: an amazing young lady named Cassandra. Before we had our daughter, we had each other for a good portion of our senior year. Paula was always smart and kool and level-headed.

She told me it was useless to fight the baseball ruling and I should pour all my energy into making sure I graduated. Tie up this big sloppy loose end once and for all, and see what the next few thousand sunrises might bring.

She was right. By way of impossible luck and maneuvering (*juking* and *dipping*?), the math was still in my favor: I had 198.5 credits on the books. Two hundred was the golden ticket to cross the Rubicon. Each class had a value of five credits. One class remaining with a final exam on deck: Mrs. Farmer's English.

I was pulling a strong C and confident the last test on her farm would till my remaining acre. The exam was two days away. I needed to do something I hadn't done in ages: study for real. I stayed home from school and hit the books like I was planning a heist. I tucked away my homicidal resentments toward the small-brained principal while I focused on the one reality I could still influence. The next day, as promised, I was there early to take the English test, loaded for bare, Bayer, and bear.

In a flurry of last-minute scramble, I forgot to bring a note from my parents to excuse the prior day's absence. Twenty minutes before the test kicked off, I went straight to the office to untangle this minor detail.

The office secretary informed me in a sterile tone that without a parent-signed letter they couldn't issue a readmit. I called home. No one answered. Secretary then told me that the only person who could grant this access was Mrs. Farmer. I raced upstairs and explained my situation to her.

With a hollow tone, she said that she was "sorry" and I'd have to get clearance from the main office. The clock was counting down. I calmly explained that she and the main office were tossing me back and forth like a football, with neither side willing to make the call. If I ran down there again, I'd be in the goddam hall when the clock struck, watching my life melt into a rotting pumpkin.

I told Farmer that the path to heroism stood right before her and begged that lady to please be reasonable. Like a dead rat, the word "sorry" limply tumbled from her mouth (again).

It was the final lie I'd suffer. The bell signaled the test to begin. *I'm sorry too.*

The floodgates exploded, cut loose from a deep and painful well.

I was *Kilgore*, with napalm on standby.

I was *Willard*, with mission clarity.

I was *ME*, the kid with the best arm on the whole fukken campus.

I had been holding the thick final exam in my right hand. In a manic half second, I balled those thirty pages into a tight sphere. The last pitch I ever threw at that school wasn't a knuckleball. It was a ninety-mile-per-hour paper fastball, right down Broadway into the center of her wooden face for a perfect fukken strike.

Ballgame.

* * *

Shortly after being "razed" by the Farmer, I made the decision to crash an event that I'd been banned from attending: the graduation ceremony. I wasn't going there to cause a scene or disrupt any part of it. No, my need to attend was personal.

From my position, I couldn't actually see the ceremony taking place down in Samohi's Greek Theatre. Sneaking crab-like through the empty administration building, I was searching for a specific filing cabinet that held something I planned on leaving with: my *cum* folder. Packed into that fat folder are the *cum*ulative records of a student's entire scholastic existence, from first grade to twelfth. Months earlier, on a routine visit to the office for truancy updates, I had seen exactly where they kept it.

That overfed binder had it all—schools, teachers, report cards, attendance, rusty lunch boxes, and chewed pencils. My plan was to extract it from the cabinet and burn it on the beach that same night. The binder's mini bonfire would sage away the crud and turn the charred page of indolence.

On the final ten feet of burglar-crawl, with the beige metal tower in sight, I could hear the names of friends I'd grown up with announced from down below. Echoed pieces of surnames, reverberating off the windows like the walls of a deep canyon: "*Ander-son . . . son . . . son, Buh-rare-ah . . . ah . . . ah.*"

With a Rawlings batting glove on my right hand, I grabbed the E–F drawer handle and gave it a mighty yank. It was locked. *Fuck.* Toppling the large case to jar the drawer loose was out of the question. Too loud, messy, and foolish.

The plan was dead. Game, set, match: Samohi. (For now.) I left the building as quietly as I'd entered. A final echoed student's name, the last kick in the ass I'd suffer in those halls—"*Este-ban . . . ban . . . ban*" was close enough to "*Este-vez . . . vez . . . vez*" to guide my exit with a giant middle finger, giving me the broom.

They expected me to spend 540 days at Santa Monica High School. Too big an ask—they should have checked with me first. I left with a 1.2 GPA and a 32 percent attendance record. I was pretty drunk when I finally received my diploma thirty years later from Tony T. and Jay Leno on *The Tonight Show*. Go Vikings!

CHAPTER 14

The following morning, the breakfast conversation with my folks was brief. I confirmed that summer school was off the table and that I wanted to spend the next three months wading headstrong into the Hollywood audition waters. I promised them both if the endeavor was a total failure, I'd switch gears and go to film school to pursue a career behind the camera. They didn't hate the plan. Mom showed her support by recommending that I have a chat with her friend Glennis Liberty.

Glennis had just quit her job as the executive assistant to Robert Redford and Sydney Pollack. She told Mom she was gonna take what she'd learned from those two titans and set her sights on becoming a talent agent. With her tidy mind and engaging personality, it seemed like a natural fit.

Save for a childhood cameo in a Dad TV movie, *The Execution of Private Slovik*, I had zero speaking credits to my name. Glennis was in a similar bind, as far as actual agenting was concerned. (Can't be a talent agent unless you've got some talent to represent.) Seated in the tiny living room of her Santa Monica apartment, we made the decision to roll the dice on each other and join forces. She'd submit her paperwork; I'd fake it until someone bought my act.

A week later, Glennis was poring over a publication called *The Breakdowns*, a bimonthly listing of all the film and TV productions gearing up to start. (Casting pal of hers slipped it to her on the sly; you had to be licensed to receive it.) It provided agents and managers a precise template for their client submissions.

After Glennis took my headshot on the front lawn of her apartment building, we needed to create a résumé to go with it. I added *Apocalypse*, *Slovik*, and a bunch of school plays I was never in and had never even read. I told her I was using Sheen as my last name, and as I watched her type the letters of the new me at the top of a blank piece of paper, I really liked the way it looked.

I'd sat with Pop the week earlier and got his blessing for the name swap. It was a much smoother father-son, Estevez-to-Sheen morph than the one Dad had suffered with his old man. I told him how important it was to honor him by carrying the name forward. With Emilio already working as an actor and using Estevez, it seemed to make perfect sense that two of his sons would be checking both ancestral boxes.

What I didn't share with Pop: Using Sheen allowed me to slam the door on the recent academic and athletic failures I felt I was connected to with Estevez. I wasn't ashamed of the name, but if this was gonna be a fresh start across new horizons, I wanted to sound different when spoken of.

Glennis circled one of the film projects in the casting bible with her trusty orange Bic pen. She looked up with a rascally grin and asked me, "How do you feel about being eaten by a giant bear?"

* * *

Auditions are a trip. My very first one took place in a small, run-down office building somewhere in the heart of Burbank. It was a long way from Point Dume, and I was about to find out if I was bringing any wisdom from all that Super 8 shit. Five feet from a video camera with a blinking red light, the excitement and nerves were high but controlled. The casting lady, a likable and salty vet named Barbara Claman, was behind the camera and talking me through the actions of that giant, pissed-off bear tearing me to shreds.

I was reading for the role of Camper Number 3 in *Grizzly II: Revenge*. I had made up my mind before I walked in: There wasn't a *wrong* way to get eaten by a bear. It also helped that I grew up on horror films and knew how to die terrified. Barbara was impressed with how committed I was, though winding up on the floor and trauma-twitching as I bled out may have been a bit much. I didn't care. I had nothing to lose. We finished the scene, she thanked me and said that I did great.

What I wanted most from that small role was on-camera experience and a SAG card. Joining that union was the golden ticket. Many of the bigger films wouldn't audition or meet with actors who didn't have one. Chris had gotten *his* card earlier from the indie film *Buzzard*, and I couldn't wait to proudly show him mine.

On the drive back to our makeshift headquarters at Glennis's apartment, all I could think about was the two actors I sat with in the waiting area before it was my turn to read. One of them, Robert MacNaughton, played the older brother in Spielberg's *E.T.*, and the other guy I grew up worshipping as Peter on *The Brady Bunch*. Are you kidding me? This was the goddam playing field moving forward? What was I supposed to say to those two—"Hey guys, perhaps you caught my latest film, *Rooftop Killer*?" I felt so unimportant and underprepared, not to mention, in *way* over my head.

Glennis was on the wall phone in her kitchenette when I walked in. After many rapid-fire *got-it*s, she hung up and spun to me. Small tears in the corners of her blue eyes threatened to spill down her cheeks as she said: "Please tell me your passport is up-to-date. You're going camping with a killer bear in Budapest!" Those words would change the course of my life.

She gave me a big hug and cracked open a coupla Coors. I couldn't believe it, a home run on my very first swing. In that casting room, on that day, *The Brady Bunch* and *E.T.* had to take a back seat. Chris and the Heaths were gonna shit!

They taught us as kids if at first you don't succeed, we're supposed to try, try again. The part they conveniently omitted was if we *did* succeed at first, then what? And in doing so, do we get to keep those two "try agains," and tuck 'em away for a rainier, less successful day? (Maybe Pop has room in that sock drawer of his.)

It was June of '83. I had landed my first job three weeks out of high school. I wouldn't leave for that job until October, giving Glennis and me the entire summer to see what else we could pry loose from this amusement park of chance and wonderment. I was in the game, and to the best of my knowledge, no one was asking to see my high school diploma.

Things were starting to cook as I made the rounds. Three or four general meetings or auditions in a single day became the norm. The instant juice I had from booking *Grizzly* sent up a signal-flare to the Hollywood casting community. There was a curiosity in the air.

Glennis was sharp and efficient. She dug into the Rolodex from her time with ex-bosses Redford and Pollack. Her outreach was impressive, her expectations realistic. She wasn't calling Spielberg and telling him Camper 3 from *Grizzly II* should be the lead in his next blockbuster. She knew a slow build, with the right choices, was the way to go. (Little bit of luck here and there didn't hurt either.)

Following another *bizzy* day of auditions, I stopped in at Chris's house to see what he was up to and give his parents a hug. Before I could exit my car, he came bursting out the front door, clutching a script and shouting, "This is the greatest fucking thing I've ever read!" The script was *Ten Soldiers*, written by John Milius and Kevin Reynolds, with Milius set to direct.

Chris went straight past hello and launched into one of the scenes for a driveway performance I swear they could've filmed. The pages were smothered in his madman-style notes, which included stick figures shooting guns. Speaking with such passion for the character of Robert, he seemed convinced they'd written the role with him in mind. I forgot to hug his parents and raced home to call Glennis with any of the film's details I could give her.

Three days after that, I was in a meeting with John Milius at his office in Century City reminiscing about *Apocalypse Now*, a film he wrote. It was the first time we'd ever met. By the end of the meeting, with *no* audition, Milius asked me if I wanted to play the role of Matt, the younger brother to the leader of the student rebels, in *Ten Soldiers*. I told him I'd be honored to do so. The title was eventually changed to *Red Dawn*.

I had my second job: a legit, big-studio action movie, with the man who also created Clint Eastwood's *Dirty Harry* franchise. My situation was changing so quickly, I felt like I was in someone else's dream. We'd film in New Mexico a month after I finished the killer-bear flick. Chris wasn't cast in the role of Robert, and I know it broke his heart. I was very careful around him, keeping my *Red Dawn* excitement respectfully contained. Everywhere else, you'd find me high-fiving anyone with a hand.

Los Angeles has never really been known for her nightlife in the same way New York is. That said, certain areas in LA's grid are known for a type of nightlife that requires a near-unattainable membership. Living up to her nickname, the Queen of the Angels made sure I found out the hard way how steep those club fees actually were.

I'd been tagging along with Emilio and his group of newly fame-minted work pals as they hit the town night after night. They were an all-star lineup of Rob Lowe, Demi Moore, Judd Nelson, and Andrew McCarthy. Rob's fiancée Melissa Gilbert was a steady presence as well. I was rolling with the "it" group, from the most popular films of the moment: *Breakfast Club*, *St. Elmo's Fire*, *The Outsiders*, to name a few. As a group, they couldn't have been nicer to me; it was the gauntlet of hysteria they incited that had me constantly seeking shelter.

As soon as we'd exit the limo, I'd be relegated by their screaming fans to the role of stray dog, bringing up the rear for their crowd-parting, bar-hopping rambles. The night always began at the Hard Rock Cafe, then sashayed its way across the landscape of the *gotta-be-seen* popular hot spots. I felt so small and left out as I watched the Emilio-steered throng, redefining what a copious and decadent bask in the limelight could look like.

Chris was a passenger as well on many of those nights. We were oarsmen in the same unknown boat, providing cover and comfort for each other when we needed it most. All of that changed when his film *Footloose* came out and was a giant hit, sending him *overnight* to the other side of the velvet rope. That one hit me the hardest—my best friend in life was suddenly *one of them*. I was torn between hoping he was ready for it and knowing deep down that he wasn't.

As those nights escalated, I remained an invisible valet carrying the bags for a clob of celebrity that had the masses hypnotized. I wanted to be told just once by their babe-squad that I mattered too. Knowing it wouldn't happen until *my* celebrated film had a line around the block required a patience I hadn't developed yet. To be in the crush of LA's insane mid-eighties club scene with Rob Lowe and a bevy of gorgeous gals was like being shipwrecked with a fat guy—you're gonna starve.

Feeling like an afterthought in those vibrant settings lit a fire in me you could see from the fukken moon. My inner bear had officially been poked.

The final audition that summer was for a film called *The Karate Kid*. My reading was nerve-racked and "stammery," and even though I left there looking for a pier to jump off, I did find it extremely kool to have gone on tape for John Avildsen, the man who directed the global smash *Rocky*. If I'd somehow done enough to plant myself in his head for something else down the line, the day wasn't a total loss.

In keeping with our rhythm, I'd meet Glennis back at her place to review my pit stops from her day-planner and, more specifically that afternoon, try to explain to her why I didn't bring the best *me* to Avildsen's casting dojo.

That time she wasn't on the phone; she was on her patio, scanning the street for me when I pulled up. Glennis couldn't contain herself when she spotted me. (My first thought was that someone had died.) She ran straight at me, almost babbling with excitement, fast-explaining they wanted me to start karate training on Monday. *Hold on a second, today's Friday, so . . .*

"Yes kiddo, congrats! You got the job! You're gonna be the Karate Kid!" She then stated: "We gotta get you out of *Grizzly*. There's a conflict with the dates."

There would be no more poking. I needed something a lot stronger than a Coors.

During the three days that I had the lead role, Glennis was pretzeling her brain to find a loophole that would allow me to trade my evil bear for a mystical sensei. While she was combing that side of the path, I went to Pop and asked him what he thought was the smoothest way to get out of my *Grizzly* commitment.

Without hesitation, he said I already gave them my word, and as a result I had to stand tall and honor it. Pop stressed that developing a reputation as someone who lives by that credo would generate the type of long-term respect one big film couldn't deliver. I knew he was right, and it pissed me off. I heeded his advice and called Glennis with my decision.

After a long walk by herself through her neighborhood, that classy lady with an identical credo agreed with Pop. The summer of awesome had its first shit sandwich. My *Karate Kid* line that would've stretched completely around the block was gonna have to wait.

With the big job gone and *Red Dawn* months away, I began to wonder how I was gonna pay the bills with a pocket full of honor. In the end, Ralph Macchio was perfect for the role, and his performance was brilliant. Go get 'em Ralph, I have a bear to feed.

Going on location in Budapest felt as old-hat as it did trial-by-fire, a topsy-turvy of uncharted yet familiar waters. A huge bonus on the trip was how quickly I bonded with my two costars, George Clooney and Laura Dern. (Can't script a more dynamic early brush with *I knew them when*.)

Flying in coach together from LA, George and I got an early jump on the bonding. Many rounds were on us, as we knocked the wheels off the drink cart. We turned the Beatles into a sextet, singing along way too loud to their greatest hits cassette tape in my Sony Walkman for nine hours. (Clooney has a pretty good voice.)

Having barely unpacked at our charmless hotel, the future matinee-idol slid perfectly into the role of protective older brother for Laura and "groovy step-uncle" for me. (I add *step* because George is only a few years older.) Clooney's other role: our de facto team leader. Hungary in '83 was still behind the Iron Curtain. George would keep the riffraff at bay when we'd go out at night, and find hot food when Laura and I couldn't. Not many folks can claim George frikkin' Clooney as their personal bodyguard on foreign soil.

Laura was the youngster in the group by about a year. The daughter of legendary actors Bruce Dern and Diane Ladd, Laura came from an on-set upbringing similar to mine. She had instincts that can't be taught—doing things on film the same way you'd do them alone in your kitchen. The first time we read a scene together, her dialogue had such an ease to it, I couldn't tell the scene had started. She was clearly paying close attention all those years to the brilliant work her folks were creating. Our teachers in life don't always have to be robed and ancient. She was a treat to be around.

George and Laura were a romantic couple in the film, my character Lance the proverbial third wheel. (The writers felt bad for me and gave Camper 3 an actual name.) The production kept delaying our scenes, which we wound up filming on the final two days we were there. The three of us rewrote all of our dialogue. Given the title of the film, you can only imagine the turds on the page we had to flush. With the limited English skills of our director, the one and only André Szöts, those edits didn't encounter much resistance.

During the downtime before we filmed our scenes, I received a call from Glennis regarding *Red Dawn*. MGM wanted me to screen-test for the role of the older brother in the film. A move like that back then was a way for the studio and the director to make sure they didn't miss something obvious. I still had the role of Matt secured, and regardless of the outcome, the screen test couldn't derail that.

The bigger news on the call: MGM was offering a three-picture deal. If accepted, I'd be under contract with them for two films guaranteed after *Red Dawn*. The salary for *Red Dawn* was scale but would jump to $100K if I signed the deal before filming began. The two films to follow (unspecified, and both with my creative consent) had guaranteed salaries attached to each one: $200K for the second film and $300K for the third. (At the time, I was making two grand a week on *Grizzly*, for a total of six kay.)

The amazing opportunity was a lot to process. I ran to George with the great news, and he was thrilled for me. We sat in the hotel bar weighing the *pro*s of the deal with glorious amounts of Hungarian whiskey. I don't remember a lot of it, but according to George the next morning, we never made it to the *con*s when they asked us to leave.

The next night, all three of us got eaten by the bear. For the record, George and Laura went first.

CHAPTER 15

It was a short two weeks at home following *Grizzly* before I had to leave for *Red Dawn*, and I still hadn't decided about the MGM deal. MGM was calling Glennis, she was calling me, I was looking for Dad.

Before I dealt with that, I made a conscious decision to let John Milius know I hadn't been miscast. I intentionally flubbed the screen test and hung onto the role I knew I was better suited for; me as the older brother trying to lead that group into battle would have been laughable.

Milius had written the famous line for *Dirty Harry*: "A man's *got* to know his limitations." I knew mine, and there was no better a time to honor those words than with that screen test. The Jed role went to Patrick Swayze, and we followed that dood into every battle.

With that behind me, I was still pondering the multi-picture deal. Dad told me I'd regret it when the studio forced me to do films I hated and couldn't get out of. I had to wonder if Pop was superimposing his own *Apocalypse* baggage on top of my situation. Years prior, he refused to sign the seven-picture deal that Francis insisted all of his talent commit to. Dad wasn't having it, telling FFC he needed to remain a free agent.

I know Pop's heart was in the right place. I took his advice and told the studio I was passing. Glennis couldn't believe her ears when I revealed my decision to thumb my nose at guaranteed work, and *that* much dough. We didn't speak for a week.

To this day, Dad never signed that contract, nor did he ever work with Francis again. After *Red Dawn*, MGM sent me to the same cornfield.

Gotta hand it to *Apocalypse*, the fukken gift that just keeps on givin'.

We nearly froze to death filming *Red Dawn*. Three months in a place called Johnson Mesa, a two-hour drive into the mountains that overlooked Las Vegas, New Mexico—the "other-Vegas," as we grew fond of saying.

The bitter chill in those windy mountains brought the cast much closer together. The misery in our case didn't just love the company, it created it. In addition to Patrick Swayze, the frozen cast included Lea Thompson, Harry Dean Stanton, and Jennifer Grey.

Two actors in the film I bonded with the strongest (and still regard as great friends) were Darren Dalton and C. Thomas Howell. Darren and Tommy had worked on *The Outsiders* together and were good friends when I met them. They went out of their way to make sure I didn't feel like just that—an outsider.

On set our trio was known as the Three Musketeers—hardly original, but the camaraderie and loyalty we shared supported the nickname. Ironically, the friendships I developed with the actual *Musketeers* (when I starred in that film years later) didn't measure up to what I had with my *Red Dawn* pals.

The Plaza Hotel was the place we called home during the shoot. The original broke ground in the 1840s and had undergone a host of facelifts over the years. In addition to the hotel's vintage charm, rumors about it being haunted swirled among the locals for decades. In Lino's pool hall across the street, we'd hear bits and pieces of the paranormal tales. We didn't give it much thought—we were too busy chasing other spirits.

For most of the shoot, the windchill was minus eighty, the actual temperature thirty below. Appearing miserable on camera in that environment required no acting. Growing up in balmy Malibu didn't help—having another friendly face from Malibu did. By pure coincidence Brown Dave's dad, Lance, was the key makeup man on the film. Two years earlier Lance had his first big break when he helped design and build the monsters for the remake of *The Thing*. His work blew our minds when Dave and I saw the movie together in Westwood on a Friday night. Not bad for a career electrician who woke up one day, said fuck it, and joined forces with FX makeup legend Stan Winston.

I started every day in Lance's makeup chair, and most of our conversations were about Dave or the icy-cold weather. We rarely spoke of Malibu; it just made us miss it that much more. I was thrilled to be working, but it still woulda been nice to feel my legs for most of the shoot. Dave visited the set several times and always felt bad when it was time to head back home to Malibu, knowing firsthand the conditions his best friend and father had to keep working through. (Five years later, on the large meadow atop the promontory where Point Dume was named, I was the best man at his wedding to actress Heather Langenkamp. For reasons none of us could ever figure out, Heather would get residual checks in the mail from *Red Dawn* for the next twenty-five years, in amounts that ranged between fifty cents and a dollar. Dave's set visits must have somehow found their way into her coffer. We'd always laugh when the three of us were having a meal and I'd say, "Dave and I will split the bill, and Heather's *Red Dawn* backend can pay for the ketchup.")

In a near blizzard white-out during a complicated sequence, the boom operator was trying to vampire-pin a lavalier mic to the inside of my camo-jumpsuit. His hands were so numb from the cold, he wound up anchoring the small mic to his thumb instead. He didn't realize he'd done so until I pointed to it. (The blood froze before it could run.)

During the combat scenes, an occasional piping-hot spent shell casing from a machine gun would find its way inside our wardrobe—scalding whatever skin it touched. As painful as that sounds, the instant heat from those sneaky blanks was almost welcomed.

The one person that didn't seem bothered by the weather was our director, John Milius. Given his passion for surfing, he was the last dood I expected to brave it like he did. I'd spot John mid-chaos, directing the action in goggles and a giant coat, like a conductor who'd traded his orchestra for bombs and mayhem. I got the sense if one of those bombs found him with a direct hit, he'd be going out exactly as he'd planned. The enormousness of his zeal was that of an anarchist poet sculpting his masterpiece with a flaming saber. We loved him.

When we weren't freezing on the set, The Three-Muskas were also loyal to the bar. (Not a lot of carding at The Plaza. The film was too valuable to their humble establishment for a little detail like underage patrons to stand in the way.)

Even then, I could pour it down with the best of 'em. My new pals caught on pretty quick that trying to match me chug for chug was an endeavor best reserved for cops, or pirates. Celebrating the completion of our first day on the movie, they quit drinking early; I didn't, and one double-whiskey at a time descended into a sad puddle of dismay.

That descent had to do with one scene in particular we'd finished earlier in the day. I was in Swayze's truck being dropped off at school on the day of the invasion. A few beats after Milius called *action*, the Stutter-Ghoul hit my brain like the face-hugger in *Alien*. The panic was instant, the fear lung-trapped. *(Breathe, Carlos, we've been here before.)*

A common trick is to add a bunch of "umms" in front of dialogue that gets stuck. Patrick was classically trained in *everything* and must have thought my "sorta words" were specific character choices not found on the page. Milius didn't say anything, and we finished the scene as best I could. It was a nightmare that I kept hidden—choked it down, like I'd done many years earlier. I wanted to scream the sun into a blackout. With that off the table, I drank myself into one instead.

Tommy and Darren didn't know the truth behind what I was actually hiding from in the bottom of those bottles. I never found the courage to say it out loud. In my defense (drunk or not), how the heck was I gonna explain, "By the way, an old foe from third grade dropped in for an unexpected visit"?

The ghoul didn't stick around past that first strafe in the truck. Made its presence known just long enough to put me on notice. That's the craziest thing about the mysterious syndrome—it creates a full-time job, having to behave like some type of sentinel to ward off its back-alley stickups. I never knew when it was coming, and I never *truly* knew why it showed up in the first place.

Be it handling weaponry or falling in love, bringing a scene off the page with any sort of passion is already difficult enough. Not being able to say certain words or sounds shouldn't be a part of the process—it's one of the main reasons I learned to drink like I did.

The magic juice would hit bottom, warm away the clench and shackles, and give that fucker the night off. The fantasies I built as a kid watching Leo and Eileen Penn dispense their woes with that same magic liquid were now my reality. They'd given me "the fix" a decade in advance. But it's no secret—every surefire solution comes with its own set of variables. I couldn't access that *fix* in the arena where I needed it the most: a film set. That was the one place where I drew the line, with no plans to cross it for a very long time.

At some point, everything's negotiable.

CHAPTER 16

Following *Red Dawn*, I didn't work for seven months. Auditions and general meetings thinned out considerably. I wasn't expecting a parade when I got home, just some quality face time with a few directors, making films that mattered. I asked Glennis if there were any updates on a film I'd read for called *The Platoon*. She told me there were none, politely reminding me what a disaster my audition was. (No need to rub it in; hard to forget Oliver Stone basically telling me that I sucked.)

I began to wonder if the town's chilly reception had anything to do with my passing on the MGM deal, or, even worse, if it was connected to my drinking or stuttering. If that were the case, Glennis would've known and sat me down. (I only *fuh-fuh-fucked* up one scene and was never hammered on the set.) Getting lost in the paranoia was useless. Getting used to the sound of crickets, a little less so.

It was during this downtime that I started seeing my high school ex-girlfriend Paula, for the late-night physical benefits. (Besides Candy in real-Vegas and the *L.A. Xpress* on Pico Boulevard, Paula was all I knew.) Her mom had a two-bedroom flat on the second floor of a building near Samohi. Paula's room had a fire escape just outside of it that I'd scale for our late-night trysts.

That went on for about a month until we dropped the birth control ball, and Paula clocked back in as a plus-one. She had just turned nineteen; I was eighteen. Not exactly the life direction, at that moment, either of us saw for ourselves. I pleaded my case, but she held firm. After a goodly amount of soul-searching, I came around a bit later.

On December 12, 1984, sometime in the late afternoon, Paula gave birth to a healthy seven-pound baby girl named Cassandra. An absolute gift to humanity. I didn't attend the birth. My "a bit later" didn't turn the corner until after the new year. We've been good since—for the most part. (Not being fukken married probably helped.)

My trusty shroom-mate Pat K was lassoed into the babysitting duties with me. We stumbled through it together while Paula attended night school. There were no shrooms in the mix, yet we did partake in the occasional bong load on Paula's patio once Cassandra had fallen asleep. (With all the carrot puree we scraped off our clothes, ya can't really blame us.) Pat was an absolute trooper and I'm sure he'd say the same about me.

My parents were extremely helpful as well during those early years, and not just with their time. Their resources filled the gaps I couldn't manage financially. Whoever penned the phrase "It takes a village" would've been kick-ass proud of our lineup. We kept the *I* out of team and set an example to be emulated gracefully.

The karma-gods took notice a few months before Cassandra was born, finally rewarding me with a job: a teen suicide TV movie *Silence of the*

Heart. My costar was Chad Lowe, a dear pal from childhood. He and his older brother Rob lived five houses away from me on Point Dume. Rob was a good friend as well, yet never to the extent as the connection I shared with Chad.

Chad's one of the good guys, and we helped each other a lot during those early lean times. He'd clue me in on projects I was unaware of, and vice versa. Chad was wholly responsible for my involvement in *Silence*—a gesture that saved the day. With a baby on the way, I was grateful for whatever work I could land.

As much as I loved working with Chad, that TV movie wasn't exactly the barn burner I envisioned as the best career follow-up to *Red Dawn*. Thankfully for me and Chad, our performances were celebrated and the subject matter revered. (It also led to my first magazine cover—a flimsy *TV Weekly* Mom still has proudly framed at home.)

They say that work begets work. Shortly after *Silence*, the traveled adage made good on its word: I landed the second lead in an indie film, *The Boys Next Door*, with Penny Spheeris directing and Max Caulfield as my costar. We played two misfits on a road trip to LA who wind up on a killing spree. Max did the killing; I was caught in the crossfire. It opened on a limited number of screens to mixed reviews and did very little business. Even when a film doesn't burn down the box office, you never know who's gonna see that flick, or how it can influence the plot twists of life.

Mom wound up framing another photo: one featuring me, Dad, and "His Airness" Michael Jordan. It looked like the kind of photo they take at an amusement park when you pose with a cutout of a famous person. The moment was captured during an episode of a short-lived

TV show called *War of the Stars* that Dad and I took part in. It was hosted by Dick Van Patten for ABC, with a theme of pitting actors against pro athletes to compete against them on their turf. The impossible card we happened to draw came in the form of Michael Jordan and a three-part competition that culminated with a two-on-one. We beat him in free throws, he *destroyed* us in horse, setting up the rubber match for all the marbles.

Like I kept telling Dad during our practices, "If we spread the floor, MJ cannot guard both of us at the same time." We did just that, he was unable to, and I hit the winning shot: an eighteen-footer from the corner. Much like that shot, being able to share the court with the greatest ever was an opportunity that magically fell outta the sky. That game wasn't just about having bragging rights for life; it was about what it represented at that stage of my journey. If the Gods weren't fully smiling on me yet, they were certainly grinning. I just had to make sure whatever smirk I offered back was good enough to fool them.

The limo ride with my parents heading home from the Jordan game was a lot different from the one driving there hours earlier. On the way back, we spent thirty minutes confirming that what had just happened was real and not an outrageous group dream. Once the pixie dust lifted, the fact that it happened on camera in front of a packed gymnasium of screaming high schoolers was alibi enough. MJ was pure class and a great sport, the way he handled being defeated by the short Sheen doods from Malibu. (He did have to shoot his free throws with his eyes closed, but c'mon, he's Michael Jordan—he's *all-seeing*.)

As much as the three of us wanted to keep the limo celebration on tilt, I had work to do and Pop was gonna help. I'd landed a small role in a film I'd be shooting in a few days and needed his input. To get a feel for the rhythm of the scene, we did a cold read that was stumbly at best. Before I had a chance to ask him about a few beats I'd highlighted, he gave me the palm-forward, eye-level, Dad-hand of *shut-it*: "Don't change a thing. What you just did is *exactly* how it needs to be played." When I explained that I'd really done nothing at all with the words, he cut me off again: "It took me thirty years to learn how to do that." I threw a look to Mom, and her eyes urged me to follow his advice. It was settled; I had my marching orders. I spent the remainder of the ride back to Point Dume hoping the director was also gonna be on board with Dad's thirty-year *nothing*.

The title was a bit odd, and the first time I heard the words Ferris Bueller's day off all strung together was from Jennifer Grey, my adorable *Red Dawn* costar. Already cast as the moody sister, she called to let me know that the director, John Hughes, loved her idea of me for the role and asked if I could make the three-hour drive to their location in Long Beach for an audition. I hugged her through the phone and said, "Count on it." I was really touched by the unexpected gesture. Jen's a doll, and one of the best eggs in the carton. She put her neck on the line with a Chad Lowe move and teed it up for me to shine. (The film biz used to be an altruistic one.)

From the edgy description of my character, I knew there was only one person sittin' on the accessories I'd need to complete the wayward delinquent look: my brother Ramon. At the time, he was in the deep end of a punk-rock phase and had all kinds of shit tucked away in that Black Flag closet of his. I wasn't wrong—it was packed with darkness and Ramon was eager to lend a spikey gloved hand.

On audition day, I drove the trusty Beemer to Long Beach decked out in his motorcycle jacket and boots, complete with cigarette ash under my eyes from Monie's Davidoff Longs. My brain was also decked out, with the scene perfectly memorized to let the brilliant John Hughes know I wasn't an amateur who just looked the part; I was an actor fully prepped to wow him.

The plan was to audition for John during the lunch break in the middle of their shoot day. I arrived at the location fifteen minutes early and was barely outta my car when I spotted Hughes walking briskly across the parking lot. I made my approach, he didn't break stride, I fell in next to him. I had decent small talk on standby about meeting him with Emilio at a screening of *The Breakfast Club* but never got a chance to spring it.

He took one short glance at me and, with clipped enthusiasm, said with a grin, "You look great kid, we'll see you in a week," and kept right on moving like a man with a full plate and no time to eat. The interaction was *so* brief, I'm not even sure I thanked him. The joyous shock from landing the gig in seven seconds turned me into a statue; I watched as he moved farther away to be joined by two PAs wearing radio headsets as they disappeared into his trailer with him. I remember thinking, *I hope Ramon's next mosh pit isn't anytime soon.*

The night before my one day on the film, I wanted to replace the cigarette ash with real fatigue and stayed up 'til 2:00 a.m., with an alarm clock set for 5:00. It went off, and like a moron I hit my internal snooze button for the next two hours. In a fukken panic on the freeway, I tested the outer limits of the Bavarian four-cylinder and still showed up two hours late.

As soon as I pulled into the parking lot, I saw a different lone figure in the distance and my knotted gut added a sheepshank. *Fuck.* When I finally walked up, the Jen waiting outside my trailer was a lot more "moody sister" than she was egg carton. Rightfully, I suppose, she let me have it at full volume. (Pretty sure "pathetic amateur" was the central theme.) I took my medicine, Ms. Grey finally stormed off. If nothing else, I gave her all the anger and disdain she'd need on camera in the police station that morning. After I rushed through makeup and arrived breathlessly on set, the first person I encountered was John Hughes, and with Jen's colossal undressing still ringing in my ears, I was cowering for more. That man walked right up to me, keenly shook my hand, and said, "Oh good, you're here. Let's get started."

And so we did.

"Drugs?"

I didn't think about *The Platoon* again until a family dinner in the summer of '85. Emilio proudly announced to everyone that he'd landed the lead role of Chris in *Platoon* and was headed back to the Philippines. Sheepishly (and stupidly), I asked him if it was the same film as *THE Platoon*, hoping like hell that it wasn't. He informed me that it was.

I congratulated him, and I meant every word of it. It was a big move for my brother, and I knew he was gonna kill it. That same night, wide awake and staring at the ceiling in my bedroom, I made a sacred promise to myself: I was gonna do whatever was needed (short of murder or extortion) to one day be in the same chair as Emilio—making an announcement of equal significance. I saw his happen live, and I could "taste the air" drenched in its value. Go do your thang, E, I'll be right behind you.

With the country teetering on edge and threatening to close its borders, Oliver's *Platoon* deal fell apart a few months before the Philippines departure. It would be a full year before he was able to strike a new deal with a different finance company. During that time Emilio had booked a couple gigs, presenting a potential conflict with the new dates. Oliver couldn't wait for my brother.

Whatever I'd done in that first *Platoon* audition (that had me tossed like a used diaper) must've left a speck on Oliver's lapel. He called me back in for a second audition. I kept it very simple—trying like hell to *not* try like hell. When I finished, all he wanted to discuss was my time in the Philippines during *Apocalypse*. Specifically the weather and whatever insights I could share about the work ethic of the local crews.

Oliver was a hard man to read, so I took his curiosity as a great sign, thanked him for his time, and left. Shortly afterward, Oliver called Glennis, telling her he had to do some homework before he made his decision.

He reached out to Spheeris to have a look at *The Boys Next Door*, David Seltzer to do the same with *Lucas*, and finally John Hughes for *Ferris Bueller's Day Off*, which hadn't yet been released. Critics and box-office grosses could fuck off; those films revealed a hidden value I would've never predicted. I was no longer the awkward kid he'd met a year ago who couldn't find his voice or rhythm. I was instead the awkward kid with a decent amount of film on him, who wasn't coming in as "green" as the character of Chris Taylor. (I'm fully hep to the irony.)

I wish I could tell you exactly where I was, and what I was doing, when I got the call from Glennis with the great news about *Platoon*. I cannot. I also wish I could share with you what the conversation was like between me and Emilio after I received that news. Can't do that either. The *only* detail I can recall with absolute clarity is the sit-down I had with Pop before I gave Oliver my final answer to the offer.

Citing everything he'd been following in the news, Dad told me that the film wasn't worth risking my life for, strongly urging that I decline the offer. Had it not been the *third* frikkin' time his advice was asking me to trade an amazing opportunity for the fear of the unknown, I might have tuned in more responsibly.

I told him if I didn't throw caution this time, I might never get to experience the consequences of autonomy and the freedom of risk. We shared a long hug. Pretty safe to say I picked the right time to declare, "I got this." We broke from the hug, and I couldn't help myself when I added, "Don't forget; I'm the guy who hit the game-winner over Jordan. The Philippines should be worried about *me*."

CHAPTER 17

"Saigon. Shhhit. I'm still only in Saigon."
—CAPTAIN WILLARD, *APOCALYPSE NOW*

"Manila. Shhhit. I'm actually back, in frikkin' Manila."
—CHARLIE SHEEN, *PLATOON*

I was already pie-eyed when I landed in the Philippines for my second tour. The fifteen-hour flight turned into a soggy airborne frat party, hosted by Johnny Depp and myself. (He had the role of Lerner, the platoon's interpreter.) As thrilled as I was to embrace a solid new friend, I made the mistake of trying to match Johnny booze-wise. That handsome fucker drank me under the tray table. (My *Red Dawn* pals Darren and Tommy would be glad to hear that I'd finally met my pirate.)

I abandoned my first-class seat to spend hours in coach with Depp, so he could chain-smoke at the back of the plane. I remember watching him slaying cig after cig, and while he *did* look James Dean–kool doing it, I stayed proud of myself for never picking up the hateful habit. (Those fifteen hours in the air would be the last time I flew anywhere as a nonsmoker.)

I'd just worked with Depp's girlfriend, a gorgeous starlet named Sherilyn Fenn, on a dog-shit sci-fi mess in Arizona called *The Wraith*. I mention it because it's one of the many awful movies I did on *both* sides of *Platoon*. The money they threw at me for those absurd projects was so tempting, I became greed-blind to how pathetic the scripts were. If I could do it over again, I'd have taken out a loan or slept in my tiny car. No one had a clue the film we were about to start would become what it did.

Upon our arrival at the Manila Garden Hotel, production informed the actors that we'd only be there for two nights. After which they'd ship us out into the bush to go get Method. Those two days were barely enough time to stash our crap, have a few hot meals, and enjoy a real bed for the last time we'd be in one for a while.

In my hotel room and knowing that time was not on my side, I opted to steal a page from the annals of Emilio and Fishburne, circa '76. Their stories over the years from these magical islands during *Apocalypse* created so much curiosity, I went ahead and arranged some female company from the concierge.

Nine minutes later, two local stunners were knocking on my door. (Were they staying at the hotel?) Faultless doesn't begin to describe their beauty.

So that's what Larry and E were always on and on about back then. (Well played, gentlemen.) Those two final nights of freedom were a naked jet-lagged blur on the vodka express to Elysium.

It was 5 a.m. In an hour I had to be downstairs ready to go, wearing the army fatigues they'd given us when we checked in. My hotel room looked like a plane crash. I was lucky at that point to be in possession of one olive-drab sock. The two beauties were incredibly helpful on that front. They organized what I needed for the trip while I showered—then hopped in the steamy enclosure with me. I remember thinking, "I've come a long way since *balut*." Our time was up; duty called. We would have all exchanged numbers but none of that shit existed yet.

Before any of us Yanks had a chance to gather our bearings downstairs with a hot cup of coffee, the entire cast was corralled into a sterile, overlit room off the lobby to be yelled at for an hour by a very serious man in uniform. The fun was over. We'd just met Oliver Stone's secret weapon.

Still reeling from the thunder of serious-man's evisceration, the whole platoon climbed aboard an ancient sweltering bus at 7 a.m. for a bumpy three-hour trip to the middle of somewhere, in the heart of nowhere.

The Philippine jungle at night can feel like the darkest place on earth. Not knowing if the object four inches from my face was a person, a tree, or an animal created a new brand of tension—primal, raw, silent. Those spectral shapes and fears lived within breathing distance every night of our crash-course boot camp for *Platoon*.

The rigorous preparation experiment was the brainchild of that serious-man-in-uniform: retired Marine captain and decorated Vietnam veteran Dale Dye. (Great guy, I just didn't know it yet.) When the film was announced, Dye approached Oliver with the pitch that if he wanted maximum realism, a pre-film training camp was the only way to go. He gave Oliver his word that the actors would emerge from his Borstal looking and sounding like real soldiers.

Oliver bit and gave the plan his stamp of approval. He knew his own input as a Vietnam vet would add immense value to whatever the

Captain was cookin' up. Over the next three weeks, we would be at the mercy of the Dye that Oliver cast.

If it was in the script, we learned it by living it. If any technical dialogue was confusing to an actor, that person became *not* confused very quickly. If a weapon was unfamiliar, that firearm became your best friend.

Every hour of every day (and most nights), Dye saddled us with challenges of mind and body. On the more intense body-days, ours were taken to the absolute brink. Humps (military hikes) in 115-degree heat and full gear ranged anywhere between five and fifteen klicks (military term for kilometers). The only water on a hump was the amount our standard-issue canteens could hold. Mastering the sip became a game of survival. Either intentionally, or because we got lost, we wound up one day on a twenty-five-klick hump.

Forest Whitaker lost close to thirty-five pounds during the training. Oliver was worried because Forest was playing a character named Big Harold. Woulda been odd to have to call him Sorta Large Harold.

We were depersonalized by only being referred to as our character names—in the camp, on the set, at the hotel. It left no room for anyone's ego or diva bullshit. When you suffer as a unit, you bond like one as well. By the end of the first week, I felt like I'd known *all* of those men for much longer than the calendar insisted. "Camp Dye" was the nickname Depp and I gave that hellscape. We never shared that with the Captain. Didn't feel like he needed any more motivation to kill us. This was already making *Apocalypse* feel like a five-star vacation.

It was 2 a.m., halfway through the grueling twenty-one days, when Corporal Drew Clark fired a palm strike into my shoulder, jolting me awake. (He was one of the three badass retired Marines handpicked by the Captain to intimidate us through every crucial detail.) I'd been asleep in the foxhole I dug ten days earlier. Clark's face was two inches from mine and painted in tiger camo. With a *shhh* finger to his lips, followed by military-precise *this way* hand signals, he led me through the dense darkness.

The other twenty-six members of the platoon (along with the brass) were sound asleep. No doubt enjoying the first night of training that didn't involve the staged camp raids or "three-on, three-off" night-duty lookout drills we'd do all night. Panther-like, Corporal Clark led me through the terrain of Luzon's lowlands to an outpost about a quarter mile from our training camp that I didn't know existed. The small, four- or five-room thatched building was manned by several members of the Philippine Constabulary, their version of the MP (Military Police).

The country was in such political upheaval with President Marcos finally out and his successor, Aquino, barely in, the military had split in half—giving rise to bands of guerrilla fighters, who struck randomly on a variety of targets.

If one of those factions stumbled onto our makeshift basecamp, they'd see thirty weathered grunts in army fatigues with M16s, .45s, and two belt-fed M60 heavy machine guns. Good luck explaining to them our little movie and fake bullets.

I'd come to find out later, the location of our training basecamp was specifically chosen for its proximity to that protective outpost. Nice to know the powers that be were thinking ahead; terrifying to know they needed to.

The commander of the unit greeted us with a giant smile and a cooler of ice-cold San Miguel beer. He'd been expecting us. Corporal Clark had set this up well in advance. I couldn't have been more grateful.

Up to that point we'd been living on MREs (meals ready to eat) and warm bottled water. The modern-day C-rations were good for energy, I suppose, but not much else. Unless you were fixing your roof and needed bulletproof meat, I didn't see a ton of residual value.

The aroma of grilled chicken from their compact mess hall inspired thoughts of me joining their unit. It was the best meal I'd ever ingested. (Sorry Mom.) Drew ate his in three bites, then shotgunned a beer and smashed the can violently into his granite forehead like a potato chip. The crowd roared.

It was 3 a.m. at that point. Reveille was at 0500. We had ninety minutes to make the most of it and still have time to re-enter the camp undetected. We both knew if we got caught, we'd be doing midday burpees for the rest of our lives.

I quickly dumped three beers down the hatch—with a goal of six. The fourth beer turned into a speed-chug between me and Drew. Beat him by half a second. Marines aren't supposed to lose drinking games. He was impressed. (My boozing skills by then had evolved to a place that didn't need to be encouraged or celebrated.)

Somewhere between beers five and six, I wound up at the ping-pong table they had, in a spirited game with the commander. (The ping-pong theme again, popping up in the most unlikely scenarios.) Beer haze aside, the two of us stayed evenly matched to the tune of eighteen-all, the sandpaper paddles heightening the speed game we both preferred.

I thought back to O.J. and what a classless bully he was, denying the kid-me a moment I'd have cherished forever. I wasn't playing a child, but I still knew the goddam life rules. My opponent lived in the jungle and opened his home for us in the dead of night. There's a time to win and a time to *read the room*. The **bold** typeface of that night's page was written on every wall: That fukken dood had a loaded Colt .45 on his belt. Final score: Commander 21, Chris Taylor 18. (*My* O.J. hand-swap was an internal one.)

The Marine corporal and I made it back to base camp and beat the bugle by seven minutes. During physical training (P.T.) after breakfast, Drew was right up in my face, screaming "sissy-maggot" to encourage my efforts. He was playing his role perfectly, dispelling any vibes that we'd bonded just a few hours ago. I had a splitting, no-sleep beer-migraine. As far as the rest of the camp was concerned, it was business as usual, with the United States Marine Corps reminding the pussies from Hollywood what fukken time it was.

Oliver would visit us every few days at Camp Dye, spend an hour or two, then leave. We didn't have a whole lot of communication with him on those visits. He was checking in on Dye's master plan for two reasons: to make sure he hadn't gone too far, or to see firsthand if he hadn't gone far enough.

Toward the end of our second week, we humped ten klicks at 0700 to an abandoned structure that sat ominously in the middle of a hidden clearing. It seemed to be some type of ancient rec center, hit with one too many typhoons. Oliver was waiting for us there with our maverick director of photography, Bobby Richardson. (He'd become the first non-union D.P. ever nominated for an Oscar.) There was a long table with thirty chairs and a script at every seat. This was our table read, a chance for Oliver to hear the script out loud for the first time with all of his talent.

I was nervous as hell but decided to go for it and meet it head-on.

Other cast members seemed to perk up when they saw how intensely I had committed to the read-through. Oliver pulled me aside afterward and complimented the passion I tapped into.

He seemed jazzed and it felt like I had his respect.

Time would tell how long I could keep it.

Our basecamp was a hundred yards across in both directions, with a ravine at the foot of it that led to a dense, unwelcoming tangle. We had a mountain range to our six and a dead forest at the base of it. At the top of the clearing sat the only structure in the meadow: a twenty-foot military tent command post for the brass to steal shade and study maps—and drink. *("Oorah.")*

Another member of Dye's crew was a man named Stanley White, our gunnery sergeant, or "Gunny" if he liked you. A Vietnam vet and close friend of Oliver's, Stanley was an active thirty-year veteran of the L.A. Sheriff Homicide Division. He was also the inspiration for a film Oliver wrote, *Year of the Dragon*. Knowing that Detective White was part of the team Drew and I had evaded on our beer-pong night added some heft to a story already packed with future lore.

Just below the apron of the clearing, the self-dug foxholes we lived in dotted our quaint meadow. From the air, those holes must have looked like a mortar barrage that ended some forgotten unit's day.

The foxholes were known as "hooches"; the dood you shared it with was your "hooch-mate." The guy who played Rhah, Francesco Quinn, was my hooch-mate. He took himself a bit seriously, but we did manage to pull some laughs from him.

I had the only wristwatch between us: a stainless Concord I'd bought in Westwood with my Ferris Bueller dough. During lookout duties, I'd roll the time forward and wake Francesco up twenty to thirty minutes early for him to begin his shift. He'd always ask, "Are you sure?"—at which point I'd raise my wrist to his face, displaying the Concord's phosphorescent proof. That ruse became some of those laughs I pulled from him. Every night.

To round out my lodging wing in the dirt-neighborhood—one foxhole over from ours was Depp's, and right below him was Kevin Dillon in his pit. Tom Berenger, Willem Dafoe, and John C. McGinley's burrows were on the other side of the command tent. When we weren't on a hump or in weapons and formation training, we stayed in our holes to rest. It was too hot, and we were too tired to do anything physical that wasn't mandatory. The vicinities of the foxholes played a hand in which platoon-mates we all built the strongest friendships with during that early phase. Location, location, location . . .

A hooch or two past Dillon was Corey Glover, who played Francis in the film. (Of course I'd wind up with a Francis back in the Philippines; how could I not?) He shared a hooch with Keith David, the actor who played King. Corey would sing his way through the endless humps, normally a move that'd be met with "Shut the fuck up" from the Marines with us on the trails. Not for this guy—his pipes were golden, his tunes rich and bluesy.

It was the only soothing element on those hikes for any of us. I pulled him aside one day and told him he should really follow that brilliant voice of his to wherever it leads. Corey explained he was the lead singer of a small rock band he formed with his pals in New York a year earlier. That "small" band became Living Colour. They sold millions of albums and won a Grammy. Being front-row-center-jungle for Corey's earliest gigs was the most hard-won ticket I ever copped for the koolest show in town.

One thing our camp never suffered a shortage of was cigarettes.

One person who relied on their steadfast availability was Johnny Depp. Anytime there was a breeze, my dirt-hole was downwind from his human Marlboro chimney. Ramon smoked when we were teenagers, and I'd grab the occasional puff of his imported Davidoffs. Didn't grab me back then, so I assumed I'd be able to take it and then leave it—again.

Depp began to offer the cigs more frequently; I began to accept them less cautiously (usually after P.T. or a meal). This went on for about a week, with Johnny's strange glee around it growing by the day. He finally clued me in—he had successfully converted one nonsmoker on each of his previous three films.

Oliver wanted me to smoke for the character. A perfect storm was forming just off my nonsmoking shores, which only added to my dilemma. Depp had his man, Oliver had his character detail, I had the nicotine curse. (When I finally quit smoking on the Fourth of July in 2019, I did the math and figured out that I had smoked *twenty-five miles* of cigarettes when lined up tip-to-butt. Thanks, Johnny; should I ever need one, I'll send you the bill for my new lung.)

By the middle of the third week, we were moving fluidly as a platoon. Each man fully connected to his responsibilities within the unit. Every piece of equipment we carried, accessed deftly in pitch-blackness if needed. The weapons we toted, from the exotic rocket and grenade launchers to the standard M16 workhorse, became extensions of our senses.

The tension was high as the camp was nearing its end. No one had showered the entire time or had any contact with the people they cared about the most.

I could see and feel a shared frequency of simmer in all of us. I watched Forest W, insane with thirst, as he tried to line up his machete on the fresh coconut he'd found in a grove we had stumbled into.

He had so much sweat in his eyes, his vision betrayed him as he reared back and drove the blade downward, straight *into his thumb* on the steadying hand. The metal against bone was audible. He dropped everything and slammed that hitchhiker into his mouth to stem the bleeding, hoping it was still attached. I watched in horror as two thick red blood-snakes shot out simultaneously from both corners of his clenched lips and all over his boots. It was a fukken mess. He's a terrific guy; I felt really sad for him. All he kept repeating as he pain-danced in a circle: "I *knew* I was gonna do it, I knew it, I knew it, I knew it." His manic distress spoke for all of us in that moment.

We had a couple of days left before "graduation"; two unique missions, one on each day, blocked the path to our infantry tassels. The first one was terrifying for most of us. We stood at the base of a *ninety-foot* wooden tower, staring up at the top platform, which the Captain expected us to rappel down from. That same distance from home to first looked a lot shorter on a baseball field. We could hear the weather-beaten structure creaking loudly as a steady wind shifted it slowly back and forth, five or six inches with each opposing breath. Almost like it was haunted and doing the crying that none of us were allowed to.

The three Marines were on the top ledge, all roped up and ready. Mark Ebenhoch and "Rock" Galotti stood on either side of Drew, with Gunny White and Dye on safety-belay down below. Dye yelled, "Go!" and in perfect unison those three lunatics flew off the ledge face-first and *sprint-rappelled* down the side of the tower. Their boots barely making contact with the tower walls, the *hiss* of the rope zipping through all six gloved hands. It was nuts. They landed to crazy applause and chants of their names. Drew unclipped, looked at all of us, and explained, "That's known as *Aussie style*. You pussies get to take your time and *bounce* your way down, backwards. Good luck, dipshits." Classic Drew. Bad, bad dood.

Dye and Corporal Galotti climbed the ladder back up to the top—to await the entire platoon and when it was *our* turn, talk us through it. We'd go one at a time, alphabetically by character last names. I was near the end of the roll call with that *T* of mine.

I watched one soldier-actor after another, and waited nervously. The cast members we expected solid showings from didn't disappoint. I could make the argument that Berenger's inner-character rage intimidated the structure into compliance. The tower ceased its yawing in the moments it took Barnes to ace it. Dafoe's grace and sinew from years of trained dance floated him to the ground, as though he'd cut a deal with gravity. The only trouble anyone got into was Forest, when he lost his footing and was stuck dangling upside down, forty feet off the deck. (My man was havin' a rough week.) They calmly lowered him; he was fine.

I couldn't help but notice that they skipped *R* for Rhah on the way to me. Turned out, Francesco was the only one of us who wouldn't give the tower a go. Dafoe took exception. I think that's the day their troubles with each other began. (Cue dramatic organ chord.)

Knowing where Forest set the bar acrobatically, my confidence was in pretty good shape to get up there and *just do it*. From the top platform, Dye would have us look into his eyes, then quietly say, "Push off the ledge." And I did. And it was incredible. For one minute. About halfway down, I came to a stop fifty feet from the soil, found Dye's eyes again, and delivered the line that was repeated by everyone for the next month: "The bouncing's not gonna happen, Sir." (The guys had a field day with that one.)

I tiptoed the next hundred steps it took to make it to the ground. Style points aside, I was proud of myself. The tower-rappel remains the only time in this life I engaged in that specific activity. Whatever it took to get me outta that camp and onto the set, I was gung ho to put in my rearview.

Graduation Mission 2: The Final Assault. The platoon was divided into three units, with each group ordered to meet up fifteen klicks away at the predetermined coordinates, where an intense simulated firefight would take place. The idea being, we'd have an opportunity to put everything we'd learned in the past three weeks on display—see how we responded in real time, making snap decisions with lives on the line. Dye stressed before we geared up and headed out, single fire *only*, no weapons set to full auto. Ammo preservation was key.

Wish I could tell you who the hell was on each team. The heat had a way of searing certain memories into the bedrock while melting other details away forever.

It played out with Berenger's team arriving first, Lieutenant Wolfe (Mark Moses) and his team getting completely lost, and my team being ambushed by the Marines. A lit and fuming smoke grenade came arcing from the tall grass, landing a *balls-eye* right into my groin. The pain of the impact flung me to the ground, the shock of it sent me past the treetops. Volleys of gunfire erupted all around me. The canister was still wedged in my crotch, off-loading its contents like a homemade Roman candle. I rose up inside the brain of a madman and sprayed the tree line with a full mag of automatic gunfire, screaming: "DIE MOTHER-FUCKERS!" Over and over, loud enough to be heard back in Manila. I had reached that place where few return from unchanged.

An early sign of the gathering "stare-scare" storm.
New York, 1967.

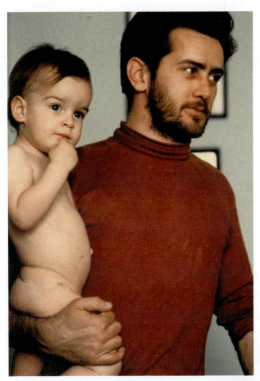

Dad's famous red shirt.
I hope he had more than one.
New York, 1965.

Mom's famous striped blouse.
My outfits must be in the washer.
New York, 1965.

"So if it's already Wednesday, that gives me 5,000 days to build my plan . . ." Circa age 4.

Dad with his boys and bombs on *Catch-22* in Guaymas, Mexico, circa 1968.

Quickly Carlos, Manson is still on the loose, so blow out those four candles and get your ass to Malibu. 1969.

Working on an early tough-guy look, circa age 8. "Camping" evidence on the clothesline at the new house.

Whatever Emilio put in my brain that day; might explain *a lot*.

Mom paid me fifty cents to sit for twenty minutes while she drew and painted my portrait. She did all four kids as a birthday gift to Dad in Colorado during *Badlands*. I was seven years old, and it feels like she could already see me as a young adult.

With an airport in the background, ⅓ of the Gypsy Express either arriving or departing.

Apocalypse with Dad, after a trip to the on-set Ifugao dentist. 1976.

Walking with Roman Coppola toward Reno's car, at KurCom. "Taxi!" 1977.

"The heads, you're lookin' at the heads. Sometimes he goes too far." Beheadings and Orange Crush—a perfect combo! 1977.

That's a *lot* of Montagnard warriors—good thing there's no shortage of mud. 1977.

Our "wishing days away" trip to Hong Kong. (I wanna see "my" photo.) Hong Kong, 1977.

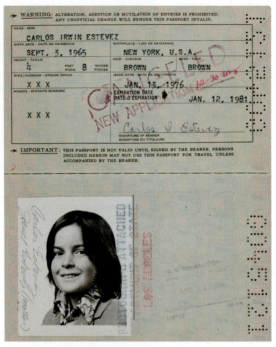

With my hair and that shirt, I look like John Bonham riding shotgun on the Partridge Family bus. 1976.

The early academic warning signs already visible as a delinquent theme was doing its best to establish a future trend, 1977. *Tonight Show* here I come!

PERSONAL DEMERIT COLLECTION

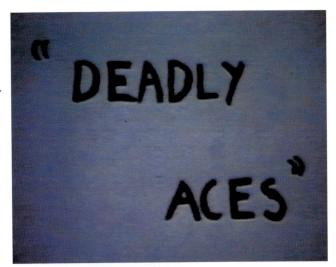

The Jacks were pretty lethal too. Title card from a PennStevez production, 1977.

A wounded but determined Chris Penn goes all in to reclaim the pot. (From the poker game, not the gully.) 1978.

Best place to hunt down a *Rooftop Killer* is with Steve Heath from ground zero: the shingles.

Bringing that PONY league "lit fuse" with really nice form. Welty beware.
Circa 1978.

Yeah. These mechanics fukken suck. As stated, my value was from the bump.
Circa 1978.

Number 5 on the Little League Astros. My "gully-joint" hat worn properly and Brown Dave in the back row far left, number 1. (He sure was.)
Malibu Little League, 1977.

That's gone! One of my "church" days during Promises.
Self-taught lefty, I'll not explain later. 1998.

BOB MARSHAK (RIP) XOXO

Final day of junior high with Rat-Packer-in-training Chris Penn, Bryn P, and half of the Heaths (the powder-blue Steve half), 1979.

With Mr. Vincent. No wonder he cried at my intervention. 1979.

As an eighteen-year-old, working on either a camera or a gun in my bedroom at home, surrounded by my film heroes.

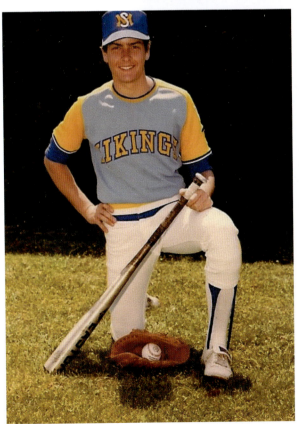

Go Vikings! I still have that Mizuno GIC-5 glove! (Oh wait, it might be an XFCB 17 Tom Seaver wing tip. I don't still have that one.)

One of our fake ID photos. Ya can't make this shit up. CHRISTOPHER SHANNON PENN

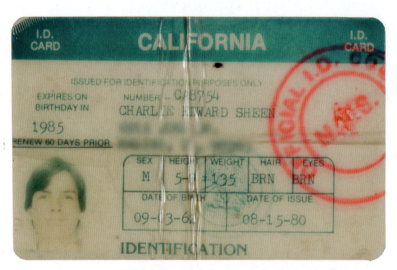

One of our actual fake IDs. I mentioned the shit lighting in those parlors, but I also spoke to the Super 8 cut and paste passion Chris and I relied on. Looking at this mess, it's obvious the cash was all that mattered.

As '80s "yearbook" as it fukken gets. Special thanks to the Men's Wearhouse. 1983. SAMOHI

Prom Day with Paula P, at the original "Malibu Lake," 1983.
RAMON ESTEVEZ

The "headshot" on the Glennis front lawn that lit the lamp, 1983. G. LIB

Most likely résumé #2, which makes those absurd theater-and-film lies even more egregious that I left them on there.

CHARLIE SHEEN

Height: 5' 10"
Hair: Dark Brown
Eyes: Hazel
Age: 18 - 25

FILM

"RED DAWN" — Starring role. Played the part of Matt. Written and Directed by John Milius.

"THE PREDATOR" — Co-starring role. Played the part of Lance. Directed by Andre Szots.

"APOCALYPSE NOW" — Extra, "Doh Long Bridge" Scene. Directed by Francis Ford Coppola.

"EXECUTION OF PRIVATE SLOVIK" — "Wedding Scene" - part of Joseph. Directed by Lamont Johnson.

"ENIGMA" — Extra - Scene where youths are demonstrating in front of museum. Directed by Jeannot Szwarc.

"MAN, WOMAN & CHILD" — Extra, "Picnic" Scene. Directed by Dick Richards.

THEATRE

"THE BOYFRIEND" — Santa Monica High School - the part of "The Boyfriend."

"ALICE IN WONDERLAND" — S.M.H.S. - part of the "Cheshire Cat."

"ANTIGONE" — S.M.H.S. - the "interpreter".

"OUR TOWN" — S.M.H.S. - part of "George."

BURT REYNOLDS DINNER THEATRE

"MR. ROBERTS" — Understudy - "Ensign Pulver"

"CUCKOO'S NEST" — Bill Bibbit

Contact: Glennis Liberty (213) 393-5078

After I'd calmed down and the threat had moved on, I lied and told the Captain that I peed blood behind a tree. He took it very seriously and ruled me out for the remainder of the mission. I lied *again* and told him how sorry I was to not be able to carry on and support my fellow troops. I was okay accepting the reality that I was done. Enough practice. We had a movie to make, and it was game time. Check that: Kickoff would be delayed even further. Our efforts had earned us a proper send-off.

That afternoon, we had a graduation party that carried deep into the night. Before it went off the rails, the Captain had each man walk up, activate his salute, then stand at ease in front of him. For the benefit of all in attendance, Dye put on quite the show. He listed our training highlights *and* shortcomings, with his great humor and peerless military wisdom. He capped off my shellacking by telling me, "Taylor: you're the *only* pencil-dick I've ever seen wear his fucking *shades* while on point leading a platoon." (It was the day after the midnight beer-run with Drew; they were Vuarnet.) We all received a special medallion he pinned to our lapels. With a snap-crisp final salute and heartfelt *congratulations*, that "serious man in uniform" declared us graduated—the first and only time in this life I'd ever achieved that status (ninth grade doesn't fukken count).

The *simmer* we'd all been carrying was finally and mercifully replaced with something else: *relief.* The respect and appreciation Dye had earned from all of us couldn't have happened anywhere else, in the way that it did. It was real, and it mattered. I could see in his thousand-yard eyes, that same respect went both ways.

Gunny White had managed to get his hands on a case of local spirits known as *lambanog*: Philippine palm liquor. That shit is so strong it's been rumored to make people go blind. Not blind-drunk, *actually* frikkin' blind. We were a thirsty group and drank way too much of it. I passed out and woke up hours later with the soirée still in full swing. (The guys were kind enough to cover me in a poncho to protect against the mosquitoes.) Everyone was still hammered when we woke up the next morning, most of the men coming-to near their foxholes.

It left us with hangovers I can't put words to as we went on our final hump, ten klicks to the bottom of a ravine. We'd have company on the other side of that ravine. What felt at first like a lambanog group-hallucination, wasn't. Fifty feet away from us stood Oliver with his small splinter crew. The cameras they manned were already rolling. A different type of ambush for sure.

Oliver wanted footage of us the exact day we said goodbye to "Camp Dye." The vision of Ollie with his equipment was a magnificent sight. Regardless of our lambanoged condition, it was one that let everyone know it was time to fight his war.

CHAPTER 18

*P*_{latoon} was filmed in perfect chronological order. My first day of shooting was the first scene in the movie; the final day of production, my last. It remains my only film experience in forty-three years to incorporate that approach. It was a brilliant decision by Oliver. It gifted the actors an opportunity to build a performance in such a way that we never had to remember what had led up to that day's work or decode how we were supposed to feel about a moment that hadn't yet happened. As the characters in the story grew weary and emotionally shattered, the actors did as well. Oliver had us marching inside of a timeline that didn't need to be explained to us; we were living it from one day to the next.

The first "motel" we stayed in, outside of a place called Los Baños, had dirt floors. While it was only a slight upgrade from the foxhole, I was so grateful to be in the tiny, hard bed they offered. It was the only lodging near the location we'd be using the following morning. The work at the airfield to capture my arrival in the film, as well as our first basecamp, went off without a hitch. Oliver was instantly pleased with my subtle choices in the scenes, which he labeled "effortless."

Back at the motel that night after work, a few of us got together and explored the small town we were in, settling into a few bars throughout the evening. We called it quits at midnight, and I was up and at 'em by 4 a.m., for the five o'clock pickup for work that morning.

We spent the whole day filming a complicated sequence, with the entire platoon on a jungle patrol, where at one point they covered my neck in red ants. (I'm bug-phobic; they were angry and weren't people-phobic.) With Doc (Paul Sanchez) trying to help out, I wound up fainting from heat exhaustion as a solid "button" to the scene.

The detailed coverage that was needed (close-ups and insert-shots) to introduce nearly every character ate up most of the day. Again, Oliver was thrilled with my work along with everyone else's. The first pieces of a puzzle he'd yearned to assemble for his entire adult life were fitting together perfectly. His excitement was contagious.

We got back to our humble digs just after sunset. The film's producer, Arnold Kopelson, was waiting for me outside my motel room. He proceeded to inform me that word had made it back to him about "you and the guys out late, tearing up the town." I had to stifle a chuckle that would have been right in his face. (This man clearly had a different take on tearing something up than I did.) He followed that with "You're not on film enough yet to not be replaced." (Didn't see it as a good time to scold him for the double negative.) Kopelson finally cleared my path, leaving me with a warning that felt like he'd rehearsed it in the mirror a few times: "We're watching you."

Message received, Mr. K. (Didn't realize we were in a spy novel.) I knew exactly where this was coming from. It began back in Arizona on the film I spoke of, *The Wraith*. I finished that movie and had only ten days before I left for *Platoon*. As much as I hated *Wraith*, I *loved* the dear friends I made while filming it: Clint Howard, Dave Sherrill (better known as White Dave), and Nick Cassavetes—a noble trio who fully embodied the art of tearing things up. Our shared commitment to "when in doubt, chug" *did* push the boundaries on several occasions.

One of the *Wraith* producers, a tragic busybody (I'm being polite), went out of his way to get ahold of Oliver behind my back and inform him that he'd hired the wrong guy for *Platoon*. That "this Sheen kid" was gonna bring him nothing but grief. It created a huge stink for me. I found out later that Johnny Depp was the runner-up for my role. If a swap was to occur, Depp was already there and prepped, having gone through the goddam training camp. (The cigarette plot *thickens*.)

My loyal agent, Glennis, had to put on the gloves to put out the fire. Oliver never brought it up. He had daily proof there were no red flags. Kopelson, on the other hand, was waiting for anything as slight as me biting into a piece of brandy-filled chocolate. I did the most prudent thing the situation called for: I ratted Arnold K to the platoon. Let them know early on, he wasn't on our side. Fuck with one, fuck with all. (Moving forward, at the bars, I started hiding my booze in coffee mugs and Coke cans.)

As the shooting progressed, and the scenes turned the pages of our very lean script, Oliver and I would spend an hour or two every few days after work recording the narration. He wanted the voice-over to have the same resonance as the rest of the film: desolate, battle-worn, homesick. The only other person with us: our sound man, Simon Kaye.

We took our time; we found its truth. I loved the process. Simon won an Oscar.

* * *

We still had a full night of work ahead of us in the underground bunker with the stoners and a difficult monkey. While we awaited a perfect sunset, Dafoe was having a rough time with the irascible capuchin on his shoulder in the scene. The damn thing was biting, hissing, and shitting everywhere, ruining take after take. Willem is one of the most patient and kind individuals I've ever spent time with, so for him to be up against it says a lot about how much effort the "organ grinder" required.

Willem was outside the bunker set, decompressing from the monkey stress in a low lawn chair, his boots perched on a dirt berm for elevation. Francesco Q was in a chair similar to his, slightly raised and facing Willem, just off his seven o'clock. I was a chair over, looking through the dialogue for the scene that night.

The only words I heard from the instantly heated exchange between them were: "Monkeys are easy" (Quinn) and "You idiot fuck" (Dafoe). I turned to get a fix on what was brewing, just in time to see Francesco cock his right leg back (while still seated) and fire the heel of his combat boot into Willem's face. The next piece of the action flew forward at ten frames per second.

That boot was the only free cheap shot Quinn would land. Dafoe exploded from his seat in a lightning lunge, twisting Francesco violently from his chair and slamming him to the ground like laundry. As lovely a man as he is, Dafoe displayed a level of insta-rage and danger I'd never want to be on the receiving end of. (I'd need a boat oar and a twelve-gauge.)

The "rescue team" of Berenger, Dye, and McGinley jumped in to pull them apart. Many bodies, tons of adrenaline. Dye was able to finally restore order. He pulled Quinn behind the latrines away from everyone and had a dialogue with him none of us would ever be privy to.

Dye then gathered the rest of the platoon, away from Francesco, and told the lot of us, "From this moment forward, Quinn is ostracized." To quote Hopper, from KurCom: "And he *meant* it." Rough day for Dafoe, rough day for all of us. Willem had a cut on his chin they were able to conceal with makeup. Outside of that, he was in solid shape. We still had to film the entire stoner-bunker scene, with both of them in it. (A crucial plot *exhale*, where both "camps" within the platoon enjoy their final moments of calm and joy.) Oliver and Dye came up with a plan that kept Quinn and Dafoe out of each other's shots. Off-camera dialogue between them I'm sure was read by Susan, our amazing script supervisor.

Francesco attacked all of us when he did that. He assaulted what we stood for and what it took to build that camaraderie. The jungle is a terrible place to unpack one's narcissism. I hope he got the help he needed after he left the Philippines. I hope the rest of his journey was a bit smoother, before he left the planet.

In the movie, it's New Year's Day 1968. The collection of scenes that spanned the next eight days of filming, to "ring in" that year, were insanely difficult for me, in both performance and subject matter. It was the baker's week from hell. Sal and Sanderson (Richard Edson and John Glover) get blown to shreds gathering intel that's rigged to a booby trap in an enemy bunker. Sanderson stumbles past me in shock, missing both arms. Manny (Corkey Ford) is abducted during the night, then strapped to a fence post with his throat slit, for all of us to discover. Seeking revenge, we infiltrate a village, where I force an amputee (who's also developmentally disabled) to "dance" by firing my M16 into the ground near his crutches. (Both conditions, the actor's reality in life.) I then have to watch in disbelief as Bunny (Kevin Dillon) clubs him to death with the butt of his rifle, as the boy's grandmother begs him to stop. In that same village, Barnes (Tom Berenger) tosses a white-phosphorus grenade into an underground hooch where a family is hiding, killing some and maiming others. He then executes a Vietnamese lady in front of her husband and daughter, because he's convinced she's hiding North Vietnamese munitions. Elias shows up and attacks Barnes in protest of the killings, unwittingly setting his own murder in motion. The decision is made to burn the village to the ground, and as we're all departing, I take it upon myself to thwart the hideous gang rape of a teenage girl by my fellow soldiers.

Kevin and I felt so bad for the kid we did that painful scene with, we pooled our per diem together and gave him all of it. Might have been close to a thousand dollars. If we'd had more, it woulda been his. His smile lit up the entire set as he wrapped us both in hugs of gratitude, with some of the fake brains still stuck to his battered forehead. Not a dry eye watched that moment unfold, ours included. Eight days, eight fukken days . . .

I was raised in these environments, always knowing how to separate make-believe from reality. This was different. My ability to maintain that distinction was becoming more difficult with each passing hour.

A few days later I was under the stars with Elias talking about losing the war. The words in that scene didn't just relate to the characters on-screen, they carried a telling weight for both of us. That was page fifty-seven. We had a ways to go.

* * *

The second half of the film would function between three remaining locations. We'd taken up residence by then in a decent hotel called Puerto Azul in the municipality of Ternate, a couple hours outside of Manila.

I had been seeing a gal named Dolly Fox back in LA before I left town for the jungle. (That's her actual name and she fully lived up to both sides of it.) Absolute knockout, really sharp, with fun and classy energy. She was also a few years older than me, which (for some reason) made her even sexier. Ms. Fox came from a set of highbrow parents and would keep me up to speed with the cultural "happenings" in her neck of the woods, the Big Apple.

On a staticky phone call with her, I jokingly asked if she wanted to come visit me halfway around the world. She didn't see any humor in my request and was on a plane two days later. Had to tip my combat helmet to her adventurous spontaneity. A legit test for both of us, to see if our LA sparks would hold up against the real heat just north of the equator.

I wasn't sure how the guys would feel about this move, or if Oliver would see it as a distraction or an asset for me. Thus far, coming home to a warm presence after work hadn't been anywhere close to our brutal landscape. I was nervous as hell about it—a new face in an established vibe always runs the risk of disruption.

Dolly was set to arrive on a Sunday, our first day off in nine days. The team plan we'd been constructing all week was to start with an all-hands raging pool party until the setting sun kicked us over to the hotel bar.

The night before all of this, a familiar face in a familiar place showed up for take two. Arnold Kopelson was (once again) blocking the door to my hotel room after a very long day. Since his last appearance, any fears he'd been coerced into having had worm-turned their way into a complete 180. Arnold hadn't lodged a single complaint since his threat. He was over the moon with the film and my performance. Given how wrong of a foot our relationship got off on, it was a huge relief to be on this side of the ball with him. He was back at my door, asking if I wanted anything from home.

I studied him for a few seconds, an assortment of impossible requests flying across my inner TV. I kept it within reason, and within the category of food: "How 'bout some hot wings from the Hamburger Hamlet?"

The Hamlet had been my favorite eatery since I was a kid, their wings prepared like no other. After high school, and throughout the early days of work and auditions, I spent so much time at their Westwood location, my friends dubbed it my office.

Arnold broke into a knowing smile and said, "I'll see what I can do," gave me an Alan Hale Jr. salute, and disappeared into the night. It was 8 p.m. in the Philippines, and Dolly was arriving in the morning.

I needed sleep, a lot of it. The person knocking at my door at 7 a.m. didn't get that memo.

It wasn't Dolly—it was Arnold's wife, Anne. She introduced herself as she handed me a weighty, bow-tied, white plastic bag. A sudden flood of Louisiana spices consumed my brain. I couldn't believe it: Hamlet's hot wings had traveled 7,000 miles to the Puerto Azul. "Courtesy of the Kopelsons," she proudly announced. Mrs. K was instantly and forever a rock star and an angel.

A few hours later, Dolly Fox was in the Philippines. We were really happy to see each other. Before her rolling luggage came to a stop, she was already sniffing the air. We'd been to the Hamlet together back home, and she immediately recognized the aroma. The pool party was in two hours. Dolly and I didn't spend that time eating lukewarm hot wings.

Seated at a long table, with no less than twenty of us drinking and carrying on, Dolly was the guest of honor and the belle of the ball. The amount of good-natured, biting humor the platoon pelted her with would have sent most packing with tails tucked. Not that girl. She was built for it, matching wits with just as much bite.

She clicked instantly with everyone, from Ivan Kane and Paul Sanchez (Tony and Doc) to Johnny Depp, the self-appointed president of her fan club.

Any concern over Dolly's visit evaporated the moment she sat down. This new face in our established vibe couldn't have been more welcomed. (Didn't hurt matters one bit that the new face was also really easy on the eyes. To a man, the guys were really proud of me.)

The wings, you may be asking? I took my chances and brought them with me to the gathering. Both boxes vanished into a hodge-podge of gratitude and wet-naps.

As the party moved to the bar, it morphed into a going-away bash for a few of our teammates. Shooting the film in chronological order did come with one downside: saying goodbye to the actors and friends who had just died in our story. That was the deal. Oliver didn't allow anyone to linger. When someone's time was up in the movie, that person was flying home as soon as Claire Simpson (our Oscar-winning editor) declared none of their footage to be damaged. Oliver wanted all of us to experience the feeling of loss from one instant to the next. It was jarring; like everything else, we just had to swallow the sadness that came with it.

Dolly's arrival, when it happened and how it did, was a huge morale boost for all of us. It felt like she brought with her a hope of sorts—that the real world and the people in it we cared about would still be there when we finished. We were so isolated, so painfully cut off from anything familiar, any glint of it was the charge we needed to stay glued to the process.

Monday was on us in a blink. The battlefield that day was dark, muddy, and loud. We got pinned down in a crossfire, because Lieutenant Wolfe (Mark Moses) misread a map and radioed an air strike directly on top of our position. I've had better Mondays.

The scene was intensely complicated. The first shot covered nearly eighty yards, with fifteen or twenty high-impact explosions wired into the jungle floor every ten feet, to go off on specific cues. We walked the route ten times then rehearsed it five. The effects team planted tiny six-inch yellow flags where all the bombs were located. When Oliver's bullhorn called "action," all of those flags were gone. It's about memory at that point, and a little bit of luck. Adrenaline has a habit of fucking with both.

The first take was as planned—total chaos. Crawling through the mud, dodging intense bombs, moving past characters howling in pain from different stages of injury. Sgt. Warren (Tony Todd) had it the worst—he was lying on his back trying to cram his intestines back into his gut. The explosions were ear-splitting. When I hit my final mark in the scene and Oliver yelled "Cut," I was yelling too.

My back was on fire. It felt like a piece of flaming peat moss from an effects bomb-tube landed down the nape of my fatigues. Still in character after *cut*, our Doc (Paul Sanchez) ran to check on me. I would have preferred the flaming moss to what he discovered. When

I dove to take cover behind a tree, my back sheared off the top of a frikkin' anthill. The angry bugs went nuts, fanning out from my butt crack to my neck. Pauly was a mensch, not stopping 'til he swatted and picked away every last one of 'em. Our "ant-scene" from the first act was now my hideous reality on steroids. (*Better Mondays* indeed.)

I wasn't the only actor rooting for Tuesday's arrival. My man with the voice, Corey Glover, hadn't clocked the bomb-flags as carefully as I did. He landed inches from one as it detonated and was badly shaken up. They tended to him as best they could afterward. Problem with that sort of thing, there's always a second take that needs to happen. Oliver had multiple cameras simultaneously filming the sequence. Close-ups and wide shots occurring in unison. Swapping someone out for a stunt double was out of the question. It was us, or it was no one.

During the next take, I paid much closer attention to that fukken anthill than I did the tiny yellow flags. Neither one got me. Corey wasn't as fortunate. Once the yips grab ahold and fear leads the charge, confidence hightails it. He didn't wind up as close to an explosion in that second take, but close enough was all it took. He had to tap out. *Shell-shocked* was a term I only knew from *Merriam-Webster*; seeing it firsthand was something else entirely. Corey was in a daze—trapped just outside of our reach, still tethered to the combat trauma.

Thankfully, finishing that battle sequence didn't involve his character. We only had a few more shots we needed to grab, to get everyone back on the freedom bus and hotel-bound for the night.

In a small clearing that sat just above the "jungle-alley" where the friendly fire kicked our asses, the scene winds up in a standoff. I'm hunkered down behind a fallen tree trunk; the NVA fighter trying to kill me is in a spider hole. My last-ditch solution would involve baseball, taunting, and hand grenades. (All we were missing was the Chevrolet.)

I remember Oliver's words verbatim: "I wanna see the great ball player you claim to be, and not some fuckin' pussy from Malibu." That was all I needed to hear. It was a blind toss with the grenade, the target easily forty feet away. I had to gauge the distance off of *feel*, as my view of the hole was blocked by tree stumps and elephant grass. *Eat this, Oliver. Malibu sends its regards.*

The first take was a perfect strike into the spider hole. The baseball term that came to mind for that level of accuracy—*dead-red*—couldn't have been more fitting. Take two: an identical result. Ollie was thrilled. It was a satisfying note to close the day on.

I needed to get down to the team bus, to check on Corey and see if by then he was anywhere close to exiting the woods. I took the empty seat in his two-pack, near the front. Such a good dood, really hard to see him that fractured emotionally. I didn't get the full impact of how deep it had hit him, until he finally tried to speak.

His usual eloquent and velvety speech cadence had been replaced with a stutter so severe, each word took about twenty seconds to chop its way out. It was shocking. The first thought that came to me was one that couldn't be said out loud. (Time and a place, right?) That thought being: *How 'bout that—I'm not alone.*

Dolly didn't spend a lot of time with me on the set. She was really mature about respecting my need to bring a different level of focus on certain days. A harder truth to express was that I didn't know her well enough yet to be comfortable with her watching me work. Anyone with an athletic background can relate to how much better we tried to play, or how kool we wanted to look, when a pretty girl was in the stands.

The film's final assault was creeping up on the schedule. The work was going to be difficult and dangerous. Dolly solved my diffidence for both of us by booking a flight to Hong Kong for a few days while we filmed those scenes. (That's where the slightly older bonus came into play—sexier isn't always defined by good looks.) It was the same flight I'd taken with Mom and Renée a decade earlier. I knew a little about how relieved she'd be feeling during take-off. I hoped other feelings would make her want to come back.

In our story, the main perimeter gets overrun. We become completely outnumbered. The chaos and carnage suffered on both sides is relentless.

In the daytime calm before that terrible storm, I had a scene with Keith David where he gets word that his papers came through and he's heading home. His farewell—being airlifted away in a chopper, screaming, "Adios, motherfuckers!"—remains one of the greatest film exits in cinema history. Watching him leave the jungle that day had everyone torn between the sadness of seeing him go and the jealousy that it wasn't us.

The massive perimeter-breach takes place at night. Signal-flares of various colors painted the combat action below in a macabre radiance as they floated back to earth. It was an endless three nights, trapped inside a fire-dance of perdition. Francis and I were in a foxhole by ourselves when it becomes obvious it's time to vacate the premises. An RPG screams into the hole and blows it to hell, as we barely make it out alive. Exposed and frantic, we drop down into a different foxhole twenty yards away to piece together a final stand.

As I jumped over the sand-bagged ridge of the new hole, I twisted the shit outta my ankle. There were way too many elements in play to stop the take. Bombs going off, flares and tracer-fire in all directions, background soldiers darting through the frame. There's a time to wave it off and a time to play hurt. On one shaking leg, with "pussy from Malibu" still fresh in my ego, Taylor has crossed over to that place where heroes forget how to die.

As my gunfire cut down one NVA combatant after another, I ad-libbed, "It's fucking beautiful, man!!" Francis right alongside me, reaching for and finding dangerous parts of himself he didn't know existed. Oliver finally yelled, "CUT," bringing the insanity to a much-needed halt.

He loved the dialogue I added, was curious about its origin. I told him it was a direct homage to Tom Cruise, lifted from his movie *Taps*, when he loses his mind at the end of the film, right before he dies. (Since Tom—one of the koolest guys ever—was good friends with Emilio, I was able to share the moment with him a year later; he was extremely flattered.)

The ankle was really starting to throb. Oliver explained that he only needed one more shot from me and Corey—a quick cut when a grenade lands at the lip of the foxhole and blows me down into the mud. I told him I probably only had one take left in me, and the sooner we could do it the better. They set it up, and Oliver yelling "action" was my final memory for the next ten minutes. In an identical situation to Corey's a few days earlier, with the bum wheel, I couldn't push off and left myself too fukken close to the grenade's iron blast pan.

I woke up to Captain Dye running a small flashlight back and forth across my eyes. My hearing was flooded, my balance upended. They lifted me outta the hole, Oliver got the shot he wanted. He told me and Corey, "Great work, men," and cleared us to go get some ice and rest back at the hotel while they stayed behind to keep filming.

Dye displayed great concern for my health after the grenade mishap and ankle injury. He handed me a cigarette as soon as he knew I was going to be okay. His only words to me would echo across many future years and situations: "It's moments like this, Taylor, why guys like us keep smoking." Sometimes it's the offhanded things we pick up that become the strongest bricks on the path forward.

Given that Corey and I were the only members of the platoon finishing early that night, the freedom bus was unavailable, as it had to remain on standby for the larger group that would kiss the sun at wrap. Not sure where it came from, or how far away it was, but they were able to literally *call us a cab*. Thirty minutes later we piled into it for the one-hour trip on that pitch-black night, headed back to the safety of Puerto Azul. And, yes, that cab was yellow.

We didn't have traditional wardrobe accommodations on the set of *Platoon*. There was a wardrobe trailer that functioned mostly for the background talent on both sides of the conflict. The main cast never stepped foot inside of it. We'd all get into our fatigues in the morning before we left the hotel. As such (and obviously), we wore those same duds home after work. Thirty minutes into the cab ride, we spotted a roadblock up in the distance. There was never a worse time to still be in those outfits than that night in the cab with Corey G.

Two heavily armed Filipino soldiers in the middle of the road signaled for our driver to pull over onto the shoulder. Behind these two men, a bug-swarmed spotlight blinding us, making the silhouette of the three-axle troop carrier barely visible. A quick scan of the backlit domes in the rear of that vehicle told my brain that those shapes were the many helmets of additional soldiers.

The two road sentries demanded that our driver step out of the cab. In absolute compliance he did so, as a third man stepped between them, immediately seizing full authority. (Had to be their commander. His uniform more decorated, his eyes more seasoned.) The first wave of dread hit me. Corey began to panic. I knew if I got sucked into that same panic with him, this detour had a good chance of becoming permanent.

Their conversation grew heated and one-sided. The commander wasn't buying any of our driver's responses. He kept gesturing and pointing at us in the back of the cab, finally throwing a hand signal to the troop truck. Six of them quickly jumped off the vehicle, jogging over to set up in a U formation behind their boss, rifles in the mid-ready position. This was going bad fast. The pain in my ankle was suddenly gone; my grenade facial like it'd never happened.

A minute ago, we were heading back to the ranch, to toast a few cold ones. Now we were in the real version of Oliver's other film *Salvador*.

Corey was becoming more unglued by the second, panic-whispering to me in the back of the cab, over and over, "*They're gonna kill us, they're gonna fukken kill us man.*"

I kept telling Corey to stay calm, that nothing of the sort was gonna happen. I didn't care if it was a lie; I'd seen more of the world than he had, and I knew if his headspace didn't right itself, things could turn tragic.

"Amerikano" was the only word I could make out from our driver's pleading Tagalog exchange with this man. I got a sense that the commander's frustration was growing—he seemed to want what the cabbie couldn't deliver: *proof*. We never brought our passports to work. No one had a trailer to stash their crap, and if the damn thing got lost, the Philippines in 1986 was the wrong place to apply for a new one.

The commander barked an order and pointed at us. Our driver stuck his head into the cab, telling us in piecemeal English that the jefe needed us to step out as well. Corey was shaking, tears beginning to pool and stream, both of our heartbeats pounding movement through our Francis and Taylor nametapes.

Outside the cab, standing there with no IDs in our muddy fatigues still caked in grime and fake blood, we must have looked like two AWOL losers from nearby Clark Air Base. The commander had his flashlight on both of our faces. Sizing us up, like he was trying to spot the one detail that would either send us on our way or put us into the ground.

Without taking his eyes off us, the commander shouted something to our driver. The driver thought about it, then shouted a few words back. I didn't speak the language, but I did speak the rhythm. The couplet between them indicated the downbeat of finality. I wish I knew our driver's name. I'd be able to include it when retelling this story in the coming years, as the hero who saved our lives. It was over. We were free to go.

The drive back to the hotel was surreal. There was a pretty large gap between the tears and the cheers. Somewhere in that space, we hoped the healing would begin. Over the next few days, Corey and I would talk about the event, almost as a way to make sure it actually happened. Other times, we avoided the topic altogether to pretend like it never did. We learned to get over things quickly on *Platoon*. We all knew from experience that whatever the next day showed up with would be enough to wipe yesterday's chalk off the board.

Dolly made it back from Hong Kong. After the week I'd just had, her return was manna. Plus, I had some pretty big news I was dying to share with her, that I stressed had to stay between the two of us for the time being.

While she was gone, I signed a "napkin in the jungle" to serve as the crude-yet-binding contract for Oliver's next film after *Platoon*. He didn't include too many details, only that it would shoot in New York, with the plot focusing on a young stock trader "seduced by the promise of quick gains," as he put it.

It was an amazing vote of confidence and statement of loyalty from Oliver. He didn't want our journey to end in the Philippines and saw something in me that inspired him enough for it to continue—in a concrete jungle.

Dolly and I spent a few wonderful days together and made the decision that she would fly back to the States while I finished the final stretch of filming on my own. A world away, we really dug what we'd found in each other. I was confident the relationship had a shot to continue nicely on the home front.

The "bar squad" at Puerto Azul after work each day (not counting Dye and his Marines) was down to six actors: Berenger, Johnny C, Corey, Ivan Kane, Frankie Q, and me. The six-pack who made it all the way to the finish line. (Quinn's gal Caroline was visiting him, so his bar sightings were nothing more than cameos. No one complained.)

The bloodbath in the church sequence a week earlier had everything to do with the hotel bar becoming a ghost-lounge. Our fictional battlefield handed many of our favorites their flying-papers—Depp, Forest W, and Tony Todd, honored on their final night with more hugs than booze. Additional Camp Dye graduates—Ace, Crawford, Fu Sheng, Morehouse, and Flash—had their tickets punched as well. Desperate to be on the exiting side of those farewell parties, my "adios, motherfuckers" moment would have to plow through the jagged teeth of the final few scenes on the schedule. These are the notes

I jotted down for those scenes, as a shorthand road map on the page for myself:

> Bunny dies, Barnes w shovel killing NVA, Junior dies, Captain Dye; "Lovely fukken war," Doc dies, Wolfe dies, John C hides, I save Barnes life, he turns on me, Jet Bomb saves me, I see the Dafoe deer, spot Barnes, and kill that maniac. Francis self-inflicted, suicide grenade?, O'Neill reassigned, I fly off in the chopper—

We'd all be leaving behind unique pieces of ourselves—on the muddy jungle floors, in the foxholes at Camp Dye, in the suffocating heat of the villages, and in the hearts of the men we struggled for and succeeded alongside of. The light at the end of the tunnel, albeit a fiery one, was finally visible.

I suppose I could describe how much I cried during takeoff from Manila, and what the LAX tarmac tasted like when I kissed it after I landed. I could also take some time to paint a picture of the car ride home with Mom, when I told her I was "now a smoker." I could do all of that, yet I'm not going to. Because I just did.

Platoon would change everything for me. It picked a fight with fame. The likes of which would spend the next thirty years trying to kill me.

CHAPTER 19

A few weeks after we wrapped *Platoon*, with my parents' blessing, I officially moved out of the home I'd lived in since I was eight. They were sad to see me go, while at the same time proud of me for having the resources to do so. In the two years since my decision to chase the dream, I'd already spent a combined fourteen months away from home on film locations. My exodus didn't carry the same set of unknowns as it did for most kids leaving the nest for the first time.

Living in hotels in strange places for months on end was more than enough rehearsal to feel confident I could handle the real thing. I had a job on the near horizon, so I knew I was good for the one-year lease I committed to. I wanted to make the move after the film *Lucas* a year earlier, yet somehow talked myself into a shiny convertible Mustang instead.

My new place sat just off PCH, eight miles north of Point Dume in a rustic multiunit beachfront building called the Whaler's Village. Judging by the name, I wasn't surprised to find the AHOY MATEY fauxseaweed-covered lifesaver hung above a doorway in the garage. (I waited 'til nightfall so the neighbor couldn't see me throw that thing in the trash.)

It was about a nine-minute drive from Casa Folks, and I knew that allowed them to sleep better. The rent was $700 a month, and for those who could afford to buy it, the deed was theirs for a clean buck forty. I wasn't one of *those*. Today that unit is close to four mil. Same beach, same mold, different shade of greed.

Dolly and I kept the fire burning that *Platoon* had started, and she joined me there shortly after I'd moved in. (I was on my own for a whopping 200 hours.) She was convinced she'd "met the one," and before I knew it, we were playing house: shopping for plates and towels, and garish throw pillows with birds on them. I wasn't looking for "the one," and was fine taking things as they came. We knew we'd have the summer together before I had to leave town again for the third film of 1986: a road-trip comedy in Little Rock, Arkansas, aptly titled *Three for the Road*. The script wasn't great but the money was. I figured we could fix it once I got there. Terrible plan that had *Wraith* written all over it.

My new place had two sets of double-decker living quarters, separated by an open courtyard that I turned into a barbecue utopia for weekend gatherings. The original crew of Chris, the Heaths, and Pat K were mainstays in the pork-smoke, blending seamlessly with the LA-based *Platoon*-mates I'd stayed in contact with. Depp, Doc Sanchez, and Corporal Clark (with the occasional drive-by from the Captain) turned my courtyard into a standing Jimmy Buffett–themed rager. With his greatest hits on a loop that summer, the Hawaiian shirts were optional, the gasoline margaritas were not.

Ferris Bueller's Day Off hit theaters right in the middle of the courtyard carnivàle, adding even more zing to the Cuervo-soaked festivities. Everyone went crazy over the movie. I was lauded by critics for my kool-drug-guy three minutes on film with Jennifer Grey. It was truly a magical time—I had my own pad (sort of), was surrounded by friends both new and old, with the freedom to enjoy it and the dough to spread some cheer. (The killer weed Chris and Pat supplied didn't hurt either.)

I was both excited by the *Ferris Bueller* praise and perplexed by it; I'd done a few leading roles by then and yet was still being asked by girls in the grocery store if I worked there. One scene in *Bueller* comes along, and those same gals began expressing how much they *loved me* in the movie, then asking if I had plans later. It was intoxicating, and a far cry from the imaginary Vons vest I was wearing the day before.

The "magic" I jealously watched happen to others had finally graced my doorstep, and the timing could not have been worse: I was trapped in a domestic straitjacket of my own design. None of it was Dolly's fault, and it was a shame that she fell into the crosshairs of my ire. I wanted to scream my frustrations into the gaudy throw pillows and fish the lifesaver outta the garbage. The tide was rising so fast I was probably gonna need it. *("Man overboard!")* I had a hunch my Arkansas "acting" wasn't gonna be limited to the character I'd be playing in the movie. My upcoming packing list would be a short one: beer Koozie—check; bad fake perma-smile—double-check.

Two days after Dolly and I arrived in Little Rock, a small group of us from the movie were invited to the governor's mansion for a photo op with future president William Jefferson Clinton. My costars Alan Ruck and Kerri Green were with me as well. Kerri was a good friend from our time on *Lucas*, and even though Alan starred in *Bueller*, we didn't have any scenes together and didn't meet until *La Petite Roche*. It was pretty surreal as Governor Clinton gave me a pair of red-

and-white Razorback shoes, intentionally tacky and modeled after the mascot of Arkansas' sports teams. I was answering a reporter's questions when Ruck overheard Clinton whisper to one of his aides: "Find out what you can about the brunette."

The brunette was Dolly, and to this day Alan swears it was an exact quote. Clearly the behavior that transformed a harmless intern a few years later into a household name had been in play long before her blue dress became famous. It was quite the moment in time to be ringside for that slice of creepy history. Years later in rehab, while watching the Lewinsky hearings play out, I shared the Clinton–Dolly story with my fellow 'habbers. I was still pretty faded on detox meds and no one believed me. I literally said out loud to the group huddled around the TV, "It's kool, I'll put it in a book one day and you can all go fuck yourselves." (And here we are.) I felt bad for Dolly to be objectified and skeeved-out like that, but still had to take some pride in "Bubba" fancying my gal. Alan gave Dolly the rundown in the bar later on that same night. To her credit, she laughed and was actually flattered. Unfortunately she didn't have much to laugh about after that.

Little Rock was the beginning of the end for me and Dolly, and it had nothing to do with the governor. As soon as we arrived on location, I realized I'd made a huge mistake by inviting her. Would have been the perfect time to give myself the space I needed, to decide if what we had was truly what I wanted. Once again, I ignored my gut and people-pleased the situation into predictable and hideous results. By the end of the first week, I felt so trapped I was ready to chew my leg off. With the help of a few new friendships and gobs of Southern cocaine, I chose a different route and chewed my brain off instead.

* * *

Prior to Arkansas, my relationship with cocaine was still in the courting phase. A couple months on the drug with a few friends in high school and a couple times during *Boys Next Door* was about as far as I'd taken it. I'd go six months without thinking about it, and it would only cross my mind again when someone else had a bag. *The Wraith* was the first film set where many *someone*s were constantly bagged-up. Bit of a game changer, and one that had me wondering for the first time if I had a problem that needed to be looked at more seriously.

Still reeling from the *Wraith* "blow"-out, I swore off that shit for the *Platoon* shoot and continued that pledge through the entire barbecue-summer. (Buffett never struck me as a cokehead.) That was fine for a while until it wasn't. The main issue with the drug for me was how cunning it was. I'd be going about my day handling a bunch of *not cocaine* things, and in the next second be launched into a hair-on-fire obsession to get that drug into my bloodstream.

Such was the case the day Dolly and I came back from the local Kmart with a hibachi for our hotel room patio. Another incident of having to "play along." Midway through grilling a slab of baby backs, I drifted into a porcine trance. Lost in the inferno beneath the meat, I knew I was gazing into the dumpster fire our relationship was sure to become. The perma-smile was gone; I was done trying to fool anyone.

I managed to establish a reliable dope connection right afterward, with a local dealer who was working through a crew member on the set. I overindulged and was scoring the stepped-on, low-grade powder twice a week. Back home we'd call the cheap shit "bug spray" for the nasty chemical aftertaste. If that was bug spray, Little Rock's was Orkin.

I wasn't snorting it as much as I was putting it in the end of my cigarettes for a move known as the *coco-puff*. Decent head rush that lasted about a minute until the next cig-tip had to be filled and lit. Looking back, as my brain became more curious about the connection between fire and cocaine, there's no doubt that combo served as the precursor to freebasing. I upped the ante further by adding porn to the mix, and *presto*—my holy trinity was complete.

Dolly would make the occasional trip to New York to go check in on her life there, and I couldn't wait for the freedom to lock myself in the bathroom with the fan running and a stack of porn mags I'd scored at 7-Eleven. Coco-puffing until sunrise and going to work after a full night of that shit became a reflection of how dissatisfied I was with my girlfriend and the job. For the sake of my health and overall sanity, it was high time I got the hell out of Little Rock before I turned that DoubleTree into a charred stump.

We finished the shitty movie, and Dolly and I were back at the Whaler's Village in time for Halloween. I didn't have to dress up as anything; I was already walking around as Harvey Dent.

The buzz on *Platoon* was becoming intense. Oliver wanted to do a limited release in December so it could qualify for the Oscars, then open it wide nationally. Emilio and his fiancée at the time, Demi Moore, saw an early cut of the film. Halfway through, Demi whispered to E, "*Tell your little brother he's gonna be a big star.*" If Demi's prediction came true, my relationship with Dolly wouldn't stand a chance. After watching the female fanfare on those endless nights out with the Emilio crew, the fantasies I built in those moments never ended at a Pottery Barn comparing fabric swatches with my best gal.

At the end of the day, Dolly was a caring and kool lady who wished me no harm, and I didn't want to wind up in a situation where I'd have to look her in the eyes and flat-out lie. The anxiety from knowing what I had to do was overwhelming, and—selfishly or otherwise—I delayed the *Dear Jane* with her for a couple weeks. Few days after my ignoble procrastination, I found myself in a hot tub with a gal named Lisa who was holding the current title of *Penthouse* Pet of the Year. Two things: One, the magazine's judges got it right, and two, I shoulda had the goddam chat with Dolly a few bubbles sooner.

CHAPTER 20

It was January of '87 and Dolly and I had parted on good terms. *Peaceful* terms sums it up more accurately. She'd found out about a few of my indiscretions, and the fact that I wasn't ducking flying CorningWare when she did supports that. A few weeks after we called it quits, I took hot-tub Lisa to see *Platoon* on a Friday night in Westwood with a packed house. Walking with her on my arm past the fired-up catcalling line that circled the block was like being in a movie on the way to the movie.

My mind was flying in a thousand directions trying to poker-face the potty mouths while taking in the frenetic adulation. I distinctly remember thinking: *I hate that I think I love this, but love that I'm pretty sure I don't*. It was a fukken trip and way too much to digest in the heat and glitter of the moment. My *line around the block* was no longer a fantasy to be scoffed at by the down-gazers; it was real and felt like a perfectly landed spinning back-kick to the temple of *Karate Kid*.

Somewhere between surviving the entrance and the final credits, I realized the theater next door was where I'd silly-cybened my balls off with Pat K and Led Z on all of those soup-brained Friday nights. Quite the journey in such a very short time.

The movie was doing gangbusters, with critics predicting Oscar gold on its horizon. The overwhelming reaction came as a huge surprise to me. I had confidence we'd made something the Vietnam vets would appreciate, yet had no idea the rest of the world would join in the celebration. If I had known, there's no chance I would have committed to the film that started three weeks after *Platoon* opened called *No Man's Land*. I'd be playing a high-end car thief who specialized in Porsches. The fly in that broth was that it was being produced by Orion Pictures, the same company behind our indie war movie. Clearly they had plans for me that put their interests ahead of mine. It became a theme with Orion that I'll dig into a bit later. (Unless when I get there it doesn't matter anymore.)

When I think of *No Man's Land*, I don't really care about the memories of the car chases and shoot-outs the experience left me with. I focus instead on the world that magically opened up around me while that mediocre film was playing in the background.

Much like being flattened in your backyard by falling space debris, nothing about the transition was gradual. It was as though I went to bed in a game of horse and woke up in the NBA Finals. I was at the best tables in the finest restaurants, spilling the rarest wine on the sharpest couture as sexy girls sent drinks over with phone numbers. The only photos anyone took were handled pre- and post- by the throngs of dedicated paparazzi, many of them on a first-name basis where a respect for boundaries still existed.

My dining groups at those lavish gorge-a-thons never ended how they started, with tables of people from all walks blending and bonding throughout the meals with drunken and regal dare. The limos filled to capacity as we spilled from the posh eateries into the nightclubs and secret after-hours hideouts. Incredible environments that granted me full access to reach out and touch the untouchables. Hanging with David Bowie in one spot, then snorting my brains out with Sam Kinison at the next. (Sam had the best cocaine in town, you just had to get to him before he did it all by himself.)

Can't fully describe it, only to say that a different language was spoken behind those guarded VIP doors. I got the sense that everyone was "in the know" but couldn't quite put a finger on what it was they all knew. So much of it had to do with privacy, and the safety within that privacy to express wild ideas without being told we were insane. The unincluded were quick to denigrate that world as a hubristic dogpile of kinky sex and fancy drugs. Did those elements have a seat or two at those neon tables? You betcha; I mean c'mon, look at the crowd we were dealing with. It was certainly a part of it but not anywhere close to being the central "it."

Bouncing like a pinball between conversations with the most unique and creative folks alive was exhilarating. At any given time, all facets of the arts-diamond were represented for me to ricochet between, from one accidental master class to another. A guy can learn a lot when the night's travels include Madonna *and* Jack Nicholson.

When I wasn't comparing handguns in the Spago bathroom with rock stars, I was front row at the Lakers and dating one of their cheerleaders: a ponytailed blonde named Suzie with a heart as golden as the team colors on her miniskirt. We went to Hawaii together and it was fun and perfect and safe.

I flew on private jets to the championship games of all four sports acronyms, usually booked the day of. They wanted me there, and that was enough motivation to high-five every single invite. I was the town's favorite new movie star, and we were both gonna have our way with each other.

Right after I finished the Porsche movie, and before I had to leave for New York to start the next one, I received an invite to a place I never imagined would finally happen. If there was any question my life was gonna be different forever, that evaporated in the fairy-mist of a gold-embossed card from Mr. Hugh Hefner—the Playboy Mansion was calling.

"*Holy caca-pants, Batman; can I wear a cape with my fancy pajamas . . . ?*"

Gotta be honest: the place was a little run-down. Maybe that was part of the charm it relied on to present itself as a den of forbidden opulence trapped in time. If so—nailed it. Once I started to ignore the cheesy gold everything and threadbare grandma furniture, the rest of the sights were jaw-dropping. Hands down the prettiest and sexiest gathering of women at one time in one place maybe ever on planet earth.

Trying to maintain my kool lasted all of no seconds. It was "schwing"-city on meth. I'd been "studying" the magazine for years and recognized almost all of the playmates at first glance. Kinda difficult (as I'm sure most would understand) to have a normal small-talk chat with any of them. As I nodded through their perfect cuteness and laughed at every joke, my mind was parked in a car at my inner drive-in with a montage of their memorized nudeness on the giant cement screen up front. In my defense, they *had* to know that was pretty much every guy's reality in those moments. (And if not, and they happen to be reading this, they do now.)

Hef knew everyone's name and spent just enough time with each person or cliquey "pod" to make us all feel welcome and special. I watched him float through the entire estate with an elegance and a charm that made it seem like his slippers were wefted from gravity-neutral silk. Good for him, because in any other situation, he'd have been viewed as some creepy old dood in PJs who wandered off the grounds of his state facility into a lavish party down the block. However, this wasn't any other situation; Hef was a god in his palace filled with goddesses.

The clock was ticking and I wasn't gonna waste another thought on how awesome or decrepit Hef was or wasn't. I spotted a childhood hero across the room I'd always dreamed of meeting. I made a beeline to introduce myself and we hit it off instantly. For several hours, baseball Hall of Famer Reggie Jackson became my date at the Playboy Mansion. The girls lost my focus for a bit as we talked baseball, family, life, relationships, and more baseball. We stayed in touch for years afterward and still regard each other as great friends.

I wanna be clear: Reggie's as classy as they come and did nothing indecorous that night. (I'm unable to claim equal upstandy-ness.) I caught the eye of a few lovelies and had to follow their orders to follow. I'd be led away, while he'd hang back, promising to keep warm whatever seat I was leaving behind.

I'll state right off the bat (and perhaps to the disappointment of some folks), there was no actual sex (that night). When a gal can tell that's not top of mind, it opens a different door into areas that aren't fueled by the stress of expectations. It created a freedom to feel like two goofy kids with stolen beers hiding from a chaperone at the big dance. In my experience, women that beautiful need a break from desperate pawing creepers, and given where we were, I knew it had to be tenfold. I used the private time we shared to discuss future plans, leaving the decision completely up to them. The plans took shape, and I wound up dating two of the women for extended periods.

It actually became comical as I emerged each time to rejoin the party and navigate my way back to Reggie. He'd subtly prod me for the fun details and when I told him the truth, he insisted I was absolutely full of shit. He joked about being my "cut man" between rounds, and having *no* cuts to fix. I was on top of the world, sneaking off with playmates at the mansion and sharing the experience with the greatest postseason slugger the game has ever known. At one point as I came around a corner to find him again, Reggie spotted me and began chanting: "Char-lie, Char-lie." It was a parody on the famous World Series chants of his name from a packed Yankee Stadium years earlier. (When people ask me what my favorite baseball story is, I've just shared it.)

It was a lot to process in the limo on the drive home. I thought back to the nudie mags in junior high I'd look through with a flashlight while the rest of the house slept. I never believed for one second those girls would ever walk off the page into my arms, and do so on the same night I bonded with a childhood hero. It was amazing and unforgettable, and like so many days and nights during my chrysalis phase, the events kept topping each other on the mind-blow scale. Knowing that night had established a much loftier bar, I guess this is the part where I'm supposed to remember thinking something in that limo like:

"My thoughts drifted toward—*now what?*"

or—

"I was so fulfilled, yet still so alone."

or even—

"I really hoped those ladies saw some part of the real me, a scared child with a fractured soul."

I thought none of that. Hef set the table and everyone involved knew exactly what the chef was cookin'. The universe had handed me an opportunity to feel as special as I'd ever felt, and there wasn't a cell in my body that was gonna reject it.

In truth, my thoughts on that drive home were about a napkin. Not the ones I had in my pocket with lipstick prints and phone numbers on them. The napkin of the hour in the back of that Cadillac was the one I had signed in the Philippine jungle. That "contract" had come home to roost, and in a very short two weeks I was due in the Big Apple to honor my side of the commitment.

The more I thought about what I'd agreed to, the more my confidence began to deflate. I didn't have a clue how the hell I was gonna fit into the world of high finance I'd be entering and believably bring the character of Joe Fox to life. Deep down I was gripped with the fear that Oliver had made a big mistake assuming what he saw on *Platoon* would translate to the concrete jungle of *Wall Street*.

I knew I needed to sit with Stone before it got too crazy and share my insecurities about the job. A therapist I'd always respected had smartly framed it as shrinking a monster by bringing it into the light. I was toying with a few opening lines to set the tone of the conversation with him, and I landed on:

"*Hey Oliver, deep down the real me is a scared child with a fractured soul. Oh also, I'm really bad with money.*"

CHAPTER 21

"Life comes down to a few moments.
This is one of them."
—BUD FOX, CIRCA '87

Wall Street is not a film I think back on fondly. It had nothing to do with anyone in the cast; top to bottom it was a lineup of legends and pros. If I'd had the opportunity to read the script before blindly agreeing to it, there's a strong chance I wouldn't have signed on. There wasn't anything about the world or the character that inspired me. For years I've had to bite my tongue when people gush over the movie, excitedly explaining how they chose a different career because of it. In those same moments I've also had to silence an inner voice that wants to scream, "I fucking sucked," when told how great I am in it. I've seen the film twice, and both times I couldn't get past how off-balance and rushed my performance felt. I look like an understudy finally getting a shot on closing night. Essential to that role was that it required a generous layer of deception and greed I was unable to deliver convincingly. (You'll notice I haven't played many bad guys in my career.)

Here's a fun fact: While hammered with White Dave at a bar years ago, we came to the math-y conclusion that the actual word count for the dialogue in *Wall Street* was *twice* as much as the combined total from all the films I'd done leading up to it. (Those bar napkins looked like the JonBenét ransom note.) Not looking for excuses, I merely mention that as an example of the blab-alanche I was buried under. Woulda been nice to have some type of a warm-up for *Wall Street* that wasn't spelled W-R-A-I-T-H.

On the macro front, working (on anything) was the last thing I yearned to be doing in the middle of the *Platoon* jamboree. I wanted to relish that fantasy parade and stay happily drunk with world-class beauties on a fancy boat in tropical waters. If that was how I needed or wanted to process all that was happening, so be it. I never got the chance to celebrate any of it on my terms, and it created a subconscious resentment that followed me to set nearly every day. Petty? Juvenile? Self-serving? I mean yeah, all of those. I was twenty-one years old, what's your point?

Then there was Oliver. Two weeks into filming and I barely recognized him as the same man I'd come to love and respect back in the jungle. *Three* weeks into filming he returned to New York after a weekend pass in LA, gripping two Oscars: Best Director and Best Picture. I was thrilled for him, for us, but also on high alert for the job to become much more demanding. I wasn't wrong, as his entire demeanor was consumed by a self-inflicted pressure for *Platoon*'s encore to be another smash. Day by day that other thing took over and contaminated his ability to enjoy any aspect of the process. The military expression "Shit rolls downhill" should have been on the T-shirts at the wrap party. If he was at the top of that hill, the cast was at the bottom and covered in it. I never got around to having that conversation with Oliver, and it would be left up to me to decide which one of us needed to be dragged into that light.

* * *

When I arrived in New York, *Platoon* was still a raging inferno at the box office with eight Oscar noms dangling from it like gold dog tags. The twinkling glitz-and-glam fame-chaos (growing in concert with my popularity) had made the trip with me to set up shop in the new area code. Honoring the amazing job in front of me while curtailing my appetites for the endless perks at my disposal stood the same chance in hell as an ice cube. I didn't want to let Oliver down in a pivotal moment for both of us. The whims of my imagination sat a phone book or a cab ride away, and I'd spend the next three months trying to make sure the movie stayed dry in my hailstorm of unfettered access.

I had a mandatory three weeks set aside for the research prep before the actual filming began. Inspired by the success of the bootcamp in the Philippines, Oliver traded foxholes for cubicles, hoping the crash course would prepare me to be entrenched in that world. His Captain Dye was a man named Ken Lipper, his Gunney White a young finance hotshot named Liam Dalton. A dood we'll call "Jarvis" was my Corporal Clark. (He was a *me* addition—not an Oliver hire.)

Lipper's business achievements and corporate credentials are too extensive to list. Ken didn't just live in that elite world, he helped create it as well. His number two, Liam (Lee to his pals), was so smooth and sharp I abandoned any attempt to mimic or emulate his mindset or trading wizardry within the first hour of being with him. Great dood, but if his world was crude oil, mine was 100 percent New York City tap water.

Over the course of those three weeks, I'd spend all day with Lee at the various top-shelf brokerage houses, attending high-level meetings with the fat cats who ran those investment firms. There was no worse feeling in those meetings than being confused by so much of it, yet never knowing the right questions to ask.

They played a game where they'd bet a dollar before lunch on whether that same dollar's value would increase or decrease (in the global markets), by the time the meal finished. The one question I did know to ask was—*How? How did that fukken dollar become more or less valuable an hour later?* When twelve versions of the answer would fill the room, it began to feel hopeless. I was so mad at Oliver I wanted to cry.

It wasn't only the daytime grind that polluted the schedule, the nighttime chores blew just as much. I'd make the trek to Lipper's house outside the city to go through the script and break down all of the technical lingo for hours on end. And when *that* wasn't enough, the literary-Oliverisms he scattered throughout the pages felt like they were written in Sanskrit. When I wasn't in either of those scenarios, I'd be on the trading floor of the NYSE or at the *fascinating* headquarters of the NASDAQ in Times Square. (At least there was still tons of porn nearby.)

The *Wall Street* training was insanely tedious and about as frustrating as one could imagine. Nothing against the gentlemen tasked with ferrying me through it, they absolutely brought their A-games. Problem was, I didn't have a game by any letter to contribute. One flowchart at a time, my focus had completely glazed over, as all of their words became the warbled echoes of Charlie Brown's unseen parents. The crash course had become exactly that, as I was skidding off the runway with both engines on fire.

Time was running out and I felt just as lost as when we started. I called an audible and decided I was gonna deliver the mountains of technical dialogue with a blistering confidence and stop caring about what any of it really meant. I was banking on the notion that if the audience felt my passion, they'd buy my act and half the battle would be won. The other half of that battle was a bit trickier: making sure Oliver and Michael Douglas bought it too. If not, fuck it; I could always give Jarvis a call and fire back up the coco-puff express. His shit was a lot cleaner than the Arkansas blend. Jarvis and I made a deal it would be restricted to weekends only. We toed that line for most of the shoot, but let's face it, with "deal" as the root word of his side gig, at some point we all had bills that needed to be paid on time.

Joe Fox wasn't a typo earlier. That was the character's name until Oliver changed it to *Bud* right before we started. Pretty hard to imagine Gordon Gekko not being able to latch onto the "*Buddy Boy*" iteration of it for the first two acts. By the third act the nickname morphed into "scumbag cocksucker" when we became archrivals. (Let's face it—I don't look like a Joe.)

Working with Michael Douglas was an absolute pleasure. I'd been connected to him for most of my childhood but had never met the man. People would constantly approach Dad out in public and tell him how much they loved him in the TV show *The Streets of San Francisco*. (We'd even call Pop "Michael" at home to continue the fun razzing.) From the very first rehearsals we did together to the days-long, complicated office scenes, Douglas was a team player and a wonderful role model. He was so prepared every day, with every word in every take, it created an air of necessary perfectionism that became contagious. I say "necessary" to highlight how much of a word hawk Oliver was with the dialogue. When Michael was delivering the brilliant "Greed is Good" speech, halfway through the third take of the master he paused, and in front of a packed ballroom said, "Hey Oliver—I'm over here." All eyes turned to Ollie, who had his face buried in the script, reading the speech for word accuracy and not watching the performance. In that moment I wanted to buy Michael Douglas a new car. Score one for the good guys.

The nights before my Gekko scenes, I rarely hit the town, and if I did, I drank half as much and called it quits at 11 p.m. (ish). When Michael won the Oscar for his performance, I took a special pride in that outcome, feeling empowered that I gave him something kool every day to work off of. (Then again, it was a role he was born to play, and he probably woulda nabbed that statue playing his scenes to a chair.)

I was also fortunate to be working with John C. McGinley again. He was Sergeant O'Neill in *Platoon* and played my forlorn pal Marv in our fictional firm, Jackson-Steinem. I was feeling so far from home, and not just geographically—John C provided a familiarity and a reassurance I wrapped my arms around. It was a lot like having an older brother in the room, with the main difference being he wasn't allowed to hit me. Whenever it got prickly between Oliver and me, John's take-no-shit approach to life became a solid buffer for the Ollie flak. (Too bad his role wasn't larger.)

The evening before day one of filming, I invited McGinley over to go through our scenes, have a few drinks, and—time permitting—see what the *Yellow Pages* had to offer date-wise. John tried to be the voice of reason, reminding me how long of a day we had in front of us and that sleep has no substitute. I made the call anyway and yawny-John split before the girls got there. Not here to brag, but he did miss out on a fantastically good time.

One of the ladies who showed up was really sweet and turned

into a semi-regular visitor. I came to find out that she had a theater background, and on more than several occasions she'd help cue me with the dialogue for scenes I'd have the following day. Her reading the Gekko lines was something I could never reenact even if I had to. Sharing the stage with her for those performances was priceless. It got to the point where I couldn't *not* hear her when I'd be doing the scene with the real guy the next day. (Add that nugget to your next Amazon watch-party of the film.)

I hope John's eight hours of sleep were worth it. We can live the stories or hear about them later from others. I choose the former.

As the film moved along and the scenes became more complicated and challenging, I couldn't seem to tap into a performance rhythm I'd been able to harness on previous movies. I'd make it through a day of filming and then spend the entire night after work second-guessing every creative choice. I couldn't *feel* the scenes when I read them, and when that happens the *inner swirl* that ignites instinct is left uninspired and dormant. (I get it—it sounds like a load of precious actor shite. Hard to put words to, kinda like someone describing what color their thoughts are.)

Oliver was growing more frustrated with my work, and I think most of his grumble was two-fold: He was pissed at himself for not revisiting (that many months later) his decision to hire me. You test-drive a car and then wait a year to buy it, it's smart chess to give it another run to make sure it still purrs. So much had happened between *the napkin* and Liam Dalton's chiseled jaw, neither of us had a chance to breathe and reflect and then plan accordingly.

I believe part two of the equation had a lot to do with the *Bud Fox* his mind created on the page not fully aligning with my choices and contributions. Rather than being more open to the style of my interpretations, he stayed rigidly glued to an image of the character he'd decided was law. It got much worse after a scene I did with James Spader.

I don't think James is capable of delivering an inauthentic moment. His skill set is on a different level, and sharing a scene with him was unforgettable. Equally indelible was the tremor of oddness I felt on the set that day, as soon as it broke the surface. Oliver began viewing James in a "what if?" manner that I could tell had a *Bud Fox* transposition at its core. It felt like the spear Albert Hall takes through the heart in the PBR on the final bend to Kurtz's Compound. I'm not a guy who imagines things for the sake of an edgier story or a sympathetic reaction. It was exactly that and I couldn't fukken believe it.

Too bad I never wound up in a high-stakes poker game with Oliver; his tells woulda made me a bundle.

After we sailed past the "innocent but corruptible" early stages in the script (the gear I think I'm pretty good at), it was the much darker beats I couldn't always find that opened the door for our struggles. I got the sense that he wanted me to capture an air of the narcissism those slimy clowns from that barfy world embodied—the same posers who were probably licking his combat boots when he was researching the film and writing the script. A huge part of a director's job relies on their ability to observe. After all that time we spent together in the Philippines, he should have realized that I wasn't *that guy*. I mean *fuck*, he coulda parked all that tortured-artist crap, and just asked me.

He was a master at getting inside people's heads and hearts, with polished tactics from the broad to the invisible. I got used to a lot of it and could usually brush it off. The stuff that did give me fits was more veiled and sneakier in design. The ear-whispering manipulations made me wanna jump out the window. He'd walk up to me after a take, with a scowl and his head already shaking in disapproval, then lean in for:

"You seem angry." (When I clearly wasn't.)

"Where are you today?" (Um, still in last night's three-way, perhaps.)

"I'm not feeling it." (When I was giving something my all.)

"I don't believe what you're saying." (Then write some better fukken words.)

I want to clarify: There was never a huge blowout, with us breaking things and storming off. The disagreements we had were handled between us with dignity, and often defused with humor. We never left a scene that didn't feel like we gave it our all, and we usually ended the day with a hug.

One of my favorite memories from *Platoon* took place at five in the morning at the hotel bar after an all-night shoot. Depp and I watched Oliver and Corporal Clark engage in a "friendly" bout of drunken hand-to-hand combat with traces of kung fu mixed in by Oliver. Some "who cares" mouth-blood from legit blows on both sides added to the spectacle. It was epic and Oliver's skills were dated but still impressive. Maybe I was just lookin' for a little more of *that* energy on our New York set. (They hugged it out too.)

I don't hate *all* of my work in the movie. There are a few moments with Dad (playing my Dad) that had flashes of promise from my end. The elevator scene stands out as our finest. He was his usual fabulous self and I was doing whatever I could to not vanish on-screen next to him. We'd been at odds over a few other things leading up to it that didn't involve the movie, and some of that energy was still on tap to be poured. He never did the famous "size of his WALLET" line in any of the rehearsals. He kept it craftily tucked away for when he knew it would have the most impact. The scene was shot with both of us in profile, making it hard to see my bug-eyed shock when it happened the first time with cameras rolling. I tried to match his intensity and learned very quickly: When Captain Willard sets the rage-bar, it's better to cower beneath it and slink back to your loser life with a great story for later.

I'd been on the receiving end of quite a few snap-screamed "wallets" growing up, and the kid me (still poking around in the dark back there) maybe saw it as a chance to finally stand up to him. It's one of Dad's best moments in the film, and I'm certain whatever *Charlie* had done to upset him that day, *Bud* wound up paying for. When personal family histories show up on-screen together, the Method approach finds a way in whether it's invited or not.

Another moment of mine I'm okay applauding is the final scene with Gekko in the park when he kicks the shit outta me. At one point Michael actually caught my chin with a punch. Being a seasoned pro and a gentleman, when he pulled me in close to keep yelling, he nano-paused between lines to whisper, "You okay?" and when I whispered back "Yes," he kept going without blowing a single line. It was so kool and smooth, I can't think back on it without smiling through the memory of the elegant pain.

On the romantic side of the *Wall Street* campus, my on-set relationship with Daryl Hannah was more like a fun blind date on Groundhog Day, night after night.

I don't present that as any type of a dig against her, it's purely my observation of the awkward straits we were thrown into. There was never any time to get to know each other away from the set, and I don't mean that lasciviously. We had one lunch in LA with Oliver (before he cast her) at a place where it was too loud to hear anything. In the few exchanges with her I could make out, I found her to be very charming and old-school friendly. Having never crossed paths again after we wrapped, my only insight into her experience on the film comes from a moment that took place during our breakup scene. (Gonna roll the dice on her approval of its inclusion.)

At the point when our argument hit its climax, I fired a bottle of vodka at the wall to punctuate my "get out" edict with a shower of exploded glass and booze. After the first take, Oliver came over and informed me that the piece of 3D art (right next to the bottle's smash-point) was an original Keith Haring that he'd purchased for eighty grand the day before. (I'm pretty sure he swung a deal on the price if it wound up somewhere in the movie.) He asked that I be extra careful with my aim and to please not blast it. Daryl overheard the conversation, and when I clued her in on my baseball background, she had confidence the Haring was in safe hands.

The second take, I nicked it—the third take, I more than nicked it. It's important to mention that the night before any of this took place, Oliver told me at wrap: Go get hammered, stay out all night, and show up sideways for the breakup scene. It was a set of directives I followed to a T. As he grew increasingly more annoyed at my wobbly aim, I didn't help matters by reminding him of his back-door role in the peril of the artwork. What Oliver didn't know was that nothing of any erratic sort was in play; I knew exactly what I was doing and was in complete control with each toss of the bottle. Daryl's a sharp gal and quietly pulled me aside between takes and asked me, "Are you doing that on purpose?"

I confirmed her giddy suspicion with a clunky wink and a drunken nod. When that info hit her brain, the smile we all fell in love with in the movie *Splash* bloomed across her face like a magician's dove taking flight. The smile told me everything I needed to know, and I remember feeling a flash of kinship between us that silently confirmed I wasn't alone in my "disturbances" from our fearless leader. I'd like to believe I elevated myself in her eyes that day and put a brief pause on us feeling like strangers on a subway. I'd made my point, I rediscovered my aim, and the Haring survived the night.

The very next evening, I found myself on the balcony of Bud's high-end condo in a silk robe trying to come to terms with the massive success his life had taken on so quickly. Daryl's character was inside and the city lights were majestically sprawled out below me in every possible direction. The mood of the scene, along with my conflicted expression, tells the audience the whole story without saying a word. The script didn't agree. When I saw the three words I was expected to whisper out loud to bludgeon the point home, I was confident they'd be cut from the script by the time we made it to that scene. They weren't. Okay, I figured we'd do a few takes with it and a couple without, and after Oliver had a chance during the editing to see how silly it was, the line would never make it into the final cut.

We didn't—and it did. (Marlon Brando would have had a hard time selling that melodramatic slop.) Near my wit's end with it, I did one take where I sang the line and another like Captain Kirk. I laughed, Oliver stared.

Looking back, I'm actually glad that awful line exists in the film. It welded itself to the funny bone of my family—and ever since, it's been the ridiculous go-to response when one of us is stumped for an answer or caught without an alibi.

Dad in particular became its most frequent patron, laughing every time as though none of us had ever heard it. While searching for a suitable coda to this chapter, I've decided there's not a better line to underscore all that I've just shared than those dopey, whispered three words:

"*Who am I?*"

CHAPTER 22

I did seven films in the two years following *Wall Street*. Eight if you count that ridiculous *Heidi* thing I was talked into by Gekko, because his brother Joel was the producer. It's a much longer (and painfully boring) story that doesn't deserve these two spaces: my page and your brain. Okay fine: The very short version is that Michael Douglas called and offered me half a mil for seven days on his brother's behalf. I'd made $600K on *Wall Street* and that was for *four months*. The Gekko-spell worked again, and I can honestly report in that instance, greed was *not* good.

I didn't realize the magnitude of the blunder until I'd arrived in Schladming, Austria, for my wardrobe fitting. They could've paid me ten mil and I still wouldn't have been able to reach up and *buy* those cartoony lederhosen off the screen on opening night. (You've all paused your Kindle to google that photo. It's kool; I deserve it.) Thanks, *other-dad* from childhood. I hope when you use the Oscar as a mirror to check your teeth, you think of me. (In Swedish fukken tights.)

I closed 1987 filming *Eight Men Out* in Indianapolis, then began '88 in New Mexico with *Young Guns* (costarring Emilio), had a month off before starting *Major League* in Milwaukee, then started '89 in the LA-based *Men at Work* (written and directed by Emilio), then went to Kamloops, British Columbia, to be directed by Pop in *Cadence* (which led to the Austrian Spyri-detour), finished that, and went to Virginia Beach and Spain for *Navy Seals*, which then sent me back to LA and San Jose for *The Rookie*, a buddy-cop film with Clint Eastwood to finish the eight-pack that began with a film that had "eight" in the frikkin' title. (That sentence was intentionally a run-on.)

The completion of that filmic odyssey sent me across a bigger finish line that just so happened to have another "8" in the mix: the *eight*-ies. That wonderful decade, an epoch of change and challenge, was officially behind me.

I ushered in the '90s with my afterburners raging at full blue. In the thumb-twirling downtime between *Navy Seals* and *The Rookie*, I stayed deep in the cups from dusk 'til dawn, trying like hell to lasso my fukken unicorn. The equilibrium I sought at all costs was predictably deteriorating into a place of unsolvable inner conflict. What I could *see* (but never describe) was the me *they* wanted versus a me I no longer recognized.

To spare her any further grief, I broke off my fourteen-month engagement to actress Kelly Preston and shacked up with world-famous porn star Ginger Lynn. She was sweet, funny, sexy, and kool, and I was hooked. We stayed drunk and perfectly high for those first few months and had more fun together than should've been achievable. (And yes, she had friends.) A few weeks before I had to go back to work, Ginger helped me shut it all down to get camera-ready for my big job with Eastwood.

The first three months of *The Rookie* went pretty smooth. The last month did not.

It was during those final three weeks when a chance encounter at a random party with my old pal Nicolas Cage opened the door to a different warehouse of mischief. I showed up with my longtime stunt-double and good friend, Eddie B., to find Nicolas there with his musician buddy Phil. Cage has an atomic wisdom and energy about him, and with both of us one step from total fission—I brought the missing neutrons. We joined forces and became hellbent on outdoing each other as we launched a quest to find the elusive Holy Grail. Not sure when or how, but we added a fifth person and with ecstasy as our rocket fuel we all wound up in Las Vegas. Barely able to count but still in need of a check-in pseudonym at The Mirage, we declared ourselves as The Jackson Five. (Gotta believe it had more to do with numbers than it did with music.) Eddie was the only one in our group who didn't drink or drug. He's most likely the reason any insane plans we hatched actually found their way to an ordered destination.

Shortened to J-5, our new club redefined the benefits of membership as we tested the ceiling of stardom against the reach of the law. We stumbled through night after madhatted night like some mobile Mardi Gras looking for the next guardrail to barrel through. I stopped caring about the job and it became impossible to conceal my sloppiness on set with Clint E. *Note to self: Don't mix Ecstasy with anabolic steroids and expect your face to stay lean.* That unfortunate combo turned my head into a bloated moon-gourd and not just on the outside. My cover was finally blown as I'd exhausted every dubious excuse to defend my giant-face syndrome. As the production drew to a close (and unbeknownst to me), Clint and Dad had joined forces and were in constant communication. Very creative duo, those two. Just how creative was yet to be unveiled . . .

I had big plans that night. I'd been running extremely hard with J-5 and we were looking forward to our trip down to Palm Springs for a Hawaiian Tropic bikini contest with me and Cage as judges for the event. I had one early commitment on my plate and I'd be done with it in plenty of time to jet down there for first-pour (of baby oil). I was on two hours' sleep but knew where I was headed wouldn't require much more. Keep my shades on, laugh at every joke, hug it out—and bail.

In hindsight, I shoulda known better—I shoulda sniffed it. Mom was at the helm as event planner, and when I say "I smelled a rat," I'm not talking about Mom. When I was told the birthday party was starting at nine-the-fuck-a.m., there would have been nothing to suspect if the celebration was for a seven-year-old and that was the time we were leaving for Magic Mountain. Those elements are a pretty safe bet that the thing is the actual thing. However, none of those items were mentioned on the invite. The day of the birth we'd be celebrating was August 3rd, and the birthday boy was a man named "Dad"—on his fiftieth.

The rat I mention didn't crawl past my nose until I was in my car and halfway to the gathering being staged at my folks' house. The acceptable window to voice any suspicion or concoct a "can't make it" alibi had long since slammed shut. Maybe if I'd parked my coke spoon and stein here and there in the months leading up to that day, I'd have been more connected to the details.

Maybe maybe maybe—if if if—repeat.

High, sober, or both, I've always stressed the importance of punctuality.

I rolled into their driveway at 8:59, knowing they could hear me before they saw me—the 427 under the hood of my candy-apple-red '67 GT-500 Shelby Mustang had that effect. Too much car for a guy in my condition. (Too much guy for a *car* in that condition.) Mom met me in the driveway, gave me a hug, then matter-of-factly asked if I was armed. It stopped me in my tracks. Such an odd question considering the theme of the day. Did Dad invite someone I had vowed to shoot on sight if we ever crossed paths again?

"Armed? As in, do I have a *gun* on me?" I asked.

"Yes sweetheart, a gun. By any chance is there one on your person?" she clarified.

"You have my word, Mom, I do not." (I didn't see any value in mentioning the loaded Sig 226 9mm in the trunk.) As I followed Mom to the door and into the house, the *hmmm*s were definitely creeping in: Dad's birthday at 9 a.m., *do you have a gun on you*, no balloon on the mailbox. The house was morgue-quiet as I followed Mom from the front hallway toward the living room. I didn't need any more clues to confirm I'd been had—if this was a birthday party, I was the king of France.

I hope when we die, we wind up in a place that offers the ability to rewatch our entire life as a movie. (Not in one sitting obviously, and from massaging recliners made out of bacon, more obviously.) I'd want to fast-forward to the look on my face when I rounded the corner into the living room and first laid eyes on that "birthday" crowd. No shit, I would have been *less* surprised if Jimi Hendrix popped out of a giant cake.

They were all seated in a fairly tight circle with only one empty chair on standby for the guest of dishonor: yours truly. A dood named Ed (who seemed Mormon-polite in a door-to-door kinda way) intro'd himself and gestured to the vacant spot. I'd been bamboozled into my first intervention and was about to step into the worst possible episode of *This Is Your Life*.

The group consisted of my entire family, and not counting Ed and his magic underwear, four others were in attendance. We had childhood pal Rob Lowe, my junior high history teacher Mr. Vincent, a gentleman named Milan (the family's trainer and former '70s Olympic athlete), and yoga master Bikram Choudhury (we had been students of his Kolkata oven in Bev Hills for over a decade). As they went around the room and each person either read their written piece or winged it on the fly, I was instructed not to speak and that I'd have the floor at the end. *(Thanks Ed, but to say what at that point? This is a big misunderstanding and ya got it all wrong? Dad's my dealer, arrest him instead?)* I wasn't just pissed off; I was ashamed and quite frankly *embarrassed* to have all eyes on me knowing how boiled-ass I looked.

While each person laid out their case for the help I desperately needed, I stayed kitten-quiet as I fought to contain the flying chairs smashing through the windows of my mind. I wanted to stand up, tell them all to get fucked, jump back into my loud car, and peel out in a cloud of *eat that*. Give 'em the show they were probably expecting. *(And then what, walk in on this same group a week later in* my *living room?)* Plan one sucked.

Midway through Emilio's share, I formed a new tact: hear everyone out, thank them for their time, then sincerely promise to mull it all over and get back to them in a few days. The good-guy move, buy some time, go hide out in Mexico. *(And then what, walk in on this same group a month later in* Bikram's *living room?)* Plan two sucked more.

As I scanned the room absorbing the words and feelings from the eclectic gang, the slow realization that I did this to myself chiseled its way in. I began to soften a bit and actually tune in to their unified message of hope and love. Rob had gotten sober nine months earlier and tried to sell me his message from a career perspective, stressing how getting sober would instantly restore my reputation. I listened to all of it and dug what he was bringin', yet stayed distracted as I kept wishing it was his brother Chad in his chair instead.

Bikram jumped in, followed by Milan, who teed it up for "Mr. V" (as we used to call him). He approached it from a place of wistful nostalgia, tapping into the Charlie he knew as a thirteen-year-old. His voice cracked at the goodness of that child still being in me, yet unable to show himself with all the booze and dope in the way. It felt like he was back at the head of my classroom again, making us feel better about the world and our place in it. I'd describe it as sobering, but that might be confusing.

My parents spoke last. They described how every late-night phone call or unexpected knock at the door had been holding them hostage in the grim grip of the unknown. The pain on their faces when speaking about the unimaginable sorrow they'd endure at my funeral hit me like a rip current in a dark ocean. Their greatest hope was for me to embrace what they'd brought to my shores that day and rediscover my value as a human being. Dad then grabbed the lowest of the hanging fruit by telling me, "*No greater birthday gift could possibly exist.*" A terrific line—but it wasn't the clincher.

What most people don't realize about interventions: It really has nothing to do with who's there or what those people have to say. When the person (the mark) walks in and sees what they've been wrangled into, the decision is made in the first five seconds if they're gonna throw in the towel or fuck it off and go chug. (I speak to this from vast experience. I went through *seven* of them.)

Per Ed's *all you* hand gesture, the floor (as promised) was finally mine. With that, as I was a half second from saying out loud, "Thank you—let's do this," the fukken phone rang, scaring the shit out of everyone. Dad jumped up and raced to it as though he was expecting the call. (Another *hmmm* moment I catalogued.) He announced from the office off the living room: "Charlie, it's for you."

No one said a word as I rose from my hot seat and crossed to join him. The group's silence was a dead giveaway that everyone was in on whatever part of the plan it would turn out to be. Pop handed me the phone, and the voice on the other end was instantly recognizable as the one and only Clint Eastwood. Regardless of the circumstances, when Captain Willard hands you a receiver with Dirty Harry on the other end, the impossible kool-factor of that is not lost on you.

Clint's known to be a man of few words. He stayed true to his style, getting right to it by telling me, "You got this, just a minor speed bump, go make me proud."

As tempting as it is to change those words on the call to "go make my day," I'm gonna stick to the original script. I thanked him and returned to the living room to announce my decision. Really hard to say no to Dirty Harry.

Tears, hugs, high-fives, and we were on the move. I'm certain the speed at which we got to the car and on the road had a lot to do with eliminating any pause for me to change my mind. *Good one Ed, you crafty turd.* It was over. I didn't have any fight left in me. I was as tired in that moment as I've ever been in this life. There was *such* relief in knowing that I could finally trade my sword for a fukken pillow and sleep like I desperately needed.

It's a baffling place to wind up, being in control of everything for so long, and then one day—not. I was told the place I was headed could *un*-baffle some of that confusion for me, and if that turned out to be the case, then Dad wouldn't be the only one receiving *the greatest gift that could possibly exist*.

In the thirty-eight-minute drive to Saint John's hospital in Santa Monica, I spent *thirty-seven* of them masterminding a way to do rehab *and* the bikini contest on the same day.

CHAPTER 23

We arrived, I checked in, family said goodbye, friendly Black nurse took over. Led me to my room, meds offered, meds declined, noted on my chart.

Pay phone; may I use it?

Down the hall on the right, Mr. Sheen. Quarters, ringing, Ginger.

They tricked me, sweetie. I'm in rehab.

Strange quiet, then: *Well, what the hell did you expect, handsome?* I loved when she called me that. In the moment I was feeling anything but.

When can I visit? Eyes burning.

Probably not tonight. I'll explain later. She got it. Told me to be safe.

Too late for that, G. Solid gal. Mature, compassionate.

More quarters. Ringing. Nicolas.

Bro, I'm at a rehab. You guys still headed down? Ice in a glass through the phone.

We are. Static, a way-off siren maybe.

I'll see you at the airport.

Charles, we can cancel.

Cancel is coming. Tonight we ride.

I slept for one hour. It felt like a picosecond.

Needed to speak with the nurse. Told her to join me out front for a cigarette at 7 p.m.

Had a hunch she was gonna dig my plan.

She hated my plan. Kept telling me I was playing with fire, and how I'd never forgive myself if something went horribly wrong down in "Bikini-ville," as she called it. Said I was tempting fate by leaving the safety of the nest to pursue the *exact fukken shit that landed me there in the first place.* Couldn't argue with her facts. She was the type of lady who'd seen and heard it all—twice. I knew I had to dig a bit deeper into the *pouch.*

"Tell ya what; you're on the night shift, right?"

"I am," she confirmed suspiciously.

"So, you'll be here in the morning, until . . . ?"

"Nine a.m. Why?" Her tolerance waning. (Launch it Sheen, wudduya got to lose?)

"If I'm not back here before 9 a.m. tomorrow morning, walking across that lawn and heading for the main entrance, I will give you one million dollars."

(In *her* afterlife bacon-recliner screening, I know she'd be looking for the close-up I was staring at.) Without another word I extended my hand for her to shake on it. She studied me. I saw something flash behind her eyes: a realization that I was as serious as the last dead face she covered with a bedsheet. She slid her hand into mine. "Deal" is all she said before she turned to head back toward the entrance. She paused at the door, "Do it for *you,* young man." And was gone.

I checked my watch: 7:15 p.m. Hospitals and cabs, a sworn combo—I hailed one.

On the short drive, I did long math for the per-hour I'd have to eat if the plan were to collapse. Certainly made the night a lot more epic. There's talkers and doers in this life. I save the talk for the shit I've already done.

As we settled into our seats for takeoff, I brought everyone up to speed with the nurse wager and how committed I was to honoring both sides of my promise. I had created a built-in insurance policy to close things out on *my* terms and still make it back to where my better brain knew I belonged.

Given everything with the brief but legendary history of J-5, it would've been depressing to not go out in style with one final hurrah. The timing of the intervention had threatened to take that from us, and with a million new reasons to do so, I was hell-bent on taking it back.

On a warm, moonlit summer night as Pop crossed the half-century mark, the pie-eyed cadre of The Nickster, Fast Eddie B, Phil the Breeze, and the MaSheen were wheels-up from Santa Monica Airport in a Hawker 600 at 8:01 p.m. It was *Bikini-ville* or bust, as the precious minutes began their expensive countdown. (I know that's only four of us, but Number 5 asked that he remain nameless in all Jacksonian lore. In case he comes up again and needs a better name than Number 5, let's call him *Doonce Capwell*.)

The trip was a bona fide Class 3 blowout. In true Jackson-Five style, our collective hippocampi were soaked in banshee-Drano before even making it to the hotel. It's no surprise that I don't have a single memory that involved a bikini from our pre-hab swan song. The contest could've been in the parking lot of a frikkin' Supercuts and I wouldn't have known the difference. The energy (and alcohol) I poured into the defiant act of *going* stomped out the experience of *went*—from our plane landing to a winner being crowned at the after-party, all of it was completely scrubbed from my data bank. I wound up as such a faded zombie, I knew of only one solution to salvage the expedition. Scoring dope in a blackout requires a special skill set that I know I have, but sadly cannot describe or teach.

I harnessed that secret sauce and somehow got my hands on a fat bag. I took my booze-coma and napalmed it with a colossal amount of cocaine. (My old pal White Dave used to bang huge rails and always say, "I'm back! Probably *dying*, but I'm back.") The night had new life and a second chance to bring a few stories home. Away from the chaos and clutter of the main event, I'd found my way back to the room White-Daving my balls off with a lovely gal who was excited to be there.

I was cokey-jitter pouring her a soda when the conversation took a sudden left turn. She confided in me that she'd just been involved in her father's drug intervention a few days earlier, and asked that I please forgive her if she seemed skittish about my partying. *(You don't say.)* I hadn't shared with her even the tiniest morsel from the earlier part of my day. I asked if one of the guys had filled her in on my plight and put her up to it to make me feel better. She stared unblinking into the very back of my eye holes and swore on her grandmother's grave that they had not.

When she described the setting for her dad's ordeal and a few of the treatment buzzwords tossed around, I was convinced she wasn't lying. It blew my Bolivian mind. I'd done everything in my power to leave that *plight* behind for a few hours, and, disguised as my greatest weakness, the damn thing followed me down there.

The beliefs I subscribe to can't be found in a book or a special building. I don't rely on an enforced code of practice to keep my antennae in receive-mode. It's allowed me to stay open and aware, mystified and curious, front and center when invited. Maybe that hotel room *was* a special building and her words that night became the book. We spent the entire evening with our bodies clothed and our hearts naked. To hear how elated her family was at their intervention when her dad said, "Let's do this," delivered a fresh perspective I could not have experienced at my own. She poured more water for me than booze. When I wanted to plow deeper into that fat bag, she convinced me the less I had to detox from in the coming days, the better off I'd be. In any other situation it would have felt like the biggest needle scratch of all time. That night was different—our meeting was no accident. As I said, front and center when invited.

When I heard Eddie's polite but firm knocking at our door, I figured he was there to make sure I hadn't drifted off into a million-dollar nap. As far as I knew, the clock was still in my favor and the troops would be lobby-rallied in a few hours. His knocks were nothing of the sort; the night was gone and we had thirty minutes to get to the airport for the flight back. I couldn't believe it—what felt like an hour was seven of them. If I'd had more time and didn't have to leave in a frantic rush, there's a real chance I might have known that young lady beyond our one cosmic night in the desert. I guess that's the real downside of chance: the circles that close, or the ones meant to stay open, never reveal that hidden truth when we sit down inside them. We're supposed to be okay with that. I'm not there yet.

Back on the plane and airborne. Hangovers from stem to stern. Phil, Eddie, and Doonce: mouths open, peepers closed. Cage and I in the two seats at the back of the bird double-shaded (windows and eyes). Our first moment of private quiet.

So, Charles (in that voice of his), *how was your night?*

Well, my man (in that voice of mine), *it had its moments.*

He turned to me, peering over his aviators. *Was the trip worth it?*

Engine hum. Brain hum.

Not really sure yet.

We both lit a cigarette.

So Nickster, how was your gal?

That fukken smile. Answer forming.

She was a . . . talker.

Clinked glasses. A shared final whiskey together.

Mine too.

We landed and they drove me back to Saint John's with a car and driver the jet company had arranged. Nic's question—*was the trip worth it?*—on a redundant loop, catching more flesh each time it scraped past the same spot in my chest. I knew the answer on the plane, and even more so in that car as we got closer to the hospital.

We parked a block away to say our goodbyes. I wanted my reentry to the facility to have a casual air about it, and screeching to a halt out front can murder that effect. Nicolas pulled me aside from the group to share a few tidbits for my ears only. He congratulated me for doing the right thing, then carefully expressed—if me shutting it down meant the end of J-5, he was hugely fine with that.

I watched them pull away and began my casual walk across the very lawn I'd promised to retrace fourteen hours earlier. I checked my Rolex: 8:44 a.m. I like those numbers—Yogi and Reggie. As long as it wasn't Maris and Martin, that kool mil would be staying in my possession. (That's one for the baseball nerds: They wore 9 and 1.)

I looked up, and there she was in her nurse smock that had "eventful night" mashed into the fabric. She was checking her watch too. She mock-frowned at the wager part of it, then broke into the brightest, most genuine smile I'd seen in ages. I gave her a hug.

"Did ya miss me?"

She laughed. "Was counting the minutes, Mr. Sheen."

"As was I, young lady, as the hell was I . . ."

She hooked her arm into mine like a regal usher, and began to lead me back toward the main entrance.

"Well, Mr. Bikini-man, how was it?"

"Ask me in a day or two. And let's go with *Charlie* from here on out."

As we walked back into the main lobby to set up shop for the next thirty days, I caught a glimpse of a squirrel pouring tea for an Egyptian werewolf on the front lawn. The Ecstasy I'd been doing was known for its trailing hallucinations.

The dance had officially begun; how many coins I had for the jukebox was yet to be determined.

CHAPTER 24

I didn't keep a journal in there, but if I had:

Day 1

Palm Springs was idiotic. I got swept up in that thing I do to put on a show and be the guy. It's exhausting. Wasted money wasted time wasted me. I hope the guys had fun because my night felt like another intervention. I know the wager nurse's name now—Deb. Do I care more about her name since I didn't have to gift her that boatload of dough? Not sure. I'm not a big sleeper. They told me it was okay to take their legal downers and crash for a couple days to get my sea legs back. That term never made sense to me. Should be land legs; I don't walk on the sea. Fuck, who cares, I'm sure I got it backwards like everything else recently. I've only met one person here who's not Deb. Old-timer named Carl. Trying to get sober in his late seventies to know his kids better. I wanted to book him a room at the Miramar instead and send over a couple girls and tell him to enjoy himself. Maybe that was just me seeing myself down the road as a "Carl" and how I'd wanna go out. I gotta stop assuming everyone wants to try my *soopah-stah* recipe. Maybe I'll be able to once I'm off the dope and booze. I feel bad for people and wanna fix them, especially girls. Drunk therapist in a bar in Carmel one night told me I had White Knight Syndrome. Said as long as there were distressed damsels I'd always feel useful. Okay fukken Steve; what's your point? Pretty sure I paid for all his booze that night. (What's the male version of *damsel*?) I wish I wasn't the only famous person in this joint. Be kinda kool if Clooney or Pacino lost their minds with the drink like I did, and had to check in so we could compare notes and work through some things only we understood. I'm not wishing terminal drunken badness on them, just lookin' for some common ground on our very uncommon fame-planet. I like the food here. Wasn't eating much the past few weeks. (Months?) I got a kick out of the orderlies' shocked expressions when they took away my licked-clean plates. I imagine I'll see more of that in the coming days with how clean my room stays. Lotta folks say it's about control. I don't agree. I like shit neat. Saves time to never be looking for things. Eyes just got too heavy to hold up. I need to spend more time with my daughter.

Day 2

Somehow they felt I was steady enough to attend my first group therapy session today. About eight of us in the room. Not nearly as dynamic or colorful as the times I've seen it in movies. They kept expecting me to chime in with an observation or some advice for the person with the talking stick. I didn't. I kept passing. They pressed me on why I wouldn't and I told 'em because it was none of my business. They didn't like that, telling me now that we're here and in this thing together, all of it is everyone's business.

I told them I didn't care about that last part. Knowing someone for a few hours and then giving advice for things that took that person years to create is entitled and invasive.

I got in a big shouting match with a girl in the group—had nothing to do with the other stuff. I shared that I felt it was unlikely I'd find any mutual connection to discuss the tricky mash-up of drugs and fame. Grumpy-girl told me I wasn't special and was just like the rest of 'em—nothing more than a run-of-the-mill, hope-to-die addict. I then asked her, if what she's saying is true, how did it feel when she also won Best Picture at twenty? The group laughed pretty hard at that one. It felt good to make her feel small. But just for about six minutes. She told some of her story. If half of it is true, her life is steaming shit. I thought about Doc Steve in Carmel. She's not hot, so she's safe from my rescue fetish. Yeah, I may have left that part out. So fukken shoot me for admitting what everyone else thinks but is too chickenshit to own. Some days here are gonna be as useless as they might be beneficial. It's hard to ask for help when someone else has raised your hand for you. Ginger is at my condo in Malibu holding down the fort. I miss her silly laugh.

Day 3

Nicolas visited today. He seemed in great spirits. Told me a funny story about leaving his fancy engraved Dunhill lighter behind in Palm Springs. He had the number of the *talker* gal he was with and called to see if maybe she had it. She did, but since her name is a match to his initials, she took it as a sign and wanted to bring it to him personally with a promise she could spend the weekend at his house. He told her "Merry Christmas" and hung up. In August. Man, did we have a needed laugh with that one. Good goin', Nina Campbell, or whatever the hell your name is. He saw it as a small price to pay to avoid other weird crap she may have been planning. When girls ya don't know that well use words like *signs, destiny,* and *fate,* it's usually a good time to yell *"Taxi,"* even if you're in a tub or on a horse. Nic told me the only hard drugs he'd ever done were during J-5. He told me he wasn't going to miss them. I said me too, and knew it was a lie as soon as it was uttered. I felt bad about the hard drugs thing but not horrible. It's all about choices. We had a cigarette together out by the bench cluster at the rear. Grumpy-girl pretended to be my friend so she could meet him. I didn't care. I still couldn't get some of the awful group-shared images of her life outta my head. It felt good to do something nice for her. Said goodbye to Nic on the lawn. He walked away, and the only fake thing I saw was a blue jay wearing a tiny diaper. The hallucinations seem to be packing their bags and on the way out. I wish I was joining them. I saw them bring in a new person near the nurse's station. I watched longer than I should have. They gave him a shot of something and I heard his pulse on the device scream its way to 200. I snuck away and didn't ask any questions. I'm not expecting him in group for a bit. I tried to make myself feel better by comparing his condition to mine when I showed up. Then realized it wasn't about that. You're in rehab dood, no one cares that your hairdo is more quaffed. We all share a similar pain and state of disrepair. But my hair does look better than his. I'll loan him a hat. I have anxiety about Ginger visiting. This is not the badass, damn-the-torpedoes energy we bonded over. I'm really worried about sober sex, but if anyone can make it awesome it's Ginger. I hope tonight's meal is something with gravy.

Day 4

Went to my first AA meeting today. It was in the cafeteria at the hospital. Didn't really understand what was going on. Was too scared to say much, but when I did, the whole room spoke back to me in unison, with prepackaged responses that felt robotic and cultish. The book they kept reading from and praising was terrible. So much ancient grammar, it felt like I was back in the first grade—in 1930. I noticed the book couldn't make it two sentences without mentioning God. I felt trapped and tricked and like some indoctrination was taking place against my will. (Where was any mention of this at my intervention?) I was so grateful for the two tubes of Rolos I had in my jacket pocket. The perfect combo of sugar, caramel, and chocolate brought the only comfort I felt during the meeting. I ate them a lot as a kid, and today they seemed the perfect chew-mates to their romper-room booze-bible. The meeting-people prayed at the beginning and prayed at the end and knew when to laugh on cue during its ninety-minute middle. There was another section dedicated to scheduled people who showed up to speak at length about getting drunk and stoned. Listening to their romanticized, drooling memories of much higher times made me want to leave the chow hall and go do everything they were describing. *Very* strange method to make fantastical claims of solution, while celebrating life-threatening chaos. As they explained how their program is supposed to work, me and my Rolos got busy on this parallel metaphor:

It's like being yanked off the street and thrown into a van with a sack over your head and taken to a secret place where they only eat mangoes. Because mangoes (you're told when you get there) are the only answer. After a few days of mangoes, you go to the head guy and tell him it's widely known that ya gotta mix in a few other items *besides* mangoes to balance a healthy diet. Head guy then tells you to shut it, that you know nothing. He says if you stop eating their mangoes, God will withhold all the gifts He has on standby for the guy who eats the most fukken mangoes.

*I'm gonna read this in group tomorrow.

Day 5

I didn't read it. No reason to give them a chance to feel threatened by it and shred my gold into tin cans. Besides, they gave us our first official assignment: We gotta list our complete drug history to include which drugs and at what ages. The third column is asking for the *why* at each stage. All I came up with so far is—*why not?* I can already hear grumpy-girl losing her shit over that one. It's due at the end of the week. The nights are getting worse. Waking up every hour overthinking all of it. I heard someone earlier talk about how our lives didn't come undone in a day, and therefore they can't be put back together in one. Makes perfect sense. Doesn't mean it makes for perfect practice.

200 BPM guy joined the group. Turns out he's a dentist named Rick. He'd frown at my love for Rolos. He shared with us how he OD'd on nitrous oxide, or laughing gas. Apparently he was over-ordering the tanks for his practice and taking them home to have parties with. Per usual it came my turn to contribute, and I told him I was glad he survived but was bummed I hadn't met him before we both wound up here.

A laughing-gas party at a dentist's house was something I never got a chance to do. Meeting these people away from their real lives doesn't give me the sense that I'm being presented with the complete person. I can tell the unspoken vibe is: Who are we really without the booze and drugs we relied on for so long? And what happens if we get off everything and meet that new person and absolutely hate him or her? It's a safe bet tonight's 2:00 a.m. awake-and-ponder moment will focus on exactly that. (It happened at 3:00 a.m., but who's counting?)

Day 6

I need to quit gambling. That's a phone call my buddy and bookie Coop won't be thrilled to receive.

I have a lot of regrets. They keep telling me not to obsess over them, and that they wouldn't call it the past if it wasn't. There're a few folks in the group working on this thing called "the steps." They told me that one of those steps deals directly with regret. I asked them point-blank: "Are these steps you mention something I'm gonna find in that ancient book?" They confirmed my suspicion, then informed me the solutions to everything I was dealing with or was afraid of could be found in the pages of that book.

I asked how that was possible if most of my problems are related to things that didn't exist sixty years ago when it was written. That drew a long stare from the counselor who ran our gripe-circle. I then asked if they offered a backup plan in the event the book and I didn't emerge as victorious. I got Rick the dentist's attention with that one. Grumpy-girl told me to stop being negative and difficult. Listening to all of that today brought one simple word into my mind: *mangoes.*

If Rick gets clean and does so well that they invite him to speak in the cafeteria, I wonder how many people in the audience will start planning a nitrous party. I didn't have the chance to bring any possessions with me for my stay. My parents put a few of my things in a bag they dropped off when I was in Palm Springs. Deb didn't tell them I had left. There's no gift shop to buy anything, so I know my stuff will all fit back into the bag it came out of. I have a plan, and it's a lot tidier than that mess in the desert. I hope Carl makes it to the Miramar. I hope grumpy-girl remembers how to smile again. I hope Rick gets his medical license back. I hope I left a mark here.

CHAPTER 25

It was noon on a Friday. I know this because I was wearing a watch with the day/date on it. They always gave us thirty minutes after lunch to go outside of our wing and get some air and sun. I knew I wouldn't have much time before one of the hospital employees asked me why I was carrying a small duffel to go sit outside. Woulda been kool if that duffel had a full set of scrubs and a surgeon's mask in it. My plan wasn't that fleshed out; it was just deodorant and a few T-shirts.

My palms were clammy and I could feel the tingles of pre-adrenaline. I spent so much time in Santa Monica growing up, I knew exactly where I was grid-wise with the boulevards and the cross streets. I didn't have much of a plan past the first stage of it. That was okay, I'd build the rest of it on the move. I surveyed the foot traffic around me; it was pretty light. The smoking benches had two or three people milling near them, but no one from my group that I'd just spent a week with. Everyone I could see was deep in their own private conflicts and passing thoughts.

No potential disrupters had eyes on me; it was time.

On the move I went. I've always criticized people in movies when they escape on foot by running like a lunatic. Draws way too much attention and I wasn't gonna be that guy. *Brisk, energetic pace like you know where you're headed*—good. *Half speed-walk, pre-run indecision gait*—bad. I made it about thirty yards across the main lawn when I heard the loud voice calling out behind me, "Bill! Yo Bill, hold up man, where you think you're off to?!" (Might have forgotten to mention I'd checked into the place under the name *Bill Butler*. He's the D.P. from *Jaws*.) I looked back, and sure as shit, hugeness was coming after me. Black dood about 6'5", 270, and my man could flat-out hoof it for his size. (Why does every orderly always have an athletic background?) In a flash, I did become the high-knees-and-elbows fleeing-movie-lunatic guy. It was on.

I came around one of the side streets near 25th, glancing back, unable to see him through the bushes I was flying past, but still hearing him. I had no idea what he was yelling, and at that point none of it mattered. As my echoey shoe-slaps approached the curb to the larger street, a city bus rolled to a stop directly in front of me as though the giant vehicle was in on it, with the perfect timing of a skilled wheelman. I barely broke stride as the massive opposing double doors *whooshed* open, and in I leaped. With no one else boarding, I turned back to see my pursuer just getting to the street as those same doors wheezed back together. Just like that—we were moving down the street, Saint John's getting smaller with each downshift. As the bus was pulling away farther and picking up speed, the orderly had stopped in the middle of the street to watch us disappear. He was wildly waving his arms and repeating the same jumble of words into the diesel plume the bus had left behind as a parting gift. I was out. I'd done it. Half of the twelve people on the bus recognized me. I slipped the driver a twenty, and cool as a cucumber, I found a seat without saying a word. I felt totally alive.

I'd find out much later what the orderly was trying like hell to tell me: I didn't have to "break out" like that, and he just wanted a signature since I was leaving *AMA, against medical advice*. I felt so fukken stupid when this information was finally shared.

I got off the bus near 4th Street and walked a few blocks to a diner on Wilshire called Zucky's. It had been there for decades and was a favorite spot of ours during high school. The move I can't really explain was the pit stop I made at a pawnshop on the way to the famous coffee house. Once inside, I saw a super-shiny saxophone hanging on the wall and decided to buy it. I don't play the sax. Maybe I just wanted off the street in case they were following the bus and tried to appear less sketchy by actually making a purchase. (Pretty sure a keychain or a pocketknife woulda served the same purpose.)

I got a table near the back of Zucky's and asked the waitress if they had a Yellow Pages phone book I could borrow. She obliged, served me some coffee, and I got to work on the next phase of my plan. Old pal of mine Scott G was working as my assistant at the time. I called him, told him where I was and to please come at once because I needed his help. He showed up a half hour later, and when he walked in to find me in a booth with two types of *phone* things, sax and book, you can bet he had a few questions for me. The only one he did ask: "They havin' a special I don't know about?" yanked a good laugh from both of us. We had just seen each other at Saint John's a couple days earlier when he dropped off a pair of glasses.

Scott was great. Didn't judge, didn't fret. He could tell I had my wits about me. We spent the next two hours researching and calling treatment centers that would take me that same day and allow me to check in as an outpatient. They could have my days, but the nights had to be governed by me.

By three that afternoon, I had enrolled myself at the new rehab, thirty minutes from Malibu in the city of Calabasas. They agreed to my terms and were counting on me to agree to theirs. I didn't leave Saint John's to go get high or reassemble J-5 to chase more chaos. I left because I still wanted to give the treatment thing a chance and do so on my terms.

I gave Scott a hug and promised my next call to him would *not* be from a diner. He flashed his trademark *hang loose* and mimicked playing a saxophone as he exited the rehab. Coming from the best drummer I've ever known, it didn't fit—but was perfectly fitting.

I hadn't been at the new place five minutes when the head therapist shook my hand, told me to have a seat in his office, then very matter-of-factly asked, "So, why are you trying to kill yourself?"

I didn't have an answer for him.

CHAPTER 26

"I loved to drink and take drugs, hang with beauties, howl with laughter and solve everything that crossed my path. I never dodged the truth or broke shit I couldn't afford to pay for. To have the run that I had and watch it all come to an unceremonious screeching halt was a seismic soul shock I wasn't emotionally prepared for."
—C. SHEEN, *TUCSON GAZETTE*, CIRCA '90

Okay, here's what the press release might have looked like:

Sheen gets out of rehab all shiny and clean, and shortly afterward goes to work on a big ol' studio comedy called Hot Shots. *He promotes a string of other films, and his press appearances on the world stage have renewed everyone's confidence in him. The rehab stint was a speed bump and it's clear his troubles are a thing of the past. Insider reports also tell us former bad boy himself Rob Lowe had promised Sheen (at a private family intervention) that his new AA life would restore his reputation. Rob's crystal ball was right as rain, as the big ol' comedy is a giant success and Sheen's star is as before—one of the brightest in the night skies of*

Hollywood. Other projects of Sheen's include a coffee-table photo book of his entire family, several lucrative Japanese commercials, as well as the purchase of his first home near Malibu. Go get 'em, Charlie, we're all rooting for ya!

Here's what was really goin' on:

I didn't get sober for me; I got sober for them. I knew the day I walked outta Camp Calabasas it was only a matter of time before I'd sneak out a side door into the alley where all things fun-and-familiar were lurking and on standby. I just wanted to get everyone off my back and outta my affairs. I felt like I was playing the role of *guy who's grateful to be clean*. I was overacting and I knew it—and that performance had me trapped in a cycle of anxiety.

I didn't feel comfortable or confident in anything I was doing, unless it was me alone in front of a TV devouring burgers and sports. Trying to navigate any complicated social setting, I could feel my body and mind literally "creaking" like some unoiled wannabe tin man. I was constantly told by all the *sobers* how AA was the only answer if I wanted to stay sane and free. So, a lifetime membership to their medieval gibberish club, and I could keep feeling the exact opposite of what they promised? Heck yeah; sign me up. (Just gotta swap out my brain with a clump of ham first.) When I'd ask about alternative modalities to decode and lick this thing, my queries were perceived as threats until I was ultimately branded a denialist. It was basically, "shut the fuck up and eat your mango."

Everything felt like a double-edged trade-off. *Hot Shots* doing really well was good for business but bad for inner-me. The me that wanted out so I could go look for the guy they fukken kidnapped. The whole charade was another straitjacket, and unlike the Dolly Fox version I'd tailored myself into, the new one was twice as thick with every buckle fastened by the hands of strangers.

After slamming the door on J-5, our quintet in many regards was still joined at the hips. Hoping to recapture the crew-vibe, we traded our silly dance moves for greaser-style leather jackets and called ourselves the Stingrays. (The stingray image on the back of those jackets was a replica of the matching tattoos we already had.) When asked, we claimed the moniker was an homage to the popular '60s muscle car. Unlike the car, we were not a finely tuned machine. Our new mission was to prove we could have just as much fun without all the booze and dope. I did appreciate the effort, but it felt like just that: an effort. In truth, it made us yearn for J-5 that much more, as our Stingrays rebranding attempt petered out into well-intentioned flatness. It reminded me of the "sober barbecues" I'd get talked into attending after AA meetings. Loathsome events at the hands of the force-fitters, where I'd wander across that day's lawn keeping an eye out for cyanide and black Nikes.

I don't believe in coincidence, or that everything happens for a reason. I prefer the middle patch that's usually floating somewhere between the two. In the early hours of another August 3, I found myself in that liminal meadow on the anniversary of the intervention. I had spent the night at Cage's house and woke up early to go inspect the fridge for a snack or some juice. I swung open the heavy Sub-Zero door and there it sat, the instantly recognizable color combo of a mondo-size *Foster's Lager*. It was completely alone at eye level, like the reveal money-shot in a commercial. There was no brooding moral debate I had to fight through to double-check my intentions. I didn't race up the stairs to Nic's bedroom to shake him awake so we could process the decision like a couple of teenage girls. Fuck all that. Lord

Foster and I were face-to-face, and his magic potion was sittin' in the wrong guy's belly. With the refrigerator door still open, bathing me in her ghoulish light, I peeled back the pull-tab and downed that wonderful can of Australian beer in three magnificent, unspilled gulps. The only sound that might've awakened Cage was the middle-earth belch I sent echoing through the halls of his castle.

I heard a guy at a meeting once say:

"There's nothing worse than a belly full of booze and a head full of AA."

Au contraire, liar-man; there was nothing *better*.

The search party for the missing actor was called off.

Happy Birthday, Dad.

The switch had officially been flipped. Out in public I had to keep the drinking below the radar. I'd tell the waitress to hide my wine in a mug and spend many dinners looking like a guy who had a real problem with coffee. It seemed like *everyone* knew I was supposed to uphold the new image, and if they didn't, their friends would share too loudly the whispered info. I did my best to keep it in check and drink just enough to have a good time, then shut it down when the next movie was starting. Instead of sailing through my usual pattern with deft aplomb, the post-rehab landscape was more like a le Carré novel.

I had to run a tight ship. To strengthen my odds, I took cocaine off the menu. It had a habit of seeking balance by doubling the level of booze consumption. Can never control or predict others, but I felt pretty confident if someone flashed a bag I'd be able to honor my resolve. For every person I came across who supported my "new" lifestyle, there were easily three or four who were thrilled to learn we could knock a few back away from prying eyes. They clearly wanted to party with the image they'd created, and not the snore-fest they feared I'd been molded into. I figured out early on how to pick out those who just wanted a story for later, versus the authenticans engaged in the value of actual-me.

From early '92 to the start of '94, I did six films that included the sequels to *Major League* and *Hot Shots*, a remake of *Musketeers*, along with *The Chase, Terminal Velocity,* and *Beyond the Law*: a true story about a cop going undercover into a biker gang. (The Stingrays woulda kicked the shit outta those sissies.) The start/stop began to wear on me with that many films in such a condensed time frame. Before long, the *stop* was being pushed off further and the *start* would arrive too soon.

In the midst of all the work, travel, and covert maneuvering, my path managed to collide with the most famous costar I'd ever wind up with. Given that she didn't appear in any of my movies, it was a crown not easily seized. Interloping shenanigans aside, it unraveled into one of the nuttiest media blitzes the town had ever witnessed. The press dubbed her "The Hollywood Madam." I just knew her as Heidi.

CHAPTER 27

July '94 Discovery-phase deposition transcript.

Assistant US Attorney: "We're noticing Mr. Sheen, the dollar amounts on your personal checks dated through the month of December, reveal a significant increase when compared to the previous months of October and November."

Mr. Sheen: "What can I say; I get a bit more generous around the holidays."

June '92. Hottest club in town was a place called On the Rox. It was an after-hours VIP cave, nestled into the top floor of the Roxy, a landmark venue on the Sunset Strip. The undersized lounge hadn't yet achieved the infamous status its legendary neighbors The Whiskey and Comedy Store had enjoyed for decades. We recognized that fact and took it as a challenge. On the Rox was a latecomer, but not a late bloomer.

Ex-friend of mine promoted the nights there when it was whitehot, so I never had to deal with a line to stand in or a table to hope for.

On an evening that felt like many others in that cramped space, I took special notice of a crowded table across the main room teeming with an unusual amount of gorgeous girls. Standing out as well was the lady who sat at the head of their table. If I had to describe her in one word, the easiest grab would be *chaperone*. I drifted toward the bar to get closer and see if maybe they had a cake in the middle of their table. A friendly "Who's the birthday girl?" never brought an air of overstep or creepy. No candles, no cake, no teed-up opening for "please join us." I spotted an old pal who always had his finger on the pulse and wasn't shy about asking him what the deal was with Fantasy Island at Table Five. Didn't matter where you were in the '90s-LA club scene, if you had a question about anything, Steve Bing had the answer.

We took up station at the bar and Señor Bing ran it all down for me. The chaperone was an elite madam named Heidi Fleiss, and the stunning cakeless harem were either in her retain or being sussed out to make that cut. The operation was high-end, the price of admission was high-dollar, the invite-only motif was high-priority. I thought back to Vegas Candy and how that felt and where it sent me. I'm still fascinated by certain memories that survive the journey and, through selective means, reappear with only their best traits intact. Candy lives on forever as a win, and I was eager to keep that streak alive. Bing got the okay from Heidi to pass along her number. The entire interaction between them lasted all of thirty-three seconds, and twenty of that was him walking. And so I called her. A lot. Like a *lot* a lot.

I remember my first conversation with her on the phone as though it were yesterday. Heidi was kool and friendly, with a relaxed sexiness that enveloped her voice. It was genuine and had a way of masking or delaying the realization of how razor-sharp she was. Intentional or otherwise, that thing worked like a charming charm. Before I knew it, I had agreed to twelve grand for two women from midnight 'til whenever and was convinced I'd pulled one over on *her*.

The feeling I'd get from the gate-buzz or doorbell when the girls arrived was like a hundred Christmas mornings all at once in my favorite age from childhood. It was the mystery of the unknown, wrapped in the giddy mischief of secrets that had to be kept in the shadows. I'm still not sure which aspect of it was more intoxicating: the women themselves or the decision to make the call. The sensation of the stomach vertigo was identical to placing a large bet with a shady bookie. Climbing inside that rush with the outside chance of opening the door to handcuffs instead of girls was a risk I was willing to take anytime I picked up that phone to deck my halls.

The women were never misdescribed or falsely represented with their age or personalities. Heidi knew the value of customer trust, and she built on that with her consistency. What most people don't understand is if you took the financial component out of the equation, the women were just as classy as the terrific gals I'd meet at clubs, bars, and parties. It never felt dastardly or corrupt. I justified the encounters as paying a convenience-tax for a guaranteed outcome the other dating scenarios couldn't offer. Maybe I blurred the lines, maybe the lines blurred me. I was having way too much fukken fun to carve out any time for soppy reflection.

The cocaine boycott didn't last. The Heidi pot was at full boil and I knew exactly what ingredient was missing. There are two camps with that shit and no middle ground. One camp lauds it as an aphrodisiac, the other does not and roundly rejects it in all realms of intimacy. You're dead-on with your guess of which one I fell into.

Yayo, as Tony Montana christened it, was always a drug for me that created a heightened attention to detail. It's been said that cocaine in the Virgo brain is like all the ants finally getting organized. (I just made that up but I think you catch my drift.) For as many micro specifics I was able to keep my mind on with that drug, there were always a few larger pieces I stupidly overlooked. One of those larger pieces was that stream we all drink from known as *cash*. I was fresh out and thought it "coke-wise" to use my checking account to settle my tab with Heidi. Silly me, I had my mind on ninety-nine other items and the list was 100. Sometimes, *careless is he who cares too much*. (I made that up too.)

My hair extensions were making me insane. *Musketeers* in Vienna was the third film in a row I had to wear them, and they'd turned into an itchy dandruff disaster. How anyone wears that shit by choice in life just walking around is beyond my level of comprehension. I flew privately back to New York for two days to promote one of the other films, and while I was there I had an appointment to get those mangy things tuned up. They were gonna be taken off when I landed and replaced in the morning, so I called Heidi from the jet to see if she had a nice girl to come visit me at the Parker Méridien. It would mark the first time the rat's nest had been off my head in *five months*, and I wasn't gonna celebrate those nine hours of freedom by myself. The lovely lady who showed up that night enhanced that freedom 'til sunup. She and I stayed in touch and saw each other for several years after that night anytime I was in the city. Heidi could tell when certain clients had taken a shine to a particular girl, and she didn't meddle or try to shake anybody down when those two had worked out their own deal moving forward. She was smart that way by never coming off as desperate or possessive. It's one of the reasons when

Fleiss got arrested in June of '93, I was pretty sure it had nothing to do with matchmaking greed.

I was in Houston, Texas, working on *The Chase* when I got the news. She'd sent a few girls to a hotel, and instead of meeting up with the alleged client, they walked in on mustaches in cheap windbreakers. The information highway I had access to was courtesy of 1993, leaving me at the mercy of AM radio and the six o'clock news for any inside track with the bust. I was with the writer-director of the film and a dear pal of mine, Adam Rifkin. He told the crew we had to take a quick break while he and I raced back to my trailer in the 105 heat to call Steve Bing. Steve and Rifkin were tight as well, and we both knew if any data had spilled to the streets, Bing would have a line on it.

We got ahold of him and he didn't have much for us beyond the standard narrative making the rounds. Before he hung up, Bing gave us a nugget that the tabloid press was on the hunt for Heidi's *little black book*. It was apparently her client-bible that held all the dirty secrets of the super-rich and famous. Bing shared that his studio-exec pals were sweatin' bullets about it being unearthed. I felt bad for Heidi and the girls but was way more panicked about my own exposure in the whole mess. I was kicking myself about those goddam checks being the only link they'd possibly have to implicate me. I began to comb through my memory for any other idiotic clues I might have left behind. It gnawed at me, I could feel it back there somewhere, begging to take that list down to ninety-eight.

—Of course. Fuck. A tunic. My hair. New York—

I didn't just use personal checks, I left behind a financial tool the bank used to promote for travel overseas: the American Express Travelers Cheque™. I'd signed about thirty of them to pay Ms. Fleiss for the Big Apple hair liberation party.

Standing in a field next to a Houston freeway in 105 with Adam, I could feel the walls starting to close in. (Lord Foster seemed so friendly in that fridge.) It's not lost on me that I shoulda been done with all things *Heidi* when I left that frozen mountain in Schladming, Austria.

I never had to appear at the trial for any of it—we cut a deal for immunity and they videotaped my testimony at a neutral office. Heidi and her lawyers were in the room with me, and I felt like such a fukken a-hole as I laid it all out like a two-bit canary.

The head-fed asked me the same question for each one of my thirty-seven exhibits:

"And what exactly, Mr. Sheen, was purchased with this check?"

To which I answered in the agreed-upon, rehearsed manner—thirty-seven times:

"Sexual services."

Every time I said those two words, I tried to imagine how it woulda sounded over the phone with Heidi if *that* was the description I used for my requests. She woulda told me to fuck off and hung up. Like a skipping record, the back-and-forth went on for an hour until the bottom of the evidence stack saw daylight. None of it felt present; I was watching myself watching Heidi stare at me with a look of betrayal and sadness. I could see with full transparency that so much more than her heart was completely shattered. To go from us having the greatest arrangement ever to that room with those people was as real as surreal gets. Strangest part in all of it was that I could tell a few of the G-men were silently wondering the same thing I was: Who the hell really got hurt in this victimless crime?

If I had it to do all over again, no chance I'd play ball like I did. Snitch is *not* a color I wear well. I was prepared to eat the misdemeanor and handle whatever consequences it brought. Problem was, they threatened to include pandering (which carries a nickel) if I didn't agree to become their "star" witness. I'll never forget the conversation during their early prep for the case that played out like a bad TV show.

Feds: "You're lookin' at five years for pandering."

Me: "But I'm just a john."

Feds: "Not if you paid the girls to be with your friends."

Me: "Who's sayin' I did that?"

Feds: "We have the proof."

Me: "Show me."

Feds: "We'll get back to you."

Called their fukken bluff but it scared the holy shit outta me. The next day we told 'em I was ready for my close-up. Turned out their entire case was built on tax evasion. They really didn't care what I'd spent the money on with Heidi; their focus was dedicated to the chunks of dough that went unreported from her side. The day they were all set to play my video testimony for the jury, Heidi's sister Shana had a complete meltdown on the witness stand. She was kicking dope with methadone and required medical aid to get herself back together. She was excused for the day, and all the press exited with her as she made her way back home like a parade leader. I caught a break but Heidi didn't.

They threw the proverbial book at her. We've never spoken since.

The press had a field *year* with my involvement in the Fleiss scandal. Hundreds of tabloid stories flooded the checkout racks, but even that tsunami couldn't touch the zenith it reached at the 1994 Academy Awards. During Whoopi Goldberg's opening monologue, in reference to the three actresses nominated for playing call girls, she posed the question, "How many times did Charlie Sheen get to vote?"

It brought down the house. Really smart joke from her writers, and honestly I didn't mind having my name spoken from that stage to a billion people worldwide. (Some crap ya gotta just own.)

The media stayed obsessed with Heidi's little black book and its unknown contents, holding Hollywood at gunpoint waiting for the client beans to spill disaster.

In some odd way, not being one of those hostages dreading their fate was a huge relief. When asked by an ambush journalist in a supermarket parking lot if I knew the names the world was craving, I didn't miss a beat with my response, "Lesson learned: don't write checks," as I ducked into the back of a limo.

The fact that I was sitting on just as much dirt as that LBB provided more humor than it did leverage. The stories about other clients the girls shared with me over a cigarette afterward were some of the kookiest I've ever heard. I coulda traded all of it for a nose job and a Swiss chalet, but that was a bridge *so* far I couldn't even see it. Too many married guys with kids to fuck around like some slimeball trying to be the man. If any of it was meant to come out, it woulda been their karma not mine. Me telling the rehab group over and over "*that's none of my business*" wasn't something that came to me in the moment. I showed up with that rule—and took it home with me when I left.

CHAPTER 28

New York, Summer of '94. The year had started out on a high note. I shot an action film in Arizona called *Terminal Velocity*. The movie was dog shit but brought with it the most dough I'd ever been paid as a film actor: six million bucks. Not too shabby for a guy the media labeled *finito* with the Fleiss fallout. (Who the hell knows, maybe the town was thanking me for keeping my stuttery trap shut.) Either way, it was an awesome milestone given my worship for the TV show I wanted to *be* as a child, *The Six Million Dollar Man*. The full-circle aspect was honored with my bad pantomimes of Lee Majors's slow-motion run in the opening credits, while my pal Adam Rifkin hummed the theme song. Incredibly silly and stupid and we probably shouldn't have done it in those restaurants. I've gotten to know Lee over the years, and never shared that story with him. (Probably better if he just reads it.)

The other employment boon in the mix was the contracts for the Japanese commercials I managed to hold onto through all the attempted character dismantling. With the help of my loyal and long-term endorsement agent, Liz Dalling, I had, at one point, three simultaneously on the air in Japan: Tokyo Gas air conditioners, Madras shoes, and Parliament cigarettes. (At the press conference in Tokyo for the cig company, I'd crammed Marlboro Reds into the Parliament box and smoked them while praising their "smooth and tasty" nic-sticks they were paying me a boatload to endorse.)

Parliament cigs would play an even bigger role in the trajectory of my personal life. While in New York filming one of their commercials in Central Park, my costar in the spot was a lovely young lady named Donna. Slender brunette with a perfect face and a disarming smile. She was smart and soft-spoken, beautiful *and* cute (my favorite combo), and had a carefree way about her I became totally smitten with. We had a few civilized dinners and drinks during our time together on the shoot.

The other moment we shared while promoting lung cancer was the same one that ninety-five million other Americans experienced at the same time. It was June 17, as we sat in my trailer and watched mesmerized on a fourteen-inch TV: O.J. Simpson's white Bronco in a slow-speed chase across the freeways of Los Angeles. Like everyone else, we were speechless and shocked as the final twisted chapter of a sports and media icon was disintegrating before our very eyes. My childhood ping-pong bully had crossed the ultimate line. I'd never known a murderer before that, and yet sadly (as we all know), thanks to twelve morons and a paper tiger prosecution, *technically* I still didn't.

After we wrapped the Parliament shoot and I flew home, I couldn't get Donna off my mind. She accepted my invite to come stay with me in LA, and we spent two fabulous weeks together like a couple of teenagers on spring break. I could feel something different with her that I hadn't enjoyed in quite some time. On the doorstep of thirty and coming out of the scandal I'd just survived, I latched onto a fantasy that I'd convinced myself would reshuffle the deck and put all the perceived wrongs behind me. Flying high on my brilliant plan, I found the courage at the bottom of a '70 Mouton magnum to take a knee and ask her to marry me. Someone much wiser once told me to never propose drunk, stressing that there was always the possibility the person could say "yes." That genius wasn't lying; Donna's response was exactly that.

It was my second proposal, and after the first failure with Kelly Preston, I was on a mission to finally make it to the altar and see firsthand how the big-whoop actually felt. I gotta give Donna a ton of credit for rolling those dice and boarding that rocket ship with me. As I look back on it, I think we were both more invested in the adventure than we were in the love thing. Guess we figured that minor detail would magically appear at some point.

I told her we needed to give it a year, and by then if we were still committed to the whole plan, we could get married on my thirtieth birthday. The added bonus for me was that I'd never forget the anniversary. That was of course assuming at some point in our future together, there'd actually be an anniversary to forget.

We spent that year together traveling between Orlando and Malibu, getting to know each other's families. I liked Donna's parents and they liked me. Her father, Jim, drank nearly as much as I did, and we closed many four-hour dinners with excessive "love you too, man" good-night hug-offs. Jim and I laughed a lot together in the face of whatever chagrin du jour Donna and her mom tried to barbecue us with. We'd often commiserate in private to discuss their constant advice for us to make healthier choices. It's not that we disagreed, we just weren't in a place to hear any of those words in English.

After awhile that shit gets old and one of two things happens:

you wave the white flag or you stand your ground. (Jim kept waving, while I stuck with stand.)

Our travel itinerary included Richmond, Virginia, as well as the various garden spots of Baltimore for a film called *Shadow Conspiracy*. The title alone tells us all we need to know. It's easily in my bottom three of all-time cinematic blunders. My review of it (were I to write one) would read something like:

> *"If a film could be liquid shit you have to drink, this one comes with a funnel."*
> —C. SHEEN, *NEW YORK TIMES*

The only standout aspect of *Shadow* was that its director, George Cosmatos, had directed Dad's film *The Cassandra Crossing*, where O.J. and I had first met. Kinda bizarre that my original O.J.-connection would be directing my first film with Donna by my side, given that I'd met her the day before the white Bronco madness. If the timing of that was an omen I stupidly missed, "oh well" is about all I can give it. It wouldn't have mattered—love and lust have a funny way of attaching blinders when you don't need them most. *Shadow Conspiracy*, for all its failures, began to lower those blinders, and the view was a lot different with those things off.

It was the first real test of our relationship to see how we functioned on location in my workplace. To put it bluntly, we malfunctioned. She didn't feel seen, and I didn't feel appreciated—the boogeyman-combo in *any* relationship and certainly not one that coulda been worked out mid-job. The wedding was a few weeks away, and the writing on every wall to rethink my decision looked like graffiti from a squatter. The signs were everywhere and my gut was at full voice, but like so many examples that preceded it, my actual voice stayed silent. I was so worried about how Donna would feel if I went ahead and postponed the big day, I completely overlooked the possibility that she might have actually agreed with me. I quashed her vote. And that was wrong.

The day finally arrived and thirty birthday candles lit the path to the altar. The JP was the Malibu judge who made my first arrest go away. On September 3, 1995, we were gonna find out if he could make the marriage charges stick. Happy birthday, dood. Enjoy your slow-speed chase.

CHAPTER 29

The wedding was a mess and the honeymoon wasn't too far behind. I kept it together during my ceremonial duties but drank way too much and crossed over into full-spectacle toward the end of the reception. Something about kicking all the lawn-lights, and pretending they were footballs going through the uprights as game-winners. I have zero memory of that neutral-zone infraction.

Donna and I were mid-flight coming back from the honeymoon and locked in a tense, snippy argument. The first leg of the two-parter had been an eight-day VIP tour of the various châteaus and vineyards in the Médoc region of southern France. For months I'd been on an insane wine jag, and selfishly used the trip as a cover story to sample the perfect Bordeaux on its native soil. She'd been dropping tropical hints as her preferred newlywed choice, but I'd already seen what Donna in a G-string did to a Hawaiian beach a few months earlier. I cast the tie-breaking vote that put me in a Versace suit with wine snobs, instead of a bathing suit with mai-tai migraines.

Many hours into cruising altitude with our squabble showing no quarter, I disengaged by taking another *walk down the aisle* to the back of the plane. Most of the 200 passengers were asleep at that point as I settled into the rear galley with a couple members of the cabin crew. I thought two double-shots of scotch would do the job, but angry math is never reliable. By the time double-shots three and four (totaling *eight*) hit bottom and got me right again, the stewardess was on the phone to the flight deck. Word of me being on the manifest had reached the captain, and his invite to visit the cockpit was extended. In that moment there's really no version of "*That's very kind, but I'm a bit too hammered and I think I'll pass.*" When boiled down, that invite is a command, and I was raised to always follow orders from anyone holding my life in their hands.

The two French pilots welcomed me inside their "office" and closed the cockpit door behind me. The A330 was so advanced for its time, a flight engineer was no longer needed to help guide the Air France jetliner. The captain and his affable copilot were big fans of *Platoon* and *Wall Street*, and I refrained from saying "I fukken sucked" when they applauded my work as Bud Fox.

The captain left his seat for us to take a photo together and I repeated the same move with his copilot. The eight shots of scotch I'd just pounded in the galley were churning their way into bloodstream bliss. I asked the captain if I could wear his fancy uniform jacket for another photo. He gladly complied, offering his pilot's cap as well to complete the look. I gestured a *do ya mind?* to his unoccupied left-hand seat, which prompted his *be my guest* sweeping hand of permission.

Down I plopped, in his uniform, into his chair.

The copilot seated next to me signaled his approval with a double thumbs-up.

We'd become a flying silent movie at that point.

The sun had just begun a horizon crest with its golden streaks filling our private space. The captain flipped down a tinted extension of the windshield visor to cut back some of the glare. Purely out of curiosity, I innocently asked both of them if "George" (the universal nickname for the autopilot) was flying the plane.

In a move that cut through all eight shots of single malt, the copilot reached up to a section of the instrument cluster and flipped a switch into the *down* position, as he informed me, "Not anymore."

Well *holy frikkin' fuck*, man. Far be it for me to ignore the fact that *someone* needed to step up and assume control. I gracefully moved both hands to either side of the steering wheel (the yoke), and instantly felt a vibration I could tell was the aerodynamic feedback from the 200-ton sky beast. *George* had turned into a dood named Carlos in a dream above the clouds. I stole a quick glance to my right at the first officer as if to say, *Um, we kool if I, uh . . . (?)*, he nodded that he was—and so I did. Leaning the yoke ever so slightly to the left, I felt like the craft was reading my mind as it adjusted with laser precision down to the tiniest measurable response.

I corrected back from that tilt to the recentered position and pulled my hands back toward my chest less than half an inch, to experience a seamless climb of maybe a hundred feet. I knew enough about the mandatory vertical separation of 3,000 feet between planes to keep us well inside the boundary. I brought her back to center and tried my hand at the right lean. Whatever I asked from the wonderful bird she spoke back to me with peerless synchronicity. It was a sensation so indescribable, I knew right then and there I wouldn't want or need to duplicate it ever again. There would be no reason to; I had arrived at terminal experiential velocity.

It's important that I make clear the entire sortie lasted all of ninety seconds. The copilot noticed my level of intensely focused joy and made the advisable decision to give the plane back to our pal *George*.

No sign of the bear, *or* the director. Also, we coulda filmed the damn thing in Malibu State Park. 1983. *GRIZZLY II: REVENGE*

Gonna have to guess that Darren Dalton took the photo. That, or C. Thomas had already plugged him with an AK and he was back in Sherman Oaks. *Red Dawn,* 1983. STEVE SCHAPIRO/ CORBIS VIA GETTY IMAGES

The Garth casting his spell, as Jen questions her casting recommendation. *Ferris Bueller's Day Off,* 1985.

PHOTO BY CBS VIA GETTY IMAGES

The Rib King and his Heath Knights of the Round Oven. My ab program clearly on the fritz.

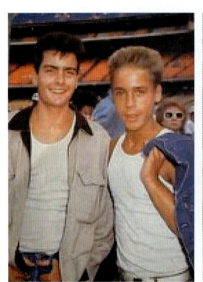

Left: With Chad Lowe at the Dodgers game, on a day off from *The Boys Next Door,* the same night I got my very first tattoo on Hollywood Boulevard, 1984. LAD STAFF

Right: I had no warning this cover was coming out. It just fell from Dad's morning paper onto the kitchen floor. They were so proud; I was the toast of the house that night. Then we all watched the show together, and afterward I felt more like the crumbs. *TV WEEKLY*

Glennis and Cassandra. One of them shaping my future—the other giving it purpose, 1985.

Brought my *Red Dawn* skills to help Dad protest something that day. The "WolverSheens" held the line.

With Paula for Cassandra's second birthday bash at the folks' house. "Family" *does* have many wonderful iterations. WENDY SHANKS

Left: In an airport in the '80s heading somewhere. Problem is, I don't remember ever working on *Miami Vice*.

Right: At the hotel during *Platoon,* really hoping I'm in someone else's room with such a Messy Marvin background. (Is that my *Red Dawn* jacket on the floor?) Busted. 1986.

Top, from left: Francis, Taylor, Doc.

Front, center: Lerner.

Mid-movie, midday, mid-thought.

Depp's great hair was very cushy. Doubt he felt the same about my arms. 1986.

This might very well be the pin that Dye graduated us with. It's either that, or it came from the PC commander during ping-pong AWOL with Drew. Either way, I'm really glad I kept it in that drawer for forty years.

A *Wall Street* scene with Pop where I tell him, "There is no nobility in poverty." Hard guy to sell that to. 1987.

When I stated that Dolly Fox "lived up to both sides of her name," my description was a fukken bull's-eye. 1986.

ALAN RUCK

In the presence of a living legend. He made my day—every day. Then he hijacked my dope. *The Rookie,* 1990. SCOTT GOLDMAN

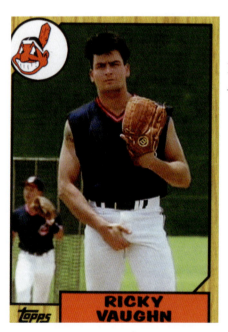

Looks like my hernia came back. *Major League,* 1998.

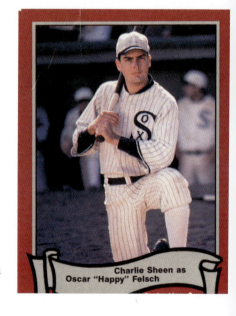

This card is the only thing I'm proud of from the movie. The Cozy Soup 'n' Burger is amazing—the meeting I had there for the film was not. *Eight Men Out,* 1987. BOB MARSHAK

Smoke break during *Cadence,* listening to either Fishburne, Pop, Brown Dave, or the lovely Kelly P. A win-win-win-win any way you slice that off-camera mystery. 1989.

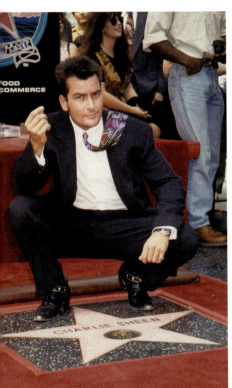

I wanted to be the first person to land on myself. One small step for (a) man, one giant promo for Versace. (I still have those fukken boots.) 1994. VINNIE ZUFFANTE (RIP)/GETTY IMAGES

Reggie's cameo in *Under Pressure.* Title shoulda been *Here's Your Refund with Interest.* Mr. October was his usual awesome self. 1996. CHRIS CHESSER (RIP)

Road trip with Pop to Cooperstown. Our baseball theme across the sands(lots) of time. Circa 1990.

Having a sweet moment with Mom. My shirt screams Buffett BBQ, but I don't think she ever braved the pork smoke or weed clouds to join us. Circa 1990.

In Hiroshima at ground zero with Mom and Scott G., 1990. I'm mid-poem and what I wrote that day brought Hopper to mind: "Feel the vibe of this place."

Our Hanes commercial, 2006. In a behind-the-scenes interview on set, Michael refused to accept the fact that Dad and I beat him years earlier in the competition. I told him I had video proof, he said he didn't care and that we lost. Can't lie—it was awesome.

Gone Fishin' –RIP Coop—x. c and t.

Hot Shots!: Topper Balboa, Brown Dave. "Ain't gonna be no rematch." 1991.

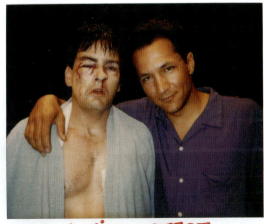

DAVE & HIS LATEST CREATION.

Twenty-first b-day in Little Rock. Alan Ruck with a heroic evac, as I was probably one drink away from needing a stretcher. D FOX

A legend sandwich. Backstage at Sam's show, circa 1989—no idea where this night wound up. It's a safe bet that they didn't know either.

J-Fiving with a '67 390 Stingray convertible, 1990. On zero sleep I wore the same outfit to the Navy Seals press junket the following morning. The twenty-five interviews I did were devoid of any terrestrial content. E. BRAUN

"Hi. We heard you were havin' a party." 1990. EDDIE B.

The "American Woman" road trip with Adam Rifkin, the Orbison Caddy, Detective Tracy's lid, and the back-seat boom-box trunk ritual. 1991. ADAM RIFKIN

With Pascal at the French Open, 1993. Our Ed Gein bathroom just a few hours in our rearview. This remains the only tennis match I've ever attended. (Cue the dramatic organ again.)

The moment of truth before entering the alien clone factory. They put Eddie B. in the same post-entry makeup, which freed me up to go blast a few rails into both noses—my own and the new fake one from Gabe and Brown Dave. *The Arrival,* 1995. BOB MARSHAK

From everything I've described about *Money Talks,* it's a no-brainer that our positions in this photo should be swapped. But holy shit, what's a guy have to do to get a waistline like that? BOB MARSHAK (RIP)

We could always count on White Dave to "man the big guns." (I mighta left out that he was a Big Bear Ace.) Dave's Howitzer that day most likely trained on the director's house. 1997.

The Brothers Mitchell (me and Emilio), celebrating a standing O at the premiere of *Behind the Green Door,* 1999. They co-directed, it had a budget of 60k and raked in 50 mil at the box office. Too bad it all ended in drug-addled fratricide. Them, not us. (Yet.)

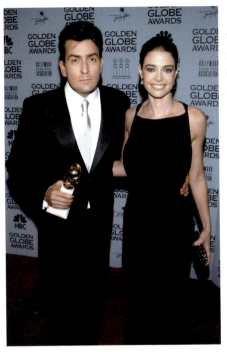

"This is for you, Alan Ruck!" (The trophy, not the girl.) C'mon D, that cracked you up. KEVIN MAZUR/WIREIMAGE

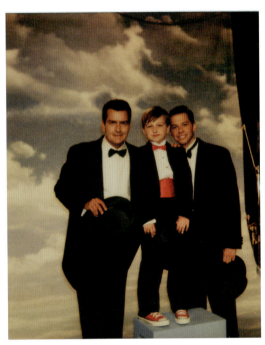

Charlie, Jake, and Alan, earliest pre-pilot days of *Two and a Half Men*. This is the day we shot the opening credits and lip-synced the "Manly Men" song. Big shoutout to Elizabeth E.G. Daily—between *Men* and *Breakfast Club*, she checked some epic boxes. 2003.

Season 2, episode 1, Sean brought his comedic genius to the C Harp men's group. I wish the world knew just how fukken funny he is. Elvis Costello is to his right, and that knee and fake Rolex belong to Coop.

Cassandra with her dad at six years old, circa 1991. Wanted her rooting for the Reds from an early age. It didn't work.

Sleep when they do—it'll be your only chance. Tiny child in giant bed is Sam. 2004.

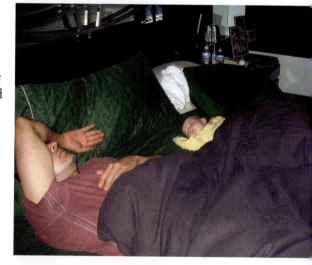

One of my favorite days ever with Lola and Sam, 2008. I lied to the customers and told them it was fresh squeezed. The girls' cuteness was the perfect distraction. We made $147 that day! MARK BURG

Hanging out at home with Sam and our special guest Crystal, the scene stealer from *Night at the Museum,* circa 2007. Well done, Eddie; the girls still smile about these days.

Crystal getting the waiter's attention for Lola. "Three bananas, I'm buyin'!"

I usually hate dopey Christmas shit, but this one with Bob and Max genuinely steals my heart. 2009.

Grandpa Charlie and his three G-daughters, 2018.
I'm gonna blink and they'll all be taking me cardigan shopping.
Enjoy every day (or at least pretend to).
PAULA P.

All photos courtesy of the author's personal collection, unless otherwise noted.

When he flipped the "life changer" switch back into its upper position, my hands were still straddling the yoke. I could feel the energy *leave* my grip as the airplane went back to its programmed business as usual.

With the help of the captain I climb-crawled out of his sacred seat and gave back the items he'd been generous to loan me. As I watched him get back into his fancy jacket and cap, it was abundantly clear that on him it was a hard-earned and noble uniform.

On me it was just a costume worn by the guy who probably just broke ten thousand laws. (But who's counting?) I thanked them for the incredible invite, and promised our "photo shoot with props" would remain entombed as top-secret from my end with our cockpit foursome. (I included *George*.)

This many years later, that promise has been broken.

Donna had fallen asleep in the time I was gone. She awoke briefly as I had to slide past her to reclaim my window seat. I gave her a kiss on the forehead and told her I was sorry about the fight.

"Where were you?" she asked.

"Took a walk, met a few people." I lit a smoke, reclined my chair.

"Anyone interesting?"

"Very. I'll tell you all about it when we land. Get some sleep, sweetie."

She did, but I didn't—sleep or tell Donna all about it. (Ever.)

The second half of the honeymoon was on the shores of Lake Tahoe at a vacation house called Bob's at the Beach. On the way there we wound up in such a verbal spat in the back of the limo, I took our wedding rings and threw them out the sunroof. Dave P., the security guard traveling with us, spent an hour looking for them with a flashlight at 2:00 a.m. on the side of the road. (He miraculously found both.) The rest of the drive was silent and awkward, with the evening breeze adding more chill to a union already in free fall. We almost called it quits that same night when we arrived at Bob's, and the decision to sleep in separate rooms mighta played a hand in waking up still married. Bob's at the fukken Beach was doing its very best to rename itself No Day at the Beach.

There were several times when I considered shutting down the booze for *her*, but that would have been a replay of the people-pleasing crap that filled all those coffee mugs with gallons of vino. I'd often drift into a state of fantasy, wishing *my* instrument cluster had a *George*-switch I could flip on when the turbulence became unbearable.

The second day on the lake I spiked my morning juice with vodka, and when Donna leaned in for a kiss and smelled it, the judgy horseshit went full splat.

I came so close to blurting out, "*The same brain that just flew our goddam airplane drunk can handle being tipsy for a fukken three-egg omelette on a balcony.*" (I'm really glad I didn't. The house came with a chef and those folks tend to hear everything.)

Not every day went like that, but the ones that did had a way of contaminating any happiness that came before. I blame myself for most of our dustups, with booze being the easiest culprit to pin it on. Our situation needed a villain to blame and a motive to convince the jury. However, the absence of a key factor could be viewed with just as much culpability. Donna and I didn't spend enough time enjoying each other with the same energy we had after that first handshake. Plain and simply put: We had forgotten how to be friends.

We somehow made it off Bob's Beach with the rings still on our fingers, and a week later I packed a few bags for Mexico City to begin filming *The Arrival*, a semi-hokey sci-fi thriller where I play a SETI scientist who uncovers a sinister alien plot. Brown Dave was my makeup artist on the shoot, and his key FX assistant was a talented Mexican dood named Gabe. The two of them transformed me with complicated prosthetics so I can go undercover into the alien clone-factory and put a stop to their global takeover. Spoiler alert: as brilliantly as those two *cloaked my Sheen*, the aliens weren't fooled and rendered me unable to thwart their evil plan. (Look it up, don't look it up, I think by now we're well past all that shit.) Actually I've spoiled nothing—no one saw the film back then and probably won't be doing so now.

I don't think it's far-fetched to attribute some of my lousy film choices to the constant stress and drama our marriage couldn't seem to escape. Donna came with me for the first two weeks of filming, and the geographic shift didn't lighten the gloomy load one bit. The more time we spent together the less we wanted to. Bottom line: As a married couple we just didn't fit, and the sooner we stopped pretending otherwise, the sooner we could both find peace and breathe again.

We never made it to our first anniversary—the one I silver-plattered to be "unforgettable."

Some marriages last forever. Many others are ripped apart by the pressure of staying together because you're *supposed to*. When all was said and done, Donna was an angel with how she handled everything. She never wrote a book, she never sold a story, she never gave an interview. The pure class and maturity that young lady upheld spoke volumes about who she is at her core. Maybe I suffocated that core, or at the very least didn't allow her the freedom to display it radiantly. Maybe if I'd just laughed more stuff away and not taken it so personally, she could have.

Maybe maybe maybe—if if if.

CHAPTER 30

Let's talk about crack. Where do I start? The word alone is fairly benign and conjures familiar images we're unfazed by—a plumber's butt, a sidewalk defect that harms your mom, an egg into a bowl of flour. Normal sights in the flip-book of life when we think of *sane* crack. *Insane* crack publishes a much different book with a host of images we avoid or try to forget: shirtless and howling, a stained gurney in a morgue, a zombie with a machete. For me, it wasn't just a word, it was another galaxy.

If you've never tried it, don't. If you're currently doing it, quit. If you used to do it and you're thinking of revisiting, do it in the middle of a crowded Starbucks and see how that plays out. Or better yet, ask your in-laws if you can bust out a few rocks at Thanksgiving after the gratitude share. It has no place in courteous society.

I first met *insane* crack with a lovely young lady named Sandy back in '92. We used to date off and on, and when it was on it was fabulous. I hadn't heard from her in a couple months and when she finally did call, there was much distress in her scratchy voice. She was in a bad spot, needing to be rescued from a gaggle of tweakers in a dope house. I swooped in to negotiate her release with an HK 9-mil concealed in my waistband. The cretins informed me that I had to clear her drug tab, which I was able to do with the two grand I had in my pocket. (I was packing a gun and a fat wad of cash, but needed to save her from people with guns and fat wads of cash. Good times.)

The drive home was quiet, and I didn't press for any details. Her appearance told the whole story—way too thin with circles under her eyes that looked like bad makeup in a cheap movie. We'd done cocaine together in the past the traditional way: straight up the ol' schnoz. I came to find out she'd been smoking it, and, while I was secretly curious about that method, seeing how it had trampled her pizzazz was not a ringing endorsement to take that plunge.

We made it back safely to my townhouse in Malibu. Sandy was so relieved to be away from that sketchy shithole, she jumped into bed naked and demanded my company. I told her it was a better plan to have a stiff drink, take a nap, and maybe cross that bridge later. She wasn't havin' it, telling me naps were for infants and to join her at once. I was torn. (There's a fine line between regret and rejoice, but sometimes ya gotta just do what you're told.)

When I climbed in beside her, she had a freshly loaded crack pipe in one hand and a lighter in the other. She handed me the paraphernalia and told me not to overthink it. My brain heard that, and *think* and *over* tapped out. I threw caution and accepted her invite to the extraordinary combo she was offering. As I took that massive first hit, Sandy disappeared under the covers and I disappeared from planet earth.

People will claim their greatest feelings in life as "my child's first steps" or "saving that kid from a fire." To quote Matt Hooper from *Jaws*: "I got that beat." Sandy and that drug rewired my frontal cortex into light-speed oneness times two.

Sorry kids, sorry wives—life can be a sneaky fucker when the narrative sprints off the page into the weeds of unredeemed nirvana.

I didn't need any more proof. Nothing would be the same after that as we decompressed next to each other in blissful silence. I knew down to my core that one of two things had to happen next: never leave the bed with Sandy and smoke that shit every day until it killed me *or* swear off of it forever and be okay leaving behind a batting average of 1.000 with that monster. As amazing as it made us feel to be so perfectly welded together, it had to stay behind for anything valuable to stay in my life.

I made a vow in that moment to my better angels that I would cozy up to the abstinence of *door number two*. I shared my pledge with Sandy and told her how much I'd love to keep seeing her but couldn't do so as a threesome. Essentially clarifying that she was welcome anytime—the crack was not. She completely understood, and after I dropped her off at her home the next day we once again drifted apart. I'd check in with her occasionally and when I didn't hear back for several months, I assumed she wanted to be left alone to figure things out on her terms. If I was to be included in those terms, she knew where to find me; I wasn't hiding.

A year later I got a call from my old pal Tommy Howell to painfully inform me that Sandy had died. Holy hell, man. It hit me really hard. I was beside myself trying to imagine her final moments on that goddam pipe. I couldn't stop thinking about our memorable night together, wondering if replacing our crack-lust with kind words would have changed anything. (Who am I kidding. The only "kind words" in that bed were *how do we get more of this shit?*)

The second-guessing we put ourselves through is always more for *us* than for the person we've lost. I never got the details, but whatever Sandy's version of *door number one* looked like must have had a hand in some of it.

It can be as simple as stay or go, left or right, and just like that it's all over because someone called "tails." The vow I made that night held true to the end of '96. Suffice it to say, however shirtless my journey was destined to become, the full story couldn't possibly be told without a goodly amount of howling.

For the record, I did mention about 100 pages ago, "At some point everything's negotiable." A sacred promise to myself was not immune to that truth.

CHAPTER 31

Across all of '97 and a few appetizers into '98, I made six movies and five of them were rancid. Thank goodness for Chris Tucker and *Money Talks*, or that lineup would have been a complete shutout. As wonderful as Chris and the entire cast turned out to be, none of them could spike-strip the booze-chariot I rode to work every day. Our first-time director, Brett Ratner, had to shoot around my wobbly moments while rearranging other scenes when he knew I was anywhere but present.

It was a career-making job for Brett, and with his troubled star flying off the rails he had to pull a rabbit from somewhere to mitigate the chaos. Wit's end doesn't really cover where I'd taken him, and he still led with compassionate solutions in place of judgment and slander. We were shooting nights and Brett came into my trailer to pitch his Hail Mary plan in earnest, disarming beggary. He carefully opened with, "Not asking you to stop, and I understand it's challenging working nights as that's usually when you're off the clock and blowing it out full tilt." His girlfriend was a notorious dopehead, so his insights weren't coming from the ancient book or some rehab therapist; they were streetwise and fluid.

He continued: "All I'm asking is that you cut it *in half*. If you need four shots to get the engine humming, go with two instead. If five or six lines of blow help you regain some focus, see if two or three will get you to that same place. If you can do this for me, I'm confident we'll finish this thing on time and on budget. Whattaya say Sheen, can I have your word you'll make a genuine effort to give this new plan a shot?"

I was touched and couldn't help but laugh at the brilliant insanity the wily young director had pulled out of his arse. I wrapped him up in a big hug and gave him my word—the "adjustments" would start that same night. Believe it or not, the relief I felt from being asked instead of told made a huge difference.

My work became solid enough to complete my scenes as I held up my shifty end of the bargain. The man they called "Ratt" brought a tree to my forest I could actually chop down. That is, of course—until my axe shattered and I wound up unable to film, with a thirty-two-hour cocaine nosebleed. The producers threatened to fire me without pay if I didn't get my act together. I love a hearty challenge, and once the bleeding stopped, I shut it down the next day and finished the film in everyone's good graces.

I never got a chance to dig down into what the hell was really going on during that movie. Mail-order psychiatry would cite unresolved funk from the sad marriage. If that was true and I had decided to unwrap it, then what?

I didn't have enough time before the next movie was starting to commit to anything meaningful that might peel that Donna onion, or begin to pump the brakes on the party bus. There was also no chance I was gonna show up to work with a traveling therapist or one of those useless, overpaid sober-companion morons. (At that point I'd be better off with a mango enema.)

I didn't view the nosebleed disaster as a sign that it was time to quit; I saw it as *proof* that the drug needed a much better delivery system. I knew I couldn't drink it, and after winding up in the medical tent at a Pink Floyd concert, I was definitely never gonna *eat* it again.

My options were down to one—the same "one" I could still see plastered to the fukken door that Sandy chose. *Sorry sweetie, but you started this.*

It got dark fast and stayed that color for a lot longer than it should have.

Films three, four, and five sent me to Scotland, Montreal, and Big Bear, California. Marlon Brando was in Montreal and I'm pretty sure we had scenes together. *Trainspotting* lied to me—it's really hard to buy dope in Scotland. I spent the entire time in Big Bear looking for one with a Hungarian accent. My career started with a bear and felt like it was lining up to die with one.

The precious Big Bear schlock with all the trimmings of a student film was called *Five Aces*. I was way too high or hungover to show up for most of it, and one of those cards, Chris McDonald renamed it *Four Aces and a Stand-In.*

Number six on the final countdown was Arizona. I wasn't there to make a movie; I was there to mook a mavie. It has no title—I've disappeared it from my soul. It had no director—just mascara on a human bandana.

The creative flame that once inspired Super 8 to the silver screen had been reduced to a crack torch lighting up porn on a computer screen. I was ready to be done with all of it.

CHAPTER 32

There's really nothing unique to speak of that I brought to the Arizona desert during that production. I was so completely beaten down by the time I arrived, I knew I should have been put on waivers three movies ago. I felt an odd, almost mystical, kinship with the bone-dry landscape—not much survives in those conditions so I guess we had that in common. A climate that drenched sweat in the daytime and froze me at night kept those promises even when I hadn't left my room. My predictable sideways behavior had become interchangeable across each film set, with the new location being the one obvious variable. My only sense of that variable usually came from the hotel stationery or the souvenirs I took from the airplane. *Oh kool, an Air-Gonzo barf bag.*

The room's elephant during that time still nudges me and can't be evoked without a heaping plate of resentment. When the various producers and directors sat with me to discuss the jobs, it does beg the obvious question: How the fuck did they not see the state of mind I was in? *(Get that man some help, you dickheads.)* It felt like I was strapped to a conveyor belt being hand-cranked by junk peddlers who stood in line to vulture the last scraps off my withered carcass. I'm not a name-namer but come on, reading this you know exactly who you are: *Shame on ALL of you.*

It adds even greater insult to the freebooting of my dire straits that the entire film slate of '97 could have been replaced with gas-station tuna sandwiches and nothing on earth would have been different. These were movies that wouldn't even make it into the dollar bin on the street in front of the video store. Cheap, useless, uninspired dreck that would never see the light of day unless the fukken sun exploded.

Yeah man, I didn't bring shit to the desert, but I did bring something home: an injectable, 80 mg per day, synthetic morphine habit.

I had a nurse fantasy for a long time. When the film ended and I left the desert, that fantasy had finally become a reality. Sexy young lady (whom we'll call *Sarah*) was a registered nurse I met at a local party close to the hotel. I asked her if she wanted to get away from all the noise and have a few drinks back at my room. She said she'd love to, and jokingly I wondered (out loud) if she'd brought her nurse's uniform with her that night. Sarah didn't miss a beat and told me it was in her car. It was then or never—I had to find out if there was any way she could bring it to the room. These days you wind up in a deposition for asking that question, that night I wound up with a lovely gal who was flattered and couldn't have been happier to play dress-up.

She had the nurse ensemble in her carry bag. The same bag that hid the dope she'd been lifting from the hospital that employed her. (The plot was thickening in my favor.) It was a drug I had never done, so I wanted to walk with it before I ran. The new kid on the block was called "new"-bain—Nubain. My sexy healthcare practitioner became known as Nurse Nubain. (Some nicknames just can't be avoided.)

I had never fucked around with heroin or needles. It scared the hell outta me for the same reason it scares the hell outta most sane people: death. Sarah explained that Nubain was an IV drug very similar to morphine, and how a small amount could be just as fun as a few stiff drinks but without the nasty hangover. She also told me that if I shot it into the muscle it would take a bit longer to kick in. Given the head-spinning visuals that stood before me, I was fine with being on Nubain's clock. Not sure if it was her white cap or the pink stethoscope that sealed the deal, but I finally said fuck it and pulled the trigger.

As it gradually washed over and through me, it was unlike anything I'd felt previously. Time didn't stand still but it didn't move forward either. I thought back to my old pal Brad W's description of opiates: *warm jacuzzi jets from the inside.* Spot on, Brad—but you did leave out that it was one hundred jacuzzis. Now please leave my fantasy.

I asked the good nurse if Nubain was something I could use to help me put down the pipe and cut back on the booze. She said it could absolutely assist in those transitions. When I heard that, it felt like I hit the jackpot—Nurse Nubain, the new freedom juice, a chance at smoother sailing. The more time we spent together the more I liked her. She was really smart and treated me with a respect that never leaned toward fawning. I felt special with Sarah and we both knew our shared feelings were genuine. We made a plan to keep the party flowing back in LA, and as a lady of her word, who took that oath, she joined me there a week after we wrapped the film.

The muscle method was no longer doing the job. I was with a pro when it came to needles and figured I couldn't have been in safer hands. She then began to administer the drug how it was intended by the evil docs at Pfizer: mainline. It was a fukken game changer. I chose a forearm vein in the middle of a tattoo to conceal the prick marks—as with every drug that needs hiding, I had to eventually decide between permanent long sleeves or a bigger tattoo. As it turned out, the only dangerous hands in the mix were my own.

Nurse Nubain didn't just steal one batch of the drug and blow through it. She was running a business dealing that shit and had a long list of VIP clients in the Phoenix and Tucson areas. *(That vibe sound familiar to anyone . . . ?)* It can roundly be said that I knew how to pick 'em. Maybe it was more about them knowing how to pick me. Either way I wasn't complaining—it's always nice to be picked by someone to do what you love.

The deal Sarah and I agreed to was that I'd only do the drug when she was in town. Best intentions for sure, but that agreement didn't survive the first week. My bodyguard, giant of a man named Zip, made arrangements at my behest for Sarah to FedEx the dope and needles in her absence. We should have honored the original plan. Getting the drug in the amounts and frequency like I did, sent my well-intentioned blueprint through the same chaos-mill that had mangled all the others.

My nurse fantasy became a lot more than I bargained for. None of that is on Sarah. Like I felt about Nicolas and influencing him during J-5—it all comes down to choices. I chose the nurse, I encouraged the outfit, I saw exactly what was in her bag. I didn't wake up with a needle sticking out of my arm, I made the decision to put it there. The series of events those choices led to would require much more attention than the expert know-how and comfort of one sexy nurse. I'd need the entire fukken hospital.

CHAPTER 33

"Escape from LA" Part 1:
Jane's Addiction

I met Jane through a friend. Easily one of the prettiest *and* sexiest women I've ever encountered. Jane was a tad offbeat and usually put her feet up on the friendlier side of nutty. She was also a part-time working girl. I asked if she'd be interested in changing that to full-time with me, and after she exclaimed "hell yes," we spent many days and nights basking in the fruits of her enthusiasm.

It was the quieter moments that exposed a different side of her character. The simple act of watching TV together brought those flaws to the surface. (A person's looks, a lousy product in a commercial, nothing life-changing.) It did have my attention, but I'd dismiss it as one wilted flower in an otherwise stunning bouquet. We also did drugs together, and to her credit, Jane was consistently able to pull it back before anyone fell asleep at the wheel. If I was going too hard, she'd always keep us on the road, away from disaster. It seemed like what we had was such a nice fit—but *fit* is a sneaky word when someone decides to throw one.

* * *

We were doing our thing. The only difference from one day to the next was the new story to tell. After a night of very little sleep, we were upstairs in my bedroom getting ready to figure out the day when Jane saw a photo of my thirteen-year-old daughter Cassandra next to my closet. She stopped in front of it, studied the picture for a few seconds, and without warning launched into a barrage of inappropriate comments that stunned me. I'd never heard anything like it. The sweet, sexy, fun person I'd gotten to know was suddenly gone, eerily replaced with a weird darkness I did not recognize. Her twisted comments led me to a stern and swift verdict: Jane had to leave my house at once. (The unease I'd been ignoring during our TV time had its lightbulb moment—her snide comments about bad hairdos and dish soap went deeper than I realized.)

I called my buddy Coop to come pick her up, and during that phone call I dropped an insult for Jane's ears, and that's when she attacked me. *(Sticks and stones, anyone?)* In a move to defend myself—my *eyes* more specifically, as she was trying to stab them with her jagged car keys—I got behind her to wrap her up and try to calm her down. Somewhere in the fracas she cut her lip, and man oh man, based on those optics the story became so radically spun you'd think I was a serial killer.

The fake stories got so ugly, there was no point in defending myself with the facts. Were I to fight the allegations, the combination of her beauty and my reputation gave their side a slam dunk of a case. I took my legal lumps, paid her 200 grand, and agreed to a restraining order of no contact inside of 100 feet. The shittiest part (once you carve out her meltdown) was that I really dug that girl. In hindsight, there were things going on with Jane that had nothing to do with me or Cassandra.

The reason I bring all of this to light is to offer a peek behind the curtain of the nonexistent epilogue. Stories don't end because you've reached the bottom of the page; there's *always* a secondary viewpoint worth listening to. The media's slanted portrayal of the situation didn't fall anywhere close to the truth, and left inquiring minds blinded by three-dollar bills 'til the cows came home and left again.

I split my time between two homes: a condo at a place called the Wilshire in Westwood and a house in Malibu Lake. About a month after the dust settled with the Jane mess, I was at the condo and when the phone rang I didn't recognize the number; I figured it was probably one of the lawyers for the probation deal I had just agreed to. (It was a two-year stretch that included community service and a very rigid order to *obey all laws*.) I picked up and it wasn't a lawyer—it was Jane. I was shocked. Part of the restraining order outlined that any telephonic communication between us would constitute a violation. Before I could hang up or pour a triple vodka, Jane lit up the line and it was a heater:

"Here's the deal, Charles, I'm down on the street in front of your building, and I am in a limo, naked, and you're gonna come down here and fuck me while we drive around—and if you don't do this right now I will call the court and tell them that you came to my place to harass me. You will go to jail."

Okay Sheen, breathe. Take a minute. This could be a trap, I mean fuck, it's already a trap, but it could be a trap trap, the really bad kind. Choose your words carefully dood, in case you're being recorded. Check the street down below, see if—hoe-lee-shit—a goddam limo. This is not a drill, people, this is real world.

Her voice yanked me back into my body: "I'm not fuckin' around, Charles, you have three minutes to get your ass down here or my next call is to you-know-who."

"Hi Jane. Nice to hear fro—"

She cut me off. "It's now TWO minutes." Her update flung me from the kitchen and out the door, banging the elevator button, still holding the cordless phone.

"Heading to you now." The elevator dinged. I tossed the handset behind me and jumped into the *going down*-box. I'd been in thousands of limos in my life. That would be the first time I entered one as a hostage.

After a steamy thirty-minute cruise through the backstreets of Westwood, the limo pulled back up to the front of my building. Every demand on Jane's list had been checked off. With the fun stuff behind us, I did use the opportunity to apologize to her for all the bullshit that came as a result of our one bad half hour together. Her response—"Don't worry about that, we're past it"—caught me off guard. I thanked her and was half waiting for her to say something similar about my daughter. It wasn't offered and I wasn't gonna push it. We tried to share a seated-in-car goodbye hug, but those always wind up like a holiday embrace with the mailman.

I got out of the limo in mild shock and watched it drive away. I was in that place again: watching myself watch something. I wasn't fully convinced yet if what had just happened was insane reality or an intense fantasy.

Back upstairs in the condo, I was having a difficult time labeling what I'd just experienced as punishment or revenge. Maybe the whole thing was about power and control, and if that was the case I was totally kool with being powerless under Jane's control anytime she chose. Just to review the rules for a second: To keep my freedom I had to weather the kinky impulses from one of the hottest gals I've ever known.

(Was I missing something? Was that the part where I was supposed to fukken whine about being manipulated or victimized by her? If so, wasn't gonna happen, that would be the biggest insult imaginable to anyone out there dealing with that hideous shit for real.)

Bottom line: I didn't have the luxury to ponder her motives. I needed to stay outta jail, and if that meant being on call for her at all hours, no sweat—not a single drop. The path to freedom can often send us through the wonkiest terrain, and if that was the vault door I had to solve, I was gonna be patient with its combination. The one advantage I did have was a slightly more refined understanding of how unpredictable she could be.

I also had a bunch of crack to keep me on my toes.

Round two of our cat-and-mouse erotic thriller was at the Malibu Lake house, a few weeks after I'd returned from Arizona. I was surprised that Jane wanted to come back there, and when I told her we could meet at the condo instead, she said the house was fine. (Her decision, her rules.) As soon as she walked in it felt nothing like the limo, and everything like before. Before mean words and unlucky actions burned it all down in less than twenty seconds. We both sensed a wisp of something in the air that neither of us wanted to define, but if pressed I knew that feeling was sadness.

That was her cue to take control again and remind me how it was gonna go. Jane wasn't there to be sad, she was there to mend the fences on her terms. I didn't have any terms; I knew the ice I stood on was still paper-thin in certain spots. My body was exhausted from all the dope and chaos, and I had to keep digging deeper to find the energy the situation required. She knew something was going on, with the amount of vodka I was chugging straight from the bottle. I explained that I was going cold turkey to get off a terrible drug I'd been shooting into my veins.

The vodka, I told her, was the quickest way to get over the hump and rinse the *other* poison outta my body. Wasn't an exact science but it sure as shit helped. The final package I got from Nurse Nubain was filled with sedatives instead of dope. I guess she wanted to be part of the solution and become *Sarah* again. Mixing downers with booze was risky as hell, but I was crawling so far outta my skin I didn't care. I was willing to do whatever it took to make it across the final bridge and avoid winding up in rehab again. I'd made it to day four and could feel I was gonna be out of the woods shortly.

Jane rode out the final throes of the detox storm with me, and when she left a couple days later, the finish line was in my sights. All alone once again in my big upstairs bedroom, my body was still chirping for even the tiniest dose of the evil freedom juice.

I would not give in. I popped another Xando and chased it with fiery gulps of Absolut Peppar. The cravings passed, I finally passed out.

If the stories they printed about my role in the Jane drama were true, there's not a snowman's chance in hell she would have come back *twice*. All these years I've known the truth, but for decades could never breathe a word about any of it. My voice in all of this could no longer stay silent.

CHAPTER 34

"Escape from LA" Part 2:
Isoptera

When I awoke the following day (at 5:00 p.m.), I was all alone in my lake house that wasn't on the lake. My bodyguard, Zip, was in a guest room on the other side of the property down near the pool. There always comes a point in any detox when it feels like the entire bloodstream has been swapped out with termites. I was in that place. I needed to make sure there weren't any wayward needles or 'bain still hidden anywhere. My search began in the office. With its superior lighting, it had become my ground zero for the needles and dope activity. If anything had been errantly left behind in there, I wouldn't need a sniffer-dog to find it.

Not five seconds into the search, hidden in the back of the first drawer I yanked open, a fresh twenty-five-gauge needle was staring at my termites. I didn't panic or try to get the good nurse on a red-eye. Without Brad's jacuzzi-juice, that needle had all the value of an unloaded pistol. However, the *pull* it created was so sudden and fierce I needed to know if any *bullets* were close by. I tore the small room apart and came up empty.

Well, not *empty* empty. I did locate a minor bindle of powdered blow that somehow had escaped the magic saucepan of Chef Boyargeeze (as White Dave used to call me).

I decided that I wanted to shoot cocaine. I had never shot cocaine and didn't know what I was doing. In the druggie films I'd watched, the characters who shot cocaine seemed to know what *they* were doing. I went to the kitchen and the bathroom to collect the items I needed and carried them back upstairs to the office. As I mimicked the preparation ritual from those movies, a line from a poem I wrote years earlier about the 27 Club was on a loop in my head: *That heated spoon of Mister Moon, cooked fast the juice of death.* Over and over, it recited itself. I flick-flicked the bubbles in the tube to get the urine-tinted liquid air-free and fancy.

Spoon Moon death, spoon Moon—

Take that, you miserable termites! Into my vein the yellow
 liquid went.
I waited. Nothing. Waited some more. Same.
I was certain that didn't happen to any of the characters in
 those cocaine-shooting films.
I had to do what I'd done in the past with other drugs. *More.*
I didn't have to wait for the second dose to kick in;
 they both hit me at the same time. The room began to spin.
My ears filled with echo that shifted into warble.
My heart rate doubled and tried to pump even faster.
My breath was tight and wouldn't travel past the bottom of
 my neck.
I fought to stand up. I got through the office doorway to the
 landing at the top of the stairs.

Any help I'd need urgently existed only at the bottom of the stairs.
Gripping the handrails on both sides, I was determined to make it down there.
The first step I tried wouldn't give me more than two inches.
My legs began to shake. The second attempt with the other foot—just as bad.
I could barely walk, much less navigate the entire staircase.
If I fainted up there, the tumble to the lower granite floor would've split my head.
With the last few cubic pockets of oxygen still available to me, I screamed his name into the void. My vision began to sparkle into black cubes.

Zip suddenly appeared. First glance was all he needed to determine my state.

He dialed a very short number then carried me down.

Zip was dumping cold water on my head when we both heard the distant siren.

I'd be going for a ride in that loudmobile, and my gut made it very clear the night wasn't drawing to a close; it was just getting started.

CHAPTER 35

"Escape from LA" Part 3:
April Showers

Nobody ever looks good in hospital lighting. Whatever the paramedics gave me in the ambulance had me in and out of the nods. Between those fade-outs, I heard a female voice ask a coworker from the doorway of my room, "Is he gonna make it? Jesus, Phil, he looks dead." (I needed a floor lamp with a frosted 20-watt bulb in the worst way.)

An irony I found most curious in the whole shit show was how it all basically came down to a registered nurse who landed me in that hospital. I'm not placing blame, just connecting dots. I finally fell asleep for twenty hours. While I was out, a host of juicy developments took place. None of which I'd be happy to hear about when that first jello arrived.

As it turned out, IV Valium wasn't the only thing the EMTs gave me in the ambulance—those lifesaving traitors also gave me the shaft. They alerted the media during the drive and sold me like a cheap hat. As a result, the place was swarming with press when I rolled in. Crazy rumors had begun to swirl that I had OD'd and punched my ticket.

Emilio heard it on the radio and refused to believe it. Dad showed up an hour after I got there and organized a press briefing to set the record straight. The word was out and I knew it would only be a short matter of time before the judge caught wind of it. That slightly amorphous *obey all laws* detail I had agreed to was gonna be a hard one to decriminalize.

The next time I awoke, my hospital room was filled with addiction shrinks—some type of crisis team that worked there. They wanted to get me straight into a rehab, and after a highly charged debate that lasted an hour, I wasn't havin' it. With the team still in the room, I asked the head MD if I had suffered a heart attack or a stroke. He informed me that neither episode had taken place. (He should have lied.) It was the weekend and I knew the court couldn't do anything until Monday. I had resigned to the fact that I was gonna be sent somewhere and was already crafting a secret plan that made room for a few concessions I needed to claw back. Unless I could spend my final thirty hours of freedom drinking away all the recent stress and trauma, I wasn't going anywhere they insisted.

I knew there wasn't any more dope at Malibu Lake to tempt me into a repeat disaster, but thankfully the place was still flush with booze. Dad somehow caught wind of my plan and his head nearly exploded. I could hear him out in the hall, asking any expert who'd listen what his options were to keep me hospitalized until the rehab transport took place. He was told he didn't have any, that I couldn't be reasoned with, and once the court got involved they'd help him in any way they knew how. Dad's face was stone, blue eyes transfixed on something way out there only he could see. I'm pretty sure that was the moment when he began to craft *his* secret plan. *(Who the heck do you think I learned it from . . . ?)*

As soon as I was able to stand and get dressed, Zip and I left the hospital and headed back to that house on the hill, above a murky man-made lake. I knew the clock was ticking.

The final booze hurrah at my home didn't really pan out how I envisioned. Getting that hammered only made me crave the pipe that much more, and I wasn't about to farm all the carpet and smoke whatever I pulled out. (Did that once with a cocktail onion, and that was lesson-learned for that move.) I also couldn't reach any of the women I'd been seeing, and one bummer after another began to stack up. Still not sure how the next piece came into existence, but around 9 p.m., I was in a car with Zip headed to Promises Malibu: the original converted five-bedroom shakedown-joint for affluent fuckups. Zip would tell me later that he and I had a heart-to-heart at the crib, and decided it was best if I got ahead of it to curry some leniency from the court in case they chose to play hardball.

He also told me that he was pretty sure my Dad would hack him up like Kurtz if he didn't get me there that night.

The Promises peeps put me in a modified garage-bedroom when I got there and fed me a steak. I ate the steak with my hands and sipped A.1. from the bottle with each bite. Good start. *Good steak.* They also fed me enough tranquilizers to put down a T. Rex. It didn't work. (Maybe T. Rexes weren't as sturdy as we've been made to believe.) I woke up two hours later and decided I needed to take a walk and get some air. The facility sits at the very top of a windy residential canyon in Malibu called Big Rock, roughly two and a half miles from the PCH. A guy named Jim was assigned to me that first night and took the walk with me. By the time he realized there was no shot at talking me out of my plan, we had reached the highway; I'd walked all the way to the bottom. In fukken pajamas.

My trusty limo driver for years, a man named Dylan, was waiting for me when Jim and I got there. (I can only guess that I had maneuvered a way to call him with the heads-up. If so, no memory of that call exists.) Jim wished me luck as I sped off into the night with Dylan in my Continental chariot. I was instantly on the phone with Zip, telling him to get ahold of a girl named April and meet us at the condo in Westwood. We made it about 500 yards when the cops lit us up and pulled us over—on the identical stretch of road where Pat K and I used to smoke the Led Zep bong loads during high school, avoiding those same cops. Seventeen years later, they finally got their man.

Someone at Promises had dropped a dime on me, telling dispatch I'd bailed from their rehab and was a threat to my own safety. (Liar.) When the cops got me out of the limousine, I told them I was on the way to a hospital to witness the birth of my second child. (Bigger liar.) They bought none of it, put me in the back of the squad car, and drove me to the psych ward at Cedars-Sinai in West LA. Once there, I wound up in a room with a psychiatrist named Stu, whom I actually knew from a few AA meetings back in 1990. Doc Stu gave me the full rundown of the power he held over me that night, with the cruelest item being the seventy-two-hour hold he could activate. I took a minute to gather myself, pointed to the telephone on his desk, and told him *that* would be the murder weapon if he didn't come up with a way to spring me. Whether he bought it or not, I guess my acting chops were still convincing enough to leave him wondering.

Twenty-eight minutes after my preposterous "tough guy" fake threat, Doc Stu and I were stepping off the elevator into my condo.

He stayed for a few minutes and made sure I was as close to okay as I could've been. Before he left, the gracious alienist looked me right in the eye. "Don't die" is all he said and was gone. I talked the hospital out of rehab, I talked the rehab into a walk, I talked Dylan into an evac, I talked the cops out of jail, I talked the head Cedar's psychiatrist into a ride home, and Zip talked April into a 2 a.m. visit on the fifteenth floor of the Wilshire with the MaSheen. As mentioned earlier: Nicknames are earned—not seized. (If I'm mistaken and didn't mention that, I did now and it's still really, really true.)

Zip and April got there twenty minutes later. She was a gorgeous petite blonde who had done a girl-girl adult film I saw and went nuts over. Through a string of seedy connections I was able to find her, and we'd been hanging out together for a couple of months. Strange thing was: That was the *only* porn April had ever done, so she wasn't all blown-out and completely fucked-up by the industry. (She also happened to be from Cleveland and loved *Major League*, so—we had that to build on.)

I had a sizable amount of crack and booze stashed away at the condo. April was too healthy to fuck around with the pipe, but she did enjoy a few cocktails here and there. We took the party into the back bedroom while Zip stayed in the central area of the place manning the helm and monitoring the comms. She and I had an amazing few hours together, and as it was winding down we sat on the comfy floor of the bathroom listening to music. Maybe it was the dope, maybe it was the speaker on the wall, but something about the pitch of the treble seemed off to me. I climbed up on the counter next to the sink, was convinced I'd spotted the problem, and decided to make an adjustment to one of the speaker cables with a knife I had close by. Someone should have hid the cutlery—the knife slipped off the wire and found the top of my left-hand middle finger and tore it open down to the fukken bone.

The blood was flying everywhere. April gasped at the gruesome sight and immediately soaked a hand towel to wrap the geysering digit. I sat down on the floor with my arm above my head as April ran to get Zip. As she sprinted off, I was left with the haunting image of myself in the mirror. Between the bloody shirt, my insane hair, the dead eyes staring back at me from a gaunt and sallow face, it seemed like I was in the room with a ghost. (I know dick about Shakespeare, but I'm sure there's some appropriate *Hamlet* quote to sum it all up perfectly.)

Fifteen minutes later the three of us were in the car on the way to an emergency room nearby. Zip had covered me in a jacket so they wouldn't 5150 me the second we came through their doors. Shortly after our motley arrival, my *FU*-finger was sewn back together by a smooth ER doc who was so handsome I wanted to strangle him. I could see how April was eyeing him and I thought: *Great, the night's hero just had to be the one dood who actually looks terrific in this hideous light. When life gets fair again, wake me; I'll be in the closet with the rest of the mops.*

CHAPTER 36

"Escape from LA" Part 4:
Sacrificial Lam

Our tidy pod made it back to the condo, my hand still numb from the pre-suture shot of lidocaine. There's always a goodly amount of medical-grade speed in any member of the *'caine* family, and with everything I had onboard from the past forty hours, I didn't know whether to shave my head or start a book club. In spite of my gorging at the pharmaceutical buffet, the sudden adrenaline crash was so intense that I passed out with the lovely April snuggled in perfectly. I'd never known a girl named May or June and that was okay, they could keep the other eleven months as long as I could have April. I felt cocooned and cared for and didn't give a shit if I had five more minutes or the whole day to enjoy it, my first pocket of bliss was gonna be more relished than Oscar Mayer's entire history.

My brain heard the violent knocks as gunshots; my visceral reality knew it was Zip's giant fist and knuckles on my bedroom door. Since April hadn't overdosed, been kidnapped, slashed, arrested, or kicked dope recently, I was really hoping she'd go unlock the door. With her nurturing qualities she certainly would have—if she was actually still in the room. *Fuck.* With a fresh set of downs came a new panic. I got my two-ton lead body to the door and Zip was already in crisis mode. In those situations, guys like Zip get that look about them, and his was one you might find at an assassination.

"The US Marshals are on their way. There's a warrant for your arrest."

"You gotta be fuck-een kidding me. What happened to April?"

"She split an hour ago, left you a note—you can read it in the car."

"We're leaving?"

"We are. I spoke to your lawyer. He's trying to negotiate a surrender but until then he wants us tucked away somewhere for the night."

"Holy fuck, Zip, where the hell are we gonna go?"

"That's the only part I can't answer. Figured you'd want some input on that front."

He wasn't wrong. I had a buddy named Kevin who lived a few floors above us with his high-profile roommate, Tori Spelling. I pointed to the ceiling and didn't make it past the *K* in his name when Zip shook his head, telling me he'd already asked them. Zip explained that Tori felt bad for me but viewed my situation as radioactive and didn't wanna go anywhere near it. (Couldn't blame her, I suppose, but shit man, who knows what story I'd be bangin' out right now if the heir to daddy's throne had said yes?)

Zip advised that we use the service elevator to avoid the fancy lobby and make a straight shot to the parking garage. I told him I needed to toss a few things in a bag and I'd be ready in five. He called out, "Make it two," as I darted away from him toward the bedroom closet. I kept the room dark and that morning even more so with how badly I needed rest. As I frantically approached the built-in dresser, my foot caught a pile of sharp, wobbly objects that sent me tumbling onto my back. It shocked the hell outta me, but I knew exactly what it was, as I lay there chuckling to myself in moronic pride.

The booby trap I'd forgotten all about was surprisingly effective. The crude landmine came from my *Platoon* research and was inspired by an evil creation known as *punji sticks*—sharp bamboo spikes the VC would place at the bottom of a hidden hole. My version replaced the spikes with the high heels various women had left behind. I concealed those shoes under a black towel on the black carpet, turning them upside down for maximum trippery and pointy pain. In the event the bad guys ever came for me, I wanted a diversion just inside the door in my bedroom that led to the service hallway.

(Crack, at times, is also the mother of invention.)

I had quite the surplus of stilettos to choose from, and I wish I could say all of those tall shoes were courtesy of actual women. The *other* source of those pumps came from an amazing sex toy I had experimented with called Real Doll. The deluxe package included extra footwear, and I guess the rest explains itself. That fukken thing was more than seven grand and if there was one person to see if those folks got it right, I felt confident I was the guy. (For the record—they did.)

Another bonus: Real Doll never took me to court.

With Zip at the wheel, I was crouched down in the back seat of my Jaguar sedan, as we made our way up the two-story underground concrete corkscrew to the main level. We cleared the exit and bounced up onto the circular driveway outside the main lobby, with the freedom of Wilshire Boulevard fifty feet away. Halfway across the beige cobblestone, we heard 'em before we saw them. The unmarked Crown Vic filled with US Marshals screeched into the mouth of the entrance, passing within three feet of our car. As their team pulled further into the cul-de-sac driveway, I was pressing so far down in the back seat I could have tasted the oil pan. Zip kept his forward gaze fixed with James Bond–kool, as he flipped the turn signal and blended into the traffic like he was heading to a Sunday flea market. I stole a peek behind me and caught the image of four large agents exiting the Crown Vic with purpose. In the words of one of my all-time favorites, Maxwell Smart: *"Missed 'em by* that *much."*

It was every shade of awesome. I had checked a box I never imagined would find its way into the cornucopia of MaSheen-chaos: I was officially on the lam.

CHAPTER 37

"Escape from LA" Part 5:
Mira on the Wall

We drove around for nearly two hours, using quiet streets and back alleys to keep our visibility low and away from the main arteries. Zip stayed in heightened contact with my lawyer as he awaited the final decision on the where and when for my surrender. We didn't park anywhere or pause for more than thirty seconds. It felt like I was stuck in a bizarre documentary, and—stranger yet—was being driven by a man who'd most likely already done many of the things my internal film was capturing. The info I was dreading finally landed on Zip's phone: Malibu Courthouse, 9 a.m. With that piece secured, we turned our attention to the next pressing logistical item: finding a place to shack up for the night so we could get the hell off the streets.

Bill was the fifth person we called and the first to pick up. He was house-sitting for my old friend Keith B, and Zip got word from Keith we had the okay to use his kick-ass Bel Air estate for the twelve hours I had left. Keith was the founder of a high-end chain of celeb-endorsed restaurants and helped me out of a jam in Chicago a few years earlier at one of their grand openings. My hotel room had been robbed, Keith made one phone call, and I had everything back in less than two hours. I couldn't fukken believe it. That's how Keith rolled—old-school—and I guarantee he was thrilled to harbor my felonious antics with the entire city on high alert to find me.

Bill greeted us warmly when we arrived and showed us the rooms where we'd be camping. I didn't have enough dope on me to do any real damage, but I knew that could change in an instant if one of my gals who delivered was reachable. I located the den with a full bar stocked for a king. I didn't want to take advantage, but since there were no padlocks on the cases, I made myself conspicuously cozy in that private saloon.

Zip wasn't drinking for obvious reasons, which left only Bill, who most likely joined me to silence my complaints about drinking alone. Bill was slow-sipping a beer which I wouldn't tolerate, and I finally got him to cave and toss back a few shots of Blat Spanish vodka. He was fine for about twenty minutes when all of a sudden he made a panicked hand-to-mouth beeline to the closest toilet to puke his guts out for an hour. (The *Blat* went *splat*.)

What Bill had failed to mention was a drug called Antabuse he was taking to help him put down the bottle. The medicine was designed to act as a sentinel, creating severe nausea when mixed with booze. Anyone taking the drug knew full well the puke thing was inescapable if they fucked off the warnings. I felt really bad that I'd tipped his scales with my frat-style coercion, but it was really on him at that point for not sharing that one very specific detail. He was in good hands with Zip's cold rags and soda water, so I got busy making sure I wound up in much better hands. (And feet, and face, and boobs, and . . .)

The witching hour had arrived, and I knew exactly which good witch would fabulously place 9 a.m. and Malibu in grave jeopardy.

We called her Red—for all the right reasons—and you couldn't find a funnier gal than Natasha. One night years ago, blasted off our faces on shrooms, we could not remember Benicio del Toro's name. For three hours we almost laughter-suffocated from the insane attempts we mangled; from *Fabreezeo Telemundo* to *Buenonoche Desperado*, we lost our melted minds. (If I see her somewhere after twenty-five years, that'll *still* crack us up.)

Tash (to friends) was a stunning redhead top to bottom whom I'd met a few years earlier through the Fleiss of it all. We didn't see each other often, but whenever we did, it always felt like the very first time. (Regardless of how much flak I still endured from the Fleiss odyssey, Heidi was the gift that redefined generosity.) Tash arrived thirty minutes after I called her, and unlike me, did show up with a bag fat enough to do some damage.

I told Zip to hold all my calls, and not to bang down the door until that very last second before go time. Tash and I wished green-Bill a speedy recovery and bolted that door so we could unlock one final night to *dis*obey all laws. Her dope was top-shelf, her attention to me was top o' the mountain. We made sure to steer clear of any mentions that involved our favorite Puerto Rican actor; that was one night I was not willing to hand over to *Baladucci Avocadopantz*.

The drive the next morning was bleak. While on the road with Zip, the images of Natasha in sensual splendor protected my thoughts from the oncoming darkly fated Malibu. They drifted; I chased what I could, then drifted away with them. The nap I stole in the car gave me the extra juice I'd need to stay upright for whatever drubbing was gonna be handed down.

Zip and I made great time getting there and used the extra hour to drop in on an old pal of mine named Saul Hudson—better known to the entire world as Slash. I'm not really sure where his house was, but I am really sure another dear friend, Mira Sorvino, was there as well. As the clock brought me closer to the inevitable, I pleaded my case to both of them that maybe I could stay on the run and keep the Madman's Ball in full swing. Mira couldn't believe what she was hearing, while Slash listened patiently until he too had had enough.

"Dood!" he chided. "I have never seen someone who needs to be in rehab more than you do. And I have seen *so* many people who needed it in the most desperate ways imaginable."

That struck me deep, but I was still pondering, fighting the obvious with potent denial. Slash pressed me harder: "If you don't go today my friend, you are going to die."

It was too much to absorb. I pulled Mira aside, seeking the comfort of her female wisdom in case Slash had missed something. (Mira and I were never intimate but did share crushes over the years in the fleeting times we spent together.) That woman took it to another level when she grabbed me by the shoulders and shook me to attention: "Listen to me, you crazy, beautiful man, I understand why you don't wanna go, but you are out of options. This isn't a game anymore, these people are playing for keeps. Look at me Charlie, *look* at me: I will sleep with you—if you just promise to get yourself to court this morning."

Her eyes were fiery and unwavering as those incredible words hit my brain. Outwardly I stayed composed; inwardly my thoughts were eating soup from a tuba. *Wait—right now? Or we talkin' more rain check-y, like after court but before rehab?*

I gave her a long hug to settle my scatter, then broke from it with, "You're beyond lovely, Mira—and I could not be more flattered by your gesture."

She stayed staring at me. The last thing I wanted was for Mira to feel rejected. I had to solve it for both of us: "I'm gonna make my way over to that courthouse and put this motherfucker behind me."

She blinked at first, and then it landed—shouts of joy and relief spilled from both of them. Held breath finally exhaled to restart and feed the brain again. Mira wiped a tear, and if Slash had one, I couldn't see it behind his bitchen shades. I hugged them both with profound gratitude, and off I went to honor my word and officially, mercifully, finally surrender. And man, did I have a good story on the drive for Zip.

CHAPTER 38

"Escape from LA" Part 6:
From FJ to MJ

Whatever Judge Lawrence Mira planned on imposing (yes, that's his actual name, pronounced *My-ruh*—go figure), I knew it was gonna hurt like hell. I didn't care. It couldn't possibly come close to what I'd already been doing to myself. There was no *maybe*. There would be no *if*. Take your best shot Your Honor, and make sure it leaves a mark.

I didn't hear a single word *other*-Mira said from the bench. Based on the gasps and groans the humorless judge drew from the packed gallery, I sensed it wasn't goin' great for Team Sheen. In all truth, I was still beaming from Mira's sexy offer. She's a world-class beauty and a terrific lady, and the fact that she stepped up in the line of fire to offer that level of support left me more touched than if it had actually happened. (Mira: If you're offended by any of this, apologies. If you're tickled by its retelling, go get 'em, you're the Queen of Hearts.)

* * *

I was immediately shuttled from the courthouse to a rehab in Marina del Rey, a city near the water just south of Santa Monica, with a harbor and many boats. That probably explained the seagull shit all over the patio tables where smoking was allowed. The place was a bit rundown. The rooms were *Cuckoo's Nest* chic and had grab bars in the shower for the guests with "fall risk" on their charts. I needed those bars for the first few days, but after that I saw them as workout gear I'd secretly use, to build back my strength for the escape plot my mind was already running with. (*To go where? Back to the condo, to wind up barricaded in a standoff with Tori Spelling as your hostage?* Yeah, it was a bad plan—but my biceps did need some attention.)

The people were friendly, the food was edible, and the nights weren't haunted by some wailing lunatic down the hall kicking benzos. They had me doped-up nicely for that first week, with food and liquids as the only commitments they expected from me. I weighed 141 pounds when I got there and I usually hover around 180. My reimagined take on the four food groups—booze, base, pills, and c-burgers—was a recipe for no recipes. (That *c* is for cheese, you gutter-brains.)

Zip showed up on day two with a few things he grabbed from my closet at the Malibu Lake house. Basic toiletries, a few T-shirts, the standard rehab essentials. As was policy, the staff had to comb through all deliveries to double-check for contraband. It was also a rule it had to be done in front of the receiving person so the staff couldn't be accused of pilfering.

Zip got most of it right, but didn't dig deep enough into the bottom of the duffel. A larger fella named Erik was doing the final scour when he pulled an object from the bag that I couldn't believe Zip had overlooked; in Erik's hand was exactly that—a hand. (Don't worry, we haven't entered the Dahmer zone.) The traveling hand came from a Real Doll. (*I may have forgotten to mention I bought two of them.*)

The one up at the lake sorta melted and came apart. As an elaborate joke months earlier, I set her up in the jacuzzi to scare the shit out of a buddy of mine. (I was too high to factor in the basic logic of really hot water and latex.) The prank was a masterpiece, but Real Doll didn't survive beyond the laughter. One thing was certain: In the long history of the rehab bag-search, it was the most unique item anyone had ever smuggled. Erik was kool, and capped it off with the great line, "Give that man a hand." I told him to go ahead and toss it (not a chance they sold Aquaphor in the gift shop).

The biggest obstacle I had to deal with was the ankle monitor the judge had imposed. Affectionately referred to by some as a LoJack, those things are a staph infection waiting to happen.

An electronic "fence" was put in place by the parole board to work in tandem with the anklet—hence creating the "green zone" for the *prisoner* (me) to roam freely inside of. (The size of my embassy basically kept me in one room on the same couch.) They were so busy acting like bullies and goons the day it was installed, they left out an extra ten feet of crucial access—rehab literally had to call the board for me to use the goddam bathroom.

My drug counselor wanted me in certain groups that sat across the border in the red zone, the parole board said I'd be arrested if I traveled that far, the court was bitching about me not making it to the mandatory AA meetings (also in the red zone), and the frikkin' rehab was telling me I wasn't engaged enough in the fellowship to experience true serenity. That three-headed genius-brigade really deserved one another.

Cluster, meet *fuck*. I was being told I couldn't go to the places that the court demanded I attend. It was like driving a car with no engine.

I felt more sane on the pipe reading poetry to Real Doll. (That never happened, just needed an *oomphy* visual.)

I got the strong sense that they wanted me to feel more like a criminal and less like a guy doing his best to heal. It was no secret which side of that fence I had more recent love for, and if outlaw was what they wanted, I barely had to dust off my fedora.

My day six was Jeff's day one. I liked Jeff. Solid guy, *crackatologist* to the core, really smart in the way most creative dopers tend to be. We had a lot in common as it related to our uncommon levels of drug use. Jeff took his last hit of crack in the parking lot and smashed the pipe in a grand show of defiance, then checked himself in. I was impressed with his ability to do so without the armada of nuclear subs and foreign spies my intake required.

He'd reached the end of the road and was grateful to find me at its final outpost. Up until Jeff's arrival, I hadn't been able to land on the same page with any of the other clients. One shattered glass tube later, my problems suddenly got a lot less unique.

Like-minded doods in a rehab are usually a really good thing. Like-minded doods in a rehab can also be as lethal as snakes in a bag. I'm not calling fukken-Jeff a snake by any means—but you will notice, his name did just suddenly change.

My day twelve was fukken-Jeff's day six, the day he woke up with rehab-fever. A condition known to sprout and spread toward the end of anyone's first week in rehab. Fukken-Jeff had it bad. The fever has another name: *obsession*. Most thoughts are harmless saplings until the waters of crave turn them into plants that become trees, and then a forest, and finally a forest fire—burning the sky into darkness. All it takes for the spiraling person to shut it down is the simple act of attaching spoken words to those runaway thoughts before they have a chance to do their thing. One of the side effects of that fever is that it never wants to be sick alone. Enter: me. On the twelfth day, I was that guy—I was his partridge. Problem was, the fukken pear tree was already engulfed.

FJ didn't have anything hanging over him with the courts. He was free and clear to fuck it all up and start back fresh the next day. My situation was entirely the opposite: I *knew* in black-and-white, uncomplicated terms, if I got high and peed dirty, I was facing the immotile reality of a year in jail. I didn't have any test blockers or fancy means to alter the results. Best I could do, if it came to that, was plead insanity.

Day twelve was the day they took me off all the meds I'd been on to manage my semi-brutal detox. Day twelve was also the day fukken-Jeff showed me the flip phone he'd been hiding from the nosy staff. Day twelve and day thirteen were not gonna have a lot in common.

It was just past midnight, and the window right before shift change gave us an extra six or seven minutes before the night crew grabbed their clipboards and began the rounds. Fukken-Jeff had been in touch with Zip throughout the day, who'd already bagged up the contents from the one drawer at the condo I knew held everything we needed to get frosty.

Zip parked a few blocks away and crept to the outside of the main wall that surrounded the rehab's courtyard where we waited. It was a still and quiet night, the light from a full moon casting long shadows from the trees across the eight feet of stucco and brick that blocked Zip from our view. Fukken-Jeff was on the phone, whispering directions back and forth with Zip on the other end. My job was to keep an eye out for any movement from the TV lounge and lobby that sat behind the glass doors next to our location—the smoking table, caked in the shit of a thousand seagulls.

I watched as a giant hand rose up into view just above the top of the wall, as Zip listened from the street side for FJ's specific guidance to the prime spot for launch. *"Okay left, little more, that's too far, go back right, there it is, more, more, half a step more, annnnnn stop."* The giant hand stopped. *"Okay, my man—TOSS it."*

The bungee-wrapped, plastic Sav•On Drugs bag came scream-skittering through that peaceful night air like a wailing newborn vampire on the back of a rattlesnake piñata. It was insane. That thing hit the deck like a dying rocket and found the only patch of wet dirt near our feet from a drizzle the day before. It was like a mud-grenade had exploded in our faces. Table-shit wasn't enough, mud was clearly missing, the Gods were letting their presence be known.

Fukken-Jeff scooped it outta the muck and quickly hid the dripping sack under his sweatshirt, whispering *"bull's-eye"* to Zip before he flipped his secret tiny phone in half and hung up. I kept my eyes on the building behind us; not a creature had stirred, not even a lab rat. Unless we were on camera from a military satellite, the coast was clear for phase two of *Operation Crack-Slop* to get under way.

Freckled in brown grime, I forced my zest toward calm as I made it back to my room, unobserved by any of the staff. I tore off my shirt and dumped it in the shower, trying to keep clues from becoming evidence. My stomach was alive with giddy anticipation, knowing my favorite drug was moments away from rejuvenating every cell I owned. With an ankle monitor and a guaranteed year hanging over me, I still viewed my reckless choices that night as a return to freedom. My temp was approaching one-oh-five; rehab-fever is a motherfucker.

FJ had taken the Sav•On bag to his quarters at the other end of the hall to sort through Zip's imported goodies. Given how quickly the plan had taken flight, I wasn't expecting Virgo perfection from Zip's end, but I did have faith he'd followed FJ's flip-phoned instructions and grabbed the Three Amigos: dope, pipe, torch. Within minutes, fukken-Jeff scurried back down the hall and slipped into my room to share the night's first hiccup—Zip had supplied us with a fat bag of rock and two lighters, but only one pipe. We'd have to take turns and treat the pipe like a baton, with the bright hallway as our double-dealing thirty-seven-meter relay.

I told FJ it was too risky and for him to go first, that I'd go second, and he could hang onto the pipe after that. We both agreed that made the most sense, and if the night stayed as planned, Zip coming back with a second pipe wasn't out of the question.

FJ followed the new plan and returned shortly to make the hand-off and activate my turn. *(Finally.)* Not sure how much that dood smoked in the brief time he was gone, but holy hell, man, his face was a red not found in nature, and his eyes looked like he had them in backwards. He was obviously locked-up and didn't say a word—because he couldn't.

As though his hands were filled with jumping beans, he gave me the hot pipe, and back to his room he headed. Fukken-Jeff was revealing himself to be a complete bust. With the clock ticking toward imminent disaster, I needed the only hit I'd have time for to land at the very bottom of me and stay there. A torch *snapped,* a rock *crackled*—Thor's hammer swung down into the center of my chest. The weightless starburst was as promised, but so was fukken-Jeff's ambush. The hallway was suddenly filled with activity and loud voices. I could hear all of it from inside the liquid church bells that had swallowed my face. My ceiling had transformed into a swirling montage of comic book animals I'd never seen before. I stayed up all night watching them, studying them, waiting for the knocks on my door that never came.

The following morning our entire wing was abuzz with chatter and stress. Word was out that a couple patients had gotten high on the premises the night before, and while they did nail one of them, the alleged accomplice was still on the loose. To spread the shakedown further, all clients were gonna be questioned and then tested. When they put the squeeze on Jeff, that guy didn't mention one letter of my name. In a blink, fukken-Jeff had become good ol' Jeff again. Like-minded doods in a rehab honor the dope code as well.

I knew exactly what I had to do. I just wasn't sure yet what the *how* looked like.

The fedora I spoke of wasn't symbolic. The one I had with me (a *Dick Tracy* model I'd bought at the airport) was an artifact from J-5's maiden night together when we declared ourselves, Las Vegas-style. In addition to the pipe, Jeff had left me with a few rocks and one of the lighters right before our night imploded. When I bought that silly hat, I never imagined I'd be using the sweatband inside the crown to conceal my dope stash. I put it on and checked myself in the mirror. Dick Tracy himself woulda been proud. (Then woulda hauled me in.)

Shortly before the group drug testing was set to commence, I found myself in the office of a lady named Betty who ran the joint.

(From the small-world files, Betty's brother was Brad, the author of the warm jacuzzi jet opioid-analogy.) Her no-nonsense lieutenant, Lori, was seated next to her. Before they had a chance to speak:

> ME: "Okay, here's the deal—I'm the missing piece in the Jeff puzzle, so please spare all the other folks the suspicion and hassle of the drug test. Also, I will have an envelope with twenty grand cash delivered within the hour to split between you, if I can have your word you'll make the relapse go away. If for some reason that doesn't work for either of you, I'm gonna leave through the window behind me, and take my fukken chances on the streets."

No one said a word. The silence was not kool, and I think they knew that. Finally:

> LORI: "Take it easy, tough guy, no one's taking bribes and no one's jumping out of windows."
> ME: "Oh. Alright, so then how do we fix this?"
> BETTY: "We need to know if there's any more drugs floating around, and if that's the case for the safety of the other residents we need them turned over to us."

That wasn't just my cue, it was Detective Tracy's as well. I made a small show of removing the yellow fedora from my mottled locks, extracted the items, and handed over the hidden stash.

> LORI: "Well there's a first. Impressive. And thank you."
> ME: "Don't mention it."

BETTY: "Two things, Charles—we are sympathetic to your situation and know for a fact that jail is not the answer to your problems."

ME: "Okay, wow, good to know, thank you, a lot. What's the second thing?"

BETTY: "Are you sick?"

ME: "I mean yeah, that's kinda why I'm here, right? But as far as *sick* sick, um, no, not that I'm aware of. Why do you ask?"

Lori produced the muddy Sav•On bag from beneath her desk. It was inside a larger clear plastic bag that she set on the table between us.

LORI: "Forgetting about the three or four random Vicodin for one sec, or the cocaine dust on everything, we really need to know why you had seventy-seven pills of the antibiotic Keflex smuggled into a rehab . . . ?"

We all went back to the staring thing. That was a really good question—*for Zip*.

I'd caught a huge break. They assured me that Operation Crack-Slop would never find its way anywhere near the court's purview. The MaSheen was gonna live to see another day and not have to strain that view through the bars of a jail cell. There was one catch though: Whether or not I was allowed to stay in the Marina didn't rest solely in the hands of those two amazing women. They had a boss (doctor something-face) and he was on a power trip by not revealing my fate until the following day. It was complicated; if his ultimate decision was to banish me, I'd need my lawyer to craft a cover story for having to leave that was so bulletproof Judge Mira couldn't disassemble it. Mira was the same man who'd dealt with Robert Downey Jr. a few years earlier, and it was a pretty safe bet any sleight of hand we came up with had already been exhausted by Bobby Dee Jay.

On the walk back to my room I passed large Erik in the hallway and a huge grin took over his face: "Dooood, I'm lookin' to score some antibiotics. You know anyone?" he asked and laughed his way down the hall. I called back to him: "Just your mom. Is that thing on her butt gone yet?" He laughed again, his middle finger the size of Zip's up and at me as he disappeared from view.

It turned out the drawer at the condo I'd sent Zip into wasn't just my illicit holdings but was also a dumping ground for all things Rx I'd been amassing and hoarding. Can't blame him for wanting to be as thorough as possible. (Kinda surprised there wasn't a size-six Manolo in that dope bag as well.) He began my journey at the Del Rey rehab with a nomadic fake hand, and ended it with a Keflex-kilo shot out of a mud-cannon.

"The Zip" was one of a kind, and the kind of one I'm honored to have known.

The final vote was unanimous: one to zero. Doctor DonkeyFace wielded his veto power and sent me packing. Betty called Promises and they agreed to take me back. As far as the story for the judge was concerned, Lori and Betty devised the perfect ruse—their psychiatric care at the Marina didn't cover the full breadth of my pathologies. Any attempts by the court to prove otherwise could not penetrate the

Iron Dome of my *HIPAA* rights. My favorite detail in that mix was the fact that I didn't spend even one living second with a psychiatrist at the Marina rehab. (Why would I need one? I had fukken-Jeff.)

The head guy at Promises met me on the lawn when I stepped outta the car. He spent a good seven minutes delivering his rehearsed speech about last chances and jail and death and so on. I went full earnest-guy and took it all in, nodded when it mattered, earnested more when it mattered more. He asked if I had any questions and I told him I only had one: "Any chance I can watch game six, Bulls–Jazz, a bit later on today?"

He gave me permission to do so and would mention in an interview years later (to some lame treatment publication) how inspired he was to see a spark in me that still cared about real shit taking place in the world. He could see it however he chose, I had twenty grand on the Bulls and didn't wanna miss the game. (It was the same twenty dimes Betty and Lori didn't accept.)

As we all know, MJ hit "the shot." It was a real moment for me. I needed to hang onto that moment, get inside of it, and stay there. I'd been tossin' up air balls for far too long. I decided that same day, June 14, 1998, it was time for me to start making a few big shots of my own.

CHAPTER 39

I spent a total of nine months at Promises, six of them as an inpatient and the other three in their outpatient program—a hybrid form of reentry into life while still logging several hours a day at the rehab. The facility had its own Jeff, a solid dood named Bill J. whom I bonded with as my roommate. It was his twentieth time in treatment and from the many scars his stories revealed, he was no doubt a firestarter. Given the right fuel, Bill was one match away from becoming fukken-Bill. Whenever he got that look, I did my best to hide the gas cans. As tempting as it was to wingman his escapades, I refused to betray the new lease I'd wrestled from the jaws of the Marina debacle.

My rules for myself at Promises were entirely different from the Marina—in that I actually had a few. *Their* rules stated that I wasn't allowed to leave the Promises premises for almost the entire first third of my term. (Might have had something to do with that 1:00 a.m. stroll to PCH in my pajamas two weeks earlier that had them on cautious alert.) Once I'd regained everyone's trust from the counselors to the judge, that leash began to loosen, both figuratively and literally. One month after Jordan hit the shot, they finally agreed to pardon my ankle and remove that fukken LoJack. It was complete overkill, but I guess every show trial has to have one or two special effects. I was grateful for the extra slack and used most of my "day passes" to pass the time with America's favorite pastime.

Reconnecting with one of my first loves in this life genuinely became the only therapy I was responding to. The omni-staunch Tony T along with a dood we called Kenny Meds (who has the best BP arm on the planet) were on time like the Navy to join me on those magical outings. Medlock used to say, "It was our day to be ten again." When anyone at the rehab asked me where I was going on those days, I'd always reply "church." Ken threw perfect strikes, my bat unloaded some rage, Tony kept us laughing.

Something in me had shifted, and as the days became months, that shift demanded it be nurtured into sharper focus. I'd been defining myself for way too long by the smoldering wreckage of my severe choices. I wore them like a badge, daring others to outdo my stupid, while caring only about shock value and spectacle—if a disaster inspired more *holy-fuck*s from my crew than the last, the pileup was a win; an early form of "likes" as it were.

The light that had once blinded me evolved into the sunlight of each new day as it broke through the shame-clouds of crack, chaos, sex, and booze. The searing truths I embraced during my stay reunited me with a hope and confidence I no longer sought at the end of a pipe or the bottom of a bottle. To finally realize those virtues had been inside of me all along, I just needed the gift of silence.

The weather in Toronto was a lot hotter than what I was expecting.

It was June 14, 1999, and, no, I wasn't gonna party like Prince recommended. Consequently, I *was* gonna party like Emilio was expecting. The two of us were in Hogtown together, starring in a movie for Showtime that E was also directing. The film was called *Rated X*, but ironically its rating was not. We were portraying the Mitchell brothers, Artie and Jim—the two genre-bending porn pioneers. In the 1970s, the brothers ushered a major shift into adult cinema that changed its commerce landscape forever: they replaced film with videotape. (Folks old enough to remember the FBI WARNING on every Blockbuster rental have the Mitchells to thank for it.) Their story had never been told cinematically, and we were there to change all of that.

During one particular scene, I was well aware that it had been a year to the day since I'd stood on that lawn at Promises and gave them my own. I'd gone seven years between sober birthdays, and the Artie Mitchell version would be my first since that Aussie in Cage's fridge took me down under. The milestone involved activities that very few could ever claim during their sober celebration: by day, I was doing fat rails of blow and slamming vodka shots; by night, I was taking a cake at a local AA meeting without telling a single lie.

The scenes we shot that day found my character Artie on a bender, snorting powdered lactose and dumping shots of Fiji Water down the hatch. It was a fukken trip.

For some reason, portraying that behavior didn't get the wheels spinnin' to dive back in for real. The fact that it wasn't at all how I used to do it kept the crave-wolves at bay and my temp at a cool ninety-eight-six. (Keep in mind I was still on probation, and would be for two more years, drug-testing every week and sometimes randomly.) I had a testing setup at a local hospital, and the results were sent back to LA for the two months I was on the film. I won't allot too much sober credit to that leash they had me on, but there were a few days during that first year when I was grateful the damn thing was in place. It never reached code-red status, but the "tickle" was just enough to know which bird the feather came from.

Rated X was my second movie with the new sober brain. The first one, *Being John Malkovich*, was only two days and didn't really count. I was driven to work to film my scenes while I was still an inpatient. One odd detail the two movies had in common was the special effects hairstyle they both called for. Often described as a *monk's fringe*, I've pictured it more as those fur headmuffs people wear during winter. In all of my previous film work, the monk-funk never made its way onto my head. To have it finally happen when it did, and do so in back-to-back roles, was as improbable as that funk showing up there one day for real. The main difference between the two *fringes* was the artistry by which they were applied. *Being John Malkovich* was a standard bald cap that looked like it was part of a bad SNL sketch. *Rated X* was an actual shave job, with an expertly trimmed receding effect by none other than Brown Dave, aka David LeRoy Anderson.

Shortly after *Red Dawn*, my man had decided to follow in his dad's FX footsteps, and it goes without saying Dave was grateful for Lance's career decision to stop changing lightbulbs. When Dave joined us in Toronto to create the monk look, he only had the one Oscar from *The Nutty Professor* (fukken slacker). A few years later, *Men in Black* landed him his second Academy Award for best makeup. I love it when the *actual* good guys win the big ones. Emilio and I had the best of the best, to transform us into those two trailblazers of cutting-edge smut.

I didn't have any female companionship during the entire shoot of *Rated X*, and I'm not blaming the sad hair. The schedule was grueling and the work too detailed and demanding to divert my focus by going there. I kept my bald head down and made the job my only priority. In a bit of an experiment, I had the prop department order the prescription in my glasses a few numbers off and wore that pair when my character was hammered in the scene. Drinks were spilled, things got bumped into, migraines awaited me at the end of those days. I didn't care—pain is temporary; film remains forever.

It also gave me the confidence to go further emotionally and well beyond where I'd normally stop or pull back. Through those blurry specs I couldn't attach faces to the shapes watching the scene, and therefore it didn't feel like they were staring at me. Sometimes ya gotta hide to be seen.

Emilio was thrilled with my work ethic from day one to wrap, and still rates my performance as the best thing I've ever done. (I can't weigh in on that, but I am okay saluting a few scenes I'm really proud of.)

It wasn't until the final night in Toronto that I decided my celibacy streak needed the closure I'd find in the matchmaking Yellow Pages of Bell Canada. In less than an hour, a gorgeous brunette rolled in to *DND* our night into the awe some would frown upon.

She was wonderful, but that level of intimacy still housed a frustrating awkwardness that I knew could be cured with substances. I *also* knew those insane thoughts were a form of sabotage from an alcove in my mind where truth didn't get a vote. The rehab folks did warn me that it would take time for my brain to adjust, but come on man, it had already been a year. My ongoing debate to appraise the value of booze and dope between the sheets was useless—multiple choices were down to two: sober sex, or no sex at all.

(Hold on, let's not get carried away here.)

If I was gonna get comfortable with it on those terms, maybe it was time to adjust the partner choice to fit the head space. It had nothing to do with judgment and everything to do with common sense; certain behaviors in specific arenas generated predictable outcomes. In other words: As long as I kept wearing hamburger-pants on safari, I couldn't complain about being attacked by a lion. In that very hotel room, on that exact night, I decided it was time to stop paying for sex.

If any of us look back on the moments that defined us or influenced major decisions, they tend to include a foreshadowing detail, either right near the surface or buried deeper for latent discovery. Case in point: I was mid-puff into a post-euphoric cigarette with my Canadian insta-girlfriend, when the young lady reached over and slapped my bare stomach with a room-filling *thwack* to get my attention. "Whattaya say, Fatso—you up for round two?" Pin drop. Ant yawn.

Wow. Jeez lady, ya had 10,000 nicknames to choose from and you went with *that*? I wanted to blow my brains out. It's amazing where one word can send a guy. (That one sent me straight to a lipo doctor about a week after I got back to LA.)

But yes, I was up for round two. I did my best not to crush her in the process.

It's pretty common for a lot of folks to gain a buncha weight after getting sober, especially when stimulants were their drug of choice. I'd always defend it by telling people I'd rather be a bit soft and alive than crack-skinny and fukken dead.

I had to shave my entire head before I left Toronto to make sure it all grew back evenly. Emilio opted not to shave his, and when I saw him at the folks' house a few weeks later, the top had grown in just enough to make his headmuff look like a punk-rock Yorkie. I followed up the gut-suck surgery with a meal-delivery plan, long before it was the barfy, en vogue, foodie thing to do. Early word on *Rated X* was strong, with my work being talked about as a proof-of-talent showcase to reignite interest and trust. I wanted to be fit and focused for whatever opportunities *Rated X* might generate. I didn't need the film to kick down every door in Hollywood, just leave 'em ajar enough for me to slip into the room and take it from there.

One of those doors opened to a man named Gary David Goldberg, the prolific TV producer and creator of the long-running hit *Family Ties*, starring Michael J. Fox. (Another MJ on my journey; add to that my first drug Mary Jane, and I think we've got a theme on our hands.)

By the time I sat down with Gary to discuss his new sitcom pilot, I'd dropped twenty-five pounds on the Zone Diet and had a full head of hair again. The pilot was called *Sugar Hill*, an updated homage to *Barney Miller*, a sitcom I loved as a kid.

Long story shorter than if I spoke it: I got the gig, we shot the pilot, it didn't get picked up. I was fukken bummed.

Gary told me not to take it too hard, and that he had another idea he needed the okay from his partners to approach me with. I really enjoyed Gary; he was genuinely funny and smart in a rough 'n tumble kinda way, and always spoke his mind like a Pall Mall—unfiltered. A week later he called to ask me how I'd feel about taking over for the health-compromised Michael J. Fox on the then-current ABC hit sitcom *Spin City*.

¡*Holy resurrection, Batman!* I was stunned, and thrilled, and asked him if I could just have twenty-four hours to sit with it. He said no problem, but not longer than that; his partners on the project needed to know ASAP. I asked who those partners might be, and he matter-of-factly told me it was Jeffrey Katzenberg and Steven Spielberg. Oh. Just those guys.

I took that phone call in a room where I'd almost died eighteen months earlier. A room where if you pressed your ear tight enough to the wall, you could still hear the distant echoes of howling anguish. Feeling as alive as I'd felt in ages, I called Gary back from that same room, twenty-three hours later. I told him I'd be honored to step in for Fox and keep Gary's terrific show on the air with our "new look" Season Five. Gary expressed how he was excited to rejoin the show and shape its new direction with me on board. Not fully sure if I'd heard that correctly, I asked him to please clarify the part about "rejoin." Gary explained that he had been fired from *Spin City*, the show he fukken created.

I didn't wanna pry too deep, but I felt it was important to know who specifically had given him the boot. After a long pause, Gary stated, "It was Mike."

CHAPTER 40

When the splashy press release dropped (informing the world I'd be stepping in because Fox had to step away), the headlines were exactly as I'd predicted:

America's comedic treasure, the modern-day Mickey Rooney, was being replaced by Bagul, the eater of children.

The media had all the exits covered and were gunning for me with both barrels. Every article about *Spin*'s torch-pass was steeped in fortune-telling arrogance with my imminent failure already penned with crystal-ball certainty. A few stories even blamed me for the show moving from New York to LA, with no mention of DreamWorks pulling that trigger. Their sweeping hit-piece campaign made it clear right off the bat, the only dissenting voice was gonna have to be my own. If I could survive their tarot-gauntlet and claw my way to center stage, I'd have the final word under those bright lights.

The episodes we started with (to be aired as shows No. 2 and No. 3) gave me time to warm up before we shot our third episode—my "pilot." The first script they sent (ep. 3) was ironically titled "Smile"—something I wasn't doing as soon as I cracked it open.

I was barely to the act break when a familiar foe emerged on the page, letting me know it was still very much in my vicinity. My hero's journey/voice-of-the-people strategy took a big fat dump in the town square. If *Spin* was gonna be my vehicle to a glorious comeback, Stutter-Ghoul was the bomb wired to the chassis.

Saturday at the condo—panic at my disco. Monday's looming network table-read sat atop the falls I'd soon be kicked over into the raging waters of sitcom television.

A pleasant gentleman had just exited the condo, leaving behind what's known as a "fluency device" he sold me for 2,000 bucks. I had it on my right ear and was staring at it in the mirror, wondering if I'd just been suckered like a chump. The battery-powered gadget looked like a hearing aid from the '60s: oversized and beige, riding the temple like a small plastic banana.

The concept behind the speech gizmo I'd just acquired utilized specific vibrations to interrupt a stutter. Any sound in the throat would activate an inner ear buzzing to give the "fear-word" a nudge. The finesse part I had to master was the low-throated *hooom* to make the thing buzz in the first place. (Last thing I needed was to turn day one into the sinus scene from *The Odd Couple*.) I was told after I made the purchase that most people used the contraption at home for a couple weeks before they felt confident with it out in the world. I had about forty hours, and there I was, trying to act normal with a giant invisible bumblebee in my fukken skull. I was a goner for sure.

The first episode involved a dental theme with the mayor and had no less than six or seven trouble spots in the dialogue. To clarify, a trouble spot is a fear-word I'd gotten stuck on in the past. My specific type of stuttering wasn't (isn't) the classic style we've all witnessed at some point, where the same letter is *buh, buh, buh* like an engine that won't turn over. The card I drew is a lot more subtle—*halting* that fear-word into a locked silence before any sound makes it to the ignition. When that happens in a film setting, it's a thousand times worse. Everyone on set knows what the word is because they're *reading* it—waiting, for what feels like forever.

Another manacle in the whole mystery was how a specific word only needed *one* event to wind up on the dreaded list. A list that also includes an entire category often overlooked as being *words*: people's names. (A stutterer's vocabulary and friend group can really begin to shrink.) My fear-fueled logic would insist that if it had happened that one awful time, it wasn't a risk worth taking anymore. Speech prison is a fucking nightmare. There is no time off for good behavior, there is no clemency. I wish it upon no one—myself most of all.

I spent the next two days debating if I should call Gary and reveal my syndrome. The fictional stories of stigma and judgment that I clung to kept the phone in its cradle. I was doing exactly what the press had done to me—concluding the unknown. I didn't want to let Gary down. I saw myself as the way back in, for both of us.

Monday arrived and so did I. With a hope that I'd find the missing courage in the eleventh hour, the bumble-buzzer was ripped off my ear and tossed in the passenger-side footwell of my car. (*Buzzkill* had a new definition.) I quieted my loud mind, and the message that came back had nothing to do with the fancy therapy of an expensive contraption. I reached a little further inside and balled my fist around the "fuck it" that I needed to corral Gary and our director Ted W. for a quick chat. They came to my dressing room—I spilled the *beh, beh, beans*. As uncomfortable as it felt to expose that part of myself, it was equally as liberating. The other side of fear is never the plank we walk to get there. Gary in particular handled it like a sniper who happened to also be driving a tank.

The read-through had all of us at three long tables they'd pushed together to form a large *U*. I was surrounded by a dream-cast of actors I'd been spending time with over the summer at various press events. Heather Locklear, Alan Ruck, Richard Kind, Michael "Boatie" Boatman, Barry Bostwick, and the *other* newcomer, Lana Parrilla, our Latina-hotness liaison.

After the intros went all the way around the table-village, Gary got everyone's attention with a few changes he needed to announce before we began. He explained nothing, just handed out the marching orders: "Couple things before we start—on page four: change New York to Manhattan, page sixteen: Heather takes Charlie's line about the delivery guy, page thirty-one: change Carter's response to *Boil it*, which makes Charlie's line *chicken* instead of ravioli. On page forty . . ." (Obviously not verbatim, but the gist is there.) On it went, until it didn't. We read "Smile," and the whole room couldn't stop doing just that.

I didn't get stuck on a single word. The roof didn't cave in on top of me. I wasn't fired when it ended. I had another separate chat with our Tom Hertz–led team of writers and brought that group up to speed as well. It's such an overused cliché, but I can honestly say that stealing back my power through surrender opened the door for a feeling of near-weightlessness. If that was all it was gonna take to remove my biggest fear from the process, there wasn't a whole lot to complain about.

In due time, that department would be brimming.

* * *

In the four years prior at Chelsea Piers in New York City, the cast had banked close to a hundred episodes together. (My sitcom tally was *one*, a guest spot on *Friends* in '96.) Stepping into a machine that finely tuned, I sponged as much as I could from my generous costars. Most of the credit for the first season going as well as it did chiefly (and rightfully) belongs to them. My new friendship with Boatman was a godsend, as was my history with Alan Ruck. (He and I still laughed about Arkansas, Dolly, creepy Clinton, and the shoes.) Heather was familiar as well, but considering we last worked together on *Money Talks*, my memories of those times were pretty vandalized. The *Spin*-Heather was perfectly raunchy and adorable and usually more nervous than I was. I didn't have the party treats she'd dip into to calm those nerves, but good gosh, she was fun as hell to watch when she did. Bostwick was an old pro who had my back in every situation. He'd often say that sitcoms were easy to do but extremely difficult to "do well."

One evening after a show, when I was walking to the car with Barry, he dropped some gold on me I still carry to this day. He shared how he never focused on the moments while he was performing them, and it wasn't until the drive home that he was able to reflect on all the little things that felt perfect—the details that filled the quiet ride with purpose and comfort.

Before he pulled away in his vintage Benz, I asked him if what he'd just described applied to every show. Barry thought about it for a second, then added a little more gold to the pile: "Not when the episode totally sucked."

I've said it before that you can't choose your gurus.

I guess the real trick is paying attention when they choose you.

CHAPTER 41

9-11-2000. It was the early stages of my Season One, and we'd all just settled in for the table read. Can't tell ya which episode it was, but I can confirm the Emmys had taken place the night before. I know this because Mike won Best Actor in a Comedy (for Season Four), and rumor had it he was already on a plane back to New York. The room got whisper-quiet as Gary began to read the screen directions from the cold open in the script.

Jarringly, like someone's car had hit the building, the doors crashed open, and in strolled MJF, gripping the shiny Emmy. The whole room broke into a chorus of cheers to salute his victory. I was really happy for him but at the same time could feel myself shrinking like that last sad balloon at a birthday party.

As the roar of the crowd began to subside, Mike walked right over to the table where I was seated and *slammed* the Emmy down—a foot from my face.

"This is for you guys," were the words Señor Fox orated. (It was easily in my top three moments of awkward McFuckness.)

I'm not an expert when it comes to spatial science, but we did have tons of it at the front of the room for him to sky-pump his golden lady. The trophy slam was a perplexing move that left a sizable dent in my enthusiasm.

A few hours later I came to the decision that I wouldn't wear any of it as a tale of woe, and instead I'd channel those feelings into another layer of armor. I parked my petty emotional bullshit and turned the focus away from the man to the trophy. I saw how spellbound the energy from that thing left everyone and wanted badly to eventually have that same experience. Let's face it—second place gets a box of steak knives; winners go home with the prom queen.

When Mike decided to reprise his role at the beginning of my Season Two, he was walking back into a community that had established its own unique rhythm. I'd found my footing and was willing to dance with whoever they put in front of me. The writers willed their skills to another level for their two prized veterans—perfect sync took notes, a waltz for the ages took flight.

Mike and I hit that stage together and my only regret is that we weren't in front of a live audience. I've toed the marks with some of the greats in this business—when it came to laser comedic timing and organic instinct, there was no one better than that brilliant dood with the fukken three-word name.

That guy did things you can't teach and taught things that can't be learned. There were times between setups when we'd have to wait a while for his meds to kick in, so he could think and breathe again. I'd have waited all night if I had to. I knew whatever Michael J. Fox was coming back with to finish the job could not be found anywhere else. Yeah, it was like that.

Everyone just assumes that I met wife number two when she guest-starred in a few episodes of season number two. Such wasn't the case, and considering that not a single living soul had tuned in to see where we *did* meet, the oversight is justified.

A few months before *Spin* kicked off, I shot an unfunny indie comedy called *Good Advice*. (The coaxing from my agent to do it was the exact opposite of the title.) As the start date was approaching, I got word that an actress they wanted had agreed to play one of the roles. When they told me who it was, I couldn't frikkin' believe it. A year earlier, my roommate at Promises had been praising this person nearly every day for six months. Bill was so obsessed, it began to feel like she was in rehab with us. In his fixated mind, "The Valley of Worship" was carved in her honor. That "her" was Denise Richards.

Denise and I really enjoyed our time on set together, not caring that the film was a dud. As I got to know her, I realized how misinformed and off base I was with my exaggerated preconceptions. She didn't enter the room with the haughty air one might expect from a former Bond girl. Her vibe was more in line with someone who shot the *Vogue* cover on their lunch break from Hardee's. It was refreshing; it was intoxicating; it was two ships passing. I was ready for the big game, but I wasn't ready for Miss America to watch me play. Future tripping or not, I knew the stakes were too high to start something I'd be expected to care about more than the job.

I kept it professional, thanked D for her contributions to the movie, and told her I hoped to see her again around the campus. It was the right call—for Season One to have the shot it deserved, I needed to stay upright on the wave of momentum I was riding.

In D's neck of the woods, she was winding down a long-term relationship that was one set of cufflinks away from its eulogy. It woulda been a force fit for both of us.

Timing is everything because it has to be.

Bill didn't agree. He told me and my timing to get fucked and that I had blown it.

The lovely Denise reappeared to join me at the *Spin* party. We were really excited to see each other again. The ease and familiarity we picked back up with was a direct result of the rapport *Good Advice* had helped us establish. Took a minute, but that indie dog with fleas eventually got us outta the woods and back on the path.

Then 9/11 happened. (No, not with Denise—the *real* event.)

It was a Tuesday. I was on my treadmill in the condo at 5 a.m. before a long day of work on our season premiere. By the time I finished, the North Tower had already been hit.

I remember sipping black Folgers as I kept an eye on the scattered updates the networks were trying to piece together. The only info available was that some type of aircraft had struck the tower in the upper floors. I knew from the size of the gaping hole in the side of the building there wasn't a chance it was a private charter.

The reports were stuck on a loop until something on the screen caught my attention that didn't belong there. I watched mesmerized as a haunting black shape entered the shot, reminding me of the shark from *Jaws*. It lumbered into its final bank and disappeared behind the South Tower. Two seconds later, a catastrophic fireball harpooned the building like a special effect from a Michael Bay film. The world changed instantly and forever, in that moment, on that day.

I called my *Spin* director Ted Dubya, insisting he turn on the TV before he had a chance to say good morning. We stayed on the phone, trying to make sense of the chaos, when the impossible happened: the South Tower collapsed.

One hundred and ten floors free-falling into pyroclastic disintegration as it disappeared into its own footprint. Massive clouds, the likes of which not seen since the volcanic eruption of Mount St. Helens, arose mightily, filling the air and suffocating the city. The words between T-Dub and myself, as we stared in horror, felt like shapeless echoes floating across the miles of copper wire that enshrined our conversation.

I was in a high-rise when it happened, and since no one really had any idea how far this thing reached, I couldn't vacate that fukken condo fast enough. Luckily, there weren't any homemade booby traps to stumble through. By then, my unit had become a certified heel-free zone. (I took the small wins where I could get them.)

The following day, we all gathered at the studio, not for work but for each other. It was like group therapy on the stage—discussing that level of reality, surrounded by all things fake. Michael Boatman and I watched solemnly as two guys from the art department removed the Twin Towers from our main backdrop. The day before, they were proudly lit and displayed; twenty-four hours later they had to disappear them. That one hit both of us hard.

Gary joined the group with his best *Gipper* in tow. Summoning Rockne or MacArthur, he reminded us that we were a New York–themed show, and the city needed us to own that. In the face of all the suffering, he wanted humor to be our message of unity.

When he finished speaking, I wanted to blow off City Hall and go take the oath for the few and the proud. If we couldn't be there in body, we could sure as hell do so in spirit (Tuesdays at 9:00 p.m. on ABC).

Couple days later, we were back in action, trying to do comedy while the whole country was crying.

CHAPTER 42

Rallying behind Gary's marching orders, we elevated the on-set camaraderie throughout every department. The network was thrilled with our clockwork delivery of every episode on schedule and budget. Combined with the level of creative quality our storylines maintained, we had their full support on all fronts. It would have been easy to fold up our tent in the middle of the chaos and ask for a few weeks off—an option never even discussed. By *Thursday* the 13th, we were plowing through the grief and fear to make sure our version of City Hall continued to serve the people.

Denise playing my love interest was a key element to those storylines. She did a great job as the sexy spy from the rival mayoral campaign, and the more time we spent together on set, the more challenging it became to hide our unchaste chemistry. We knew, but didn't care, how thoroughly we'd trampled the line that separates the person from the character. Let's not forget my curiosity roots with Dee-nice could be traced all the way back to Promises. Anyone who spent that much time "imagining" the banquet would ultimately have to make a choice when it finally manifested: be a moron and fukken starve or sit the hell down and eat.

Perfectly in line with how sobriety had *Urkel'd* my kool-factor, our first date was baseball-themed and took place at my condo. It was October 4, and Barry Bonds had the world's attention as he sat one home run shy of tying Mark McGwire's single-season record of seventy. I carefully explained to D that if we were at a restaurant unable to watch, the main thing on my mind would be the game. (The main thing I could say out loud.) She completely understood and loved the idea of joining me to celebrate my passion for baseball. We ate our Zone meals from plastic bowls and hung on every pitch when Bonds was at the plate.

He was 0 for 1 with three walks, but Denise stayed enthusiastic as the game crossed the three-hour mark—setting the stage for Bonds's final at bat in the ninth. (My last chance to go from zero to hero.) On the third pitch, we lost our shit when Barry cranked a moonshot that landed twenty rows deep into the upper deck at Enron Field. As soon as he connected, it was a great sign when Denise yelled louder than I did—it was a yell that vindicated my risky, dorky date plan.

As we were saying good night at the elevator, D grabbed my face and pulled me into a long passionate kiss. The Baseball Gods had sprinkled some magic on our night.

I was no longer thinking about the game.

A week after home run number seventy, D spent the night. Two weeks after that, we enjoyed a lovely week in Hawaii at the *Hana Lana Kapana*. Two months later, with my Billabongs still reeking of coconut oil, I took a knee and asked Denise to marry me. (You happy *now*, fukken-Bill?)

Impulsive or otherwise, our dash to the altar wasn't fueled by pink cloud infatuation or a runaway fantasy that ran outta gas. I was three-and-a-half years sober, and for the first time in years, my feelings were accessible and based in reality. I can declare with certainty, that big swirling glob of mysterious elation was the love I had for my favorite Hardee's employee. My motivation to tie the knot wasn't connected to the usual emotional suspects—it was galvanized by the life-changing events of 9/11.

A few months before I took that knee, outlandish disasters, the displacement of continuity, and catastrophic upheaval were no longer hyperbolic neurotic figments of doomsday preppers or constructs of nihilistic woo-woos. All of that shit came knocking on America's front door, and when we went to answer, it blew up the whole fukken house. On September 10, I was fine; by the morning of the 12th, I didn't wanna die alone.

We announced our engagement, and the town gave us a standing O. A month later I got another one at the Golden Globes, when I took home the award for Best Actor in a Comedy Series. During my speech I played a great joke on Alan Ruck, who was in the hospital at the time with pneumonia. I thanked everyone from the show, and it seemed as though I'd unfairly omitted Ruck. Looking like I was done, I quickly turned back to the mic: "Hey Alan Ruck—this is for YOU," as I held the trophy skyward.

The following morning in Ruck's hospital room on the other coast, his doctor dropped by with Alan's test results in his hand, paused dramatically at the door, and proclaimed, "Hey Alan Ruck—these are for YOU," as he pushed his chart skyward, exactly as I'd done with the Globe. Alan would tell me later it was one of his favorite moments ever. Emmys and balloon shrivel? I dig the Ruck stuff a lot more. It still matters to both of us.

On April 30 in '02, the season finale of *Spin City* aired. The show left everyone on a cliff-hanger, and not just with the storylines but also in the plot of life. We had no official word yet from the network if a third season was in the cards, which would have translated to a *seventh* season for the show overall. The producers had planned a ritzy wrap party on our stage at Radford Studios, which potentially would carry a twofold purpose. If we got picked up for another season, it would have been your basic "have a nice summer, see ya in the fall" shindig. If that turned out *not* to be the case, then it would have provided a venue for a very kind and hardworking group of talented people to say their sad goodbyes.

Before I could choose which side of my brain I'd need to show up with, I was yanked from that decision like a child wandering toward traffic. The person responsible for my jolty arm-grab was none other than Giorgio Armani himself. His people had reached out to Denise with an offer to design her wedding dress. (As a bonus they extended the same for my tuxedo.) With GA's tight schedule, it meant we'd have to leave for Italy on the red-eye the same night the *hello/goodbye* party was set to take place. D expressed how it was every girl's dream to have her wedding gown designed by a world-famous fashion icon, and the once-in-a-lifetime opportunity could not be missed because of a ho-hum standard wrap party. Ho-hum, you say?

It had been confirmed that Spielberg would be in attendance at the *Spin* party. I saw it as a perfect opportunity to handle everything show-related I wanted to address. I'd have the moments of closure I'd earned with my amazing cast and crew, as well as five or ten minutes with the greatest filmmaker of all time. Perhaps I'd even be able to maximize the encounter by dropping a few subtle hints about future work beyond the show, whether it got picked up or not.

It will come as no surprise to anyone that I lost the Italian debate like that O.J. ping-pong game. Trying to wrestle that custom Armani away from her was like trying to pry Alex Kintner from the jaws of Spielberg's famous shark. I had to bitterly accept from the very get-go our family-pants doctrine was no longer the one I'd written. (It was impossible to not take it personally.) We'd built our relationship *inside* a situation I was responsible for creating. The fukken shit I'd gone through and the odds I overcame to get there should have eclipsed the selfish want for a shiny wedding accessory from a stranger.

"Welcome to marriage sir. Right this way, may I take your soul?"

Italy was a linguine-and-clams beating. Armani was pretty kool, but maintaining the jet-lagged plastic grin on my face the entire time felt like angry facial hemorrhoids.

We got through it—and made it back home. Gary DG was an absolute rock star, offering his beautiful home for our intimate wedding in the hills overlooking LA. We danced to Journey—and got through that too. Honeymoon in Turks and Caicos—check. Back on the mainland and pretty darn happy about a buncha shit—check. Getting a lousy phone call, and suddenly really unhappy about a buncha shit—check.

Spin City had officially been canceled.

Out of a job with two mortgages and a wife to support—double check.

CHAPTER 43

My favorite restaurant in Malibu in the late '80s was an Italian bistro called Anthony's. The place was falling apart, so the owner asked me for a loan to overhaul the entire operation. I obliged, told Anthony to keep the change, and became his partner and co-owner. The new-look joint was a fun hang that stayed modestly profitable for a short spell. (Different story for another time, but Anthony wound up burning me worse than the shitty veal he used to serve.)

What I did enjoy about being an owner (before it went bad) was the safe environment it provided when I wanted to go there on a date. No photographers, no douchebags throwing chairs. Fun fact: When I was engaged to the lovely Kelly P, she had an entrée named after her on the Anthony's menu, Shrimp Kelly. (That was one dish my larcenous partner didn't burn.)

A few months after the restaurant was revamped, I met a girl named Brandi and invited her to dinner at the spot. Gorgeous gal from the Midwest—as friendly as she was pretty. We didn't hang out that often, but the times we did were exceptional and memorable. So memorable in fact, that when the stunning face on a magazine cover at a local newsstand stopped me dead in my tracks, I knew instantly it was Brandi.

It had been about a year since I'd seen her, and I would occasionally wonder how things had worked out for her. The magazine was *Penthouse*, so, maybe not exactly what she'd planned—but there are much worse hands to draw in that casino.

Roughly fifteen years later, I was on location in Hawaii a few months after *Spin* was canceled, working on *The Big Bounce*—a dreadful film my old pal Steve Bing was producing. It was a remake from the '60s, and the original had been rated as one of the worst films of all time. No idea why Bing wanted to exhume that corpse and attempt a reanimation—but he did, and I showed up to woefully join the party. (The bag of dough Bing gave me was much bigger than the small role I gave to his movie.)

The film was nicknamed "The Turkey at Turtle Bay" (it wasn't but it is now), and I had ten shoot days left when D flew back to LA, leaving me to finish the gobbler on my own. After work during one of those ten days, I was in the gym at the much nicer resort next door to our hotel. Doing my usual treadmill with ESPN in the headphones, I spotted a gorgeous blonde porn actress I recognized instantly. (To prevent her life from blowing up this many years later, we'll respectfully call her Nancy.)

I'd grown extremely fond of Nancy during the vast research I'd conducted on her industry, at a time when the crack rocks were still poppin'. I do recall that she was part of a control group that yielded breakthrough results for the combined effects of porn and crack on the brain and other organs. I guess the impact of that combo didn't wreak too much havoc on my memory.

We made eye contact a couple times in the gym, and other than being flattered by her glances, I didn't give it too much thought. I got back to my room, showered, fired up my first-generation (seventeen-pound) Sony VAIO PC, and proceeded to give Nancy *way* too much thought. Time caved in on itself, and when I finally looked up, I'd been lost in space perusing her website for several hours. It was an empty quest and I knew it; I was chasing the false freedom those cyber halls could no longer provide. Unless there was dope in the mix, recapturing that glory was an Alice burger with a side of white rabbit.

I was about to log out and see what the hotel's SpectraVision had to offer, when I spotted a link to what appeared to be Nancy's personal email. I clicked on it and wrote the following: "*Hi Nancy. Was that you in the gym earlier today? c.*" My cursor hovered over the send command. If my attempt to reach out was made public, would they be able to pin it on me with a simple lowercase *c*? Were the clues of *gym* and *today* specific enough for the adultery-cops to show up with a battering ram at my door? Why I was willing to risk it I still don't know. What I do know is that the sender box was blank when I finally clicked the damn thing to *whoosh* it into the hands of fate. (Or someone's hands, and hopefully the nice, manicured ones I'd been staring at for hours.)

The next morning I awoke to my phone ablaze with activity, and none of it from the lithe and sultry Nancy. It was Denise and she was on one. Easily twenty predictive texts of *CALL ME, CALL ME NOW.* My first thought was that I'd somehow accidentally included D on the fukken email. I've done a ton of stupid shit in my day, but nothing as careless as that. (At least not when sober.) Still unsure if the email was responsible for all the commotion, my gut knew the timing of the uproar was too specific to be anything else.

Every suspicion was confirmed when I sucked it up and answered D's call. Very quickly she made the texts seem like a love letter. Not a good time to interject anything as I held the phone half a foot from my ear and let D unleash her blistering drone strikes. I half-listened, half-scrambled to fabricate an alibi during the onslaught. The first three I built were implausible, the next few didn't make it past "Here's the deal."

I was headed so deep into the doghouse, I'd need a bowl with a lowercase *c* on it.

Good news/bad news: Denise did burn her source. While it was a bit satisfying to discover the connection, it was also a forehead-slap to learn that the traitor was a relic from my past. Somehow, Denise had become friends with a gal who was also tight with Nancy. Nancy forwarded my email to that person, who in turn sent the damn thing straight to D. All of my tracks were covered by using Nancy's internal server, but there was no way to account for the pit stop in the middle: Brandi. Yes, *that* Brandi: my Anthony's date from '88 and *Penthouse* model extraordinaire. I was shocked. We had parted on great terms (or so I thought) with no score left dangling to settle that many years later. I guess some folks just choose to do that stuff, because they completely suck at minding their own business.

Denise coldly informed me that we'd "deal with it" when I was done with the movie. I spent the remaining days on that island in a preoccupied state of hopeless, impending doom. The flight home was equally dour. I stared out the window the entire time at the endless blue of the ocean below. Picking at the crust of a food thing on my tray table, I couldn't seem to dislodge the one question that stayed trapped in a nagging loop of thought: Would that awful future moment have been the same if the fukken dish on the Anthony's menu had been changed to Shrimp Brandi?

A lot of things in life are connected. Some strands make their final destination known within minutes, while others may take years or decades to reveal their future landing spot. Cause and unknown effect follow us everywhere; just because the weather is tropical doesn't mean we can't find snow if we go looking for it.

Back in LA and into the meat grinder of total mistrust, I followed the advice of a therapist I'd been seeing since I left Promises: "*Know more, say less*" (as a stutterer, I'd been doing that my whole life). Pretty solid words, and given that the probation period was gonna hover somewhere in the neighborhood of 200 years, I'd have time to keep working on both. The situation was every branch on the penance tree, and obviously my fault.

On the alibi front, I told Denise that Nancy had been up for a part in *Rated X*, and I was merely reaching out to say I was sorry she didn't get the job—three years after the fact. I'll admit it was dubious, but it was also a test to see if the nefarious back-channel-Brandi was still an operational threat. (I hope she wound up working at a bot farm in the Philippines.)

I've been married a total of three times (you'll meet the third wife here shortly), and I need to clarify that I never cheated on any of them. Others may claim different, but I don't care about those muck-vendors or the fiction they spew; I know the number and it's zero. (That said, the "addendum" to that zero are the times when I was legally separated. That number was *not* zero. It was numbers *with* zeroes.)

* * *

It was time to land a decent gig and become the hero of the house once again.

Denise may have been side-eyeing me as a philandering dickhead, but the one thing she could never question was my professionalism and talent. I'd been working with a manager named Mark Burg for a few years, and his new assignment was to put the word out that *Spin* was a warm-up, and I was looking for my next multi-camera show. Mark was aggressive and rubbed a lot of people the wrong way, but as he'll tell you himself, if he wasn't pissing people off then he wasn't doing his job properly.

Essentially, Mark and I presented as the perfect balance of good cop, bad cop. He'd beat 'em up on the deal, and I'd stroll in to nice-guy away all their venom.

We transformed the condo into a setting that felt very much like a high-level casting office. The difference being, I was no longer auditioning; that hot seat was reserved for TV writers and showrunners to plop down into and pitch their wares. For an entire month after *The Big Bounce*, we must have read thirty scripts and sat through fifteen presentations. We knew the *Spin* momentum had a shelf life, but there was too much at stake to settle for fine, or *okay*. We weren't there to make friends or get taken by a charlatan. I weeded from the top, and Mark went deep into the dirt to get the roots. Patience was the key, memorable content was the goal.

A mission that began with oodles of optimism whittled our once-voluminous prospect list down to *nada*. Mark expressed that it might be time to shelve the plan temporarily and set our sights on a kool film instead. I agreed and we pulled the plug on the condo-casting marathon, with Mark telling me he'd report back with any decent feature scripts that came across his desk.

In a downcast mood, on the same driveway where I'd evaded the feds a few years earlier, we said our goodbyes in front of the Wilshire on Wilshire. As I watched Mark drive away, I couldn't help but feel like the entire month had been a big fat failure. In reality, that cool California winter evening was the telling calm before the gnarliest fukken storm of my life.

CHAPTER 44

2*003–05.* I barely had time to lick my condo-casting wounds, when Mark got a call from Warner Brothers to discuss a new sitcom they were producing for CBS. A few days after that phone call, I was in an office seated across the desk from a man named Chuck Lorre. Chuck's dog had died earlier that same day, and while the atmosphere in the room didn't exactly scream *comedy*, the concept for his show certainly did. His concise description told me everything I needed to know—it felt like an updated version of *The Odd Couple*, with the addition of a kid being the *updatey* part.

Having just suffered through a baggage carousel of overwritten garbage, it was refreshing as hell to finally hear a pitch that honored a proven traditional formula. Lorre's idea reminded me of the sitcoms I fell in love with as a child, in that they were everyday stories about complicated people. I cared so much back then about the characters in the situations—they barely had to leave their fake houses to deliver years of comedy and comfort to mine.

At the end of the meeting (in a vote of raw confidence), Chuck asked me to commit to his show right there in the room. As much as I wanted to say yes, I couldn't do so without first reading the script. I could tell that my response bugged him, but I also saw a tinge of respect prowling behind the shadow of that bug. I was told they'd send the script after the weekend, and as I was leaving the office, I asked Chuck if the show as of yet had a title. He said they were thinking about calling it *Two and a Half Men*—five words that stopped me dead in my tracks. I turned back to him from the doorway, looked him right down Broadway, and replied with five of my own: "Kool. Sounds like a hit."

The script showed up, and by the act break on page seventeen, it was Charlie's *one line* to that kid (Jake) that sank the hook. When I realize his value as the perfect chick magnet and tell him, "You're even better than a dog," I knew I'd found what I was looking for. The humor was edgy, and the story had a ton of emotion without being sappy. I didn't have a clue which actors they had in mind to fill out the cast, but those characters on the page already had a heartbeat.

The actual heartbeats in the actors who brought those roles to life were as vibrant and talented as anyone could have hoped for. From Holland Taylor and Melanie Lynskey to Marin Hinkle, Angus T. Jones, and the late, great Conchata Ferrell—anywhere Chuck pointed his camera was a guaranteed capture of their magic. After they signed Jon Cryer to play my brother, the material found another gear. The first time we read the scenes together out loud as Charlie and Alan Harper in Chuck's office, there was a vibe in the room that signaled something special was afoot. The serendipitous, imperfect cohesion I had with Jon was the type of accidental gold that comedy writers dream of harnessing. We never had to plan anything ahead of time or figure out the rhythm; we just traded jabs, and the footwork took care of itself. In that medium there is no comedy without conflict, and inside that laughter is where much conflict finds resolve. (Eventually.)

* * *

When Chuck and I first met we were both coming up on five years of sobriety. We got along great and worked in terrific concert with each other. He saw how easily I slid into the character and began to write more to those strengths, never losing sight of the poetic irony I brought to it: playing drunk all day, then driving home safely after work. Pains me to think about the future shit we could've done together had I not launched myself to Mars—literally. (I guarantee the street they named after him on the Warner's lot would have been a few stop signs away from Sheen Boulevard.)

Before we shot the pilot, I gave my "stutter speech" (my least favorite oxymoron) to Chuck and his writing partner, Lee. *Spin* had empowered me to stop shying away from it, and they both seemed willing to have my back. There were a few moments early on when the ghoul got me, but we were able to sneak past it with a couple word-trades. Jon was a champ with that stuff and even volunteered once or thrice to alleviate my struggle and take the whole damn line. It's worth pointing out: My stand-in on the show, Jimmy M, is also a stutterer. We'd compare notes and most of the time have the same fear-words underlined in the script. It didn't solve shit for either of us, but it was pretty kool to have a fellow ghoul-mate close by.

I'd be thrilled if this book wound up serving as a type of clarion call, announcing my brain glitch to the world. To walk into a high-stakes job in the future and have my new workplace already aware of this awful curse would be a gift like no other.

I shot the *Men* pilot in February of '03, and a few weeks later was in Vancouver working on the spoof comedy *Scary Movie 3*. (Never watched the first two, didn't feel like the third installment required much research.) Denise was also in the film, and through the high-tech use of a fridge calendar, we were confident our daughter Sam had been conceived during the shoot.

On March 19 in Vancouver, I was watching the shock-and-awe campaign blow Baghdad off the map, when I got the call that *Two and a Half* had been picked up for series. The theme that followed me everywhere had struck again—the genesis of a personal life-changing moment, symbolically coinciding with an event that affected everyone. It'd be nice one day to buck that trend and get my Oscar job when the only news story is a postal strike, or a hippo somewhere giving birth to a fukken walrus.

Our freshman season, for me, was by far the most exciting out of the eight I'd leave behind in total. When we debuted, the deck was stacked heavily against us: The entire landscape was undergoing a drastic shift toward reality programming. The networks had fallen in love with the novel formula of delivering prime-time hits at a fraction of what they'd been spending on scripted shows. Reality-greed for CBS was good, but it created more pressure for *Men*. We had to prove ours was a bet worth their wager.

At the TV up-fronts that year (a highbrow event to secure ad dollars), a few catty journalists treated us like we were lucky to be there. Much like in the lead-up to *Spin*, the press had picked a side, and we were in the challenger's corner. Chuck's advice was to ignore all of it. He knew better than any of us the secret weapon we had in our possession. He wasn't wrong: We debuted to fifteen million viewers and reminded everyone that "show" *always* shits on "tell." It felt great to win a fight every week without throwing a single punch—our "little engine that could" continued its ratings ascension with a bullet.

The narrative continued that our "piddly farce" had snuck into the dance, and we were running on the fumes of borrowed time. We didn't care, killing it like we owned the joint from one Monday night to the next. Riding high Tuesday mornings, I'd come to work expecting a not-so-scary clown with an espresso cart and a basket of sugary treats. I would have also been fine with a few balloons on the stage door, and a high-five tunnel on the set—like we used to do on the baseball field. Okay, just a hand-drawn sign in blue Sharpie that read, CONGRATS! WE BEAT *FRIENDS*! woulda done the job. Nothing resembling any of that was ever waiting for me.

It was business as usual, and that *usual* didn't make room for espresso clowns.

The on-set energy had no interest in laurels—its sights remained fixed on the momentum of *what's next*. It's worth pointing out that Chuck's MO, his style of leadership, was based in commonsense guidelines for accountability inside the job. Basically: Do the fukken thing we hired you for. His embedded approach from day one was as consistent as the sun attending dawn. For lack of a better word, if those were Chuck's "rules," I did a great job following them for the first two seasons. After that (I think it's safe to say), I built my own high-five tunnel and filled that gauntlet with lots of sugary treats.

Winding up on a hit show, and spending that much time away from home, inevitably created the "double-family syndrome." A strange duality-portal between both worlds, where my attention had to be undivided in each camp. At times it was like having a full-time job away from my full-time job, but that begs the question, which one was away from which? I had to make sure D didn't feel excluded or threatened by my television family. I'd often downplay the victories at work so they never felt more important than her prenatal vitamins or that night's baked chicken. And forget the weekends, holy hell man, if I could claw back *half* of them—I'd be in my twenties again.

We had somehow managed to put my *Big Bounce* email blunder behind us, and overall, our good days together outweighed the troubled ones. When we were alone, Denise had a goofy side to her that I found quite disarming. But our "alone" changed forever in Vancouver. If I couldn't get served at Hardee's anymore, I'd settle for Carl's Junior. I won't say all of that changed, but a lot of it went somewhere else on March 9, 2004, when our beautiful daughter Sam came into our lives. Amazing baby, very challenging year.

As a nineteen-year-old with Paula and Cassandra, I wasn't able to experience the joys of raising a tiny child full-time. Sam would change all of that. Waking up before the roosters every morning and then learning a mountain of dialogue after work, I was miffed that Denise still believed we should split the middle-of-the-night feedings *right down the middle*. Sure, I suppose, but last I checked I wasn't exactly blessed with a milk-rack quite like hers. But that's kool, right down the middle—no sweat. As it turned out, eschewing much-needed sleep for the 3:00 a.m.-ers with Sam were some of the best times I've ever had. Tucked into our moonlit alcove with my noble dad-duties, Sam wasn't the only one being nourished.

I sold the condo and the Malibu Lake digs, and we moved into Al Jolson's old estate in a San Fernando Valley suburb called Encino. (Worked out a private sale with Katey Sagal, terrific lady but, good gosh, I wish she had taken better care of the place.) I spent most of Season Two renovating every square inch of the 1940s ranch-style property. It was a lot to undertake and became a breeding ground for the conflicts in our marriage. (There were other elements obviously, but it's classless to rehash and relitigate that nonsense. Our kids deserve better.)

As the show grew in popularity, I became less popular at home. I did my best to keep all of that noise separate from the work environment, but as anyone who's been through that fire knows, denial is not the cure for depression. It was around that time that I met a pill dealer at a local diner and became willing to try *his* cure. That drug, Norco (Vicodin 2.0), had a way of convincing me it was the missing ingredient in a variety of scenarios. The house overhaul was a prime example of that, but then again so was the supermarket, the car wash, the ballgame, dog park, gym, and the day I blew thirty grand on a Panama hat. (It didn't fit as well as Detective Tracy's. Hat karma is a real thing.) Those sneaky 10/325s found their way into just about everything, and created even more friction on the home front. The only place I wasn't doing them was at work, which ultimately became much harder in a constant start/stop detox-cringe for months at a time.

By the middle of the audience show, I'd be in full withdrawal, sweating like a Bonnie Brae junkie. My last dose was usually around 11 p.m. the night before, creating a jonze-gap of more than twenty hours before I'd feel whole again. If I could just grind through that final scene, Dylan would soon be driving me home while I devoured the four or five ovals I had stashed in my pocket. Chomp, crunch, soda chug. In under five minutes they'd bum rush the blood barrier with a swan dive into my dope-starved brain. As Brad's jacuzzi factory churned the ripples of relief, my opiate straitjacket was snugly fastened.

It was a hideous trap I had created for myself, but the alternative was a bridge I'd wind up jumping from. The bottom line was that the pills made my stutter a lot worse, and on top of that, there was too much AA on the stage to keep it under wraps. The combo of those two red flags motivated me to finally shut it down—and return to hardcore sports gambling.

In the midst of all the domestic prickle, Denise got pregnant with our second daughter (and not accidentally). Regardless of where D and I stood, we both agreed it would be better for Sam if she wasn't an only child. We were hoping it would jar us back into seeing the larger picture, a new one that didn't feature the two of us at the center of its frame. Wrong again. When the tenderness two people once shared gets smashed into a million pieces, the most painstaking restoration becomes hopeless—in certain light, even the tiniest cracks remain visible.

On a Wednesday night as I was learning lines for the next day, a big Black dood came to the door and served me divorce papers. (He was a huge fan and very friendly.) The homework he interrupted was the episode about Alan's Porsche. That Wednesday night in my Encino kitchen was three months before Lola was born. Lola was an amazing baby; divorce was a really mean adult.

Watching my summons deliveryman disappear into the dark was a check my brain couldn't cash. In my experience, the main feeling in that situation, between sadness and rage, is something I can only describe as *discarded*. When a stranger hands over a piece of paper that states you no longer matter, it's like being a single-use item tossed into a landfill. All the therapy in the world is gonna have a hard time reattaching the hero label to that empty plastic bottle.

*   *   *

2006–08. I was asked (by a judge) to leave the beautiful house I'd renovated to perfection. The night I packed up my shit and vacated the premises "in a timely manner," the glow of the lights escorting my exit made me think of one person: Holland Taylor. A few months earlier I'd been on set with my TV mom (one of my favorite humans ever), and we were comparing the most oddball or unique people we each had in our phones. When I showed her the contact name *Holly Streetlamp*, Holland could not stop laughing and declared me the winner. I explained that *HSL* was a vendor I had used to acquire the beautiful '50s-style lampposts that lined my Jolson driveway all the way to the main gate. Ms. Streetlamp lit my departure from an oasis I had hoped to occupy for decades. Well done, Holly, sorry we didn't last.

I love culture shock when I encounter it by choice; I don't love it when it's accidental or enforced. I went from the lap of customized luxury to shacking up in a one-bedroom at the corner of Vineland and Ventura. (It sounds scuzzy because it was.) I lived behind a 7-Eleven that seemed in better shape than my building. It was only six minutes from the studio, but I managed to be late almost every day. The new wrinkle was a madam I'd started working with to maximize the freedom of fresh singledom. (My on-the-job tardy slips were seldom the result of a broken alarm clock.)

After work one day, Denise decided to drop in unannounced at my 7-Eleven apartment. She had Sam with her, claiming it was a bathroom emergency. Luckily they had to buzz me from the lobby, just enough time to rush the girl I was with outside onto the balcony, slamming the drapes as D knocked on my door. I felt like I was on a reality show. They never saw balcony-girl. It was really great to see Sam.

I mention that encounter because it marked the last time I'd see Sam (or baby Lola) without the lawyers or a court *allowing* me to do so—for the next year and a half. Those jackals preach unity, with the currency of sorrow, to get rich through division. The most debilitating anxiety never came from the legal conflicts I could see and touch, it was the surprise *gotchas* that drained all of my chi. Not lost on me was the paradoxical essence of Chuck's version versus mine when it came to "what's next."

As the show wore on (and the pills came back), it was more like two and a half personalities I had to embody. Sober-guy for Chuck, friendly-guy for my costars and crew, half-a-whatever-guy left over for me. Fear-guy, mostly. Fear I'd be exposed or randomly drug-tested by the network, then have to face everyone in the AA men's group we had on Fridays. Nobody insisted I attend our sober work-huddle, but to beg out of it usually came with passive leers of suspicion. *(Talking to you, Lee.)* I guess the irony with the whole setup is the fact that they did have something on me to hold in suspicion. Keeping secrets from your boss is one thing, concealing a workplace dope habit while reading Chapter Five from the ancient book is another level of performance. Pain pills and AA are an exhausting combo. If anything, they create more pain than they alleviate.

CHAPTER 45

It was during the writer's strike of '07 that I had the pleasure of hanging out with Matthew Perry a few times. He hosted a private men's group at his condo, and through our mutual connection, the invite was extended. (He spoke publicly of said group when he was still with us, so I'm not violating any code.) Matt and I shared a deeper truth we saw in each other—we were both, as Bobby Dee Jay used to say, "veterans of the unspeakable." (Those who've been through it recognize fellow graduates at a glance.) I was fascinated by Matt's ability to turn every frown upside down. I've never met anyone who more masterfully used humor as a deflector-shield to keep you just enough over *there*. I dug every minute we spent together—and over *there* with Matthew was much better than most people's front and center.

Matt and I wound up at a party one night, where I was introduced to a friendly gal in a blue dress on the dance floor. She was looking for someone to light her cigarette (not a metaphor). Her name was Brooke and we were quite taken with each other. She had a carefree vibe I really dug, and a few puffs into that Marlboro, Brooke informed me she too was a member of the sober club. We went on a couple dates and even attended a few AA meetings together. For most people it would have been the perfect opportunity to spill the pill beans. I didn't see it that way, and for good reason, I chose to keep it all under wraps. With the divorce not yet finalized and a renegotiation of my *Men* contract fast approaching, there was way too much at stake to fuck around with "honesty in all my affairs." On that note, I don't see the value in another cook's *tour d'amour* of which we already know the outcome—a year later Brooke and I got married. (Too bad Google didn't have Gemini back then.)

I'll admit, I was convinced she was the one who was gonna show me how to finally do it right and make it stick. (When I get shit wrong I'm never off by inches, it's usually measured in planets.) The one question I get asked a lot is why was I in such a hurry to get married again. I've had a long time to come up with an answer, and I'm still not sure if I'm satisfied with where I've landed. I think half of it had to do with B, and the other half was more about loneliness and fear. I was feeling so overwhelmed, beat down, and outnumbered in my life; I didn't want to keep fighting those battles alone.

2009–11. B and I got straight to it and had twin boys, Bob and Max. They were born early and had to stay at the hospital for a month like Bruce Dern in *Silent Running*. I lived at the hospital with them while doing the show, barely going home in between to shower. I missed several dress rehearsals and was learning my dialogue in the NICU. I got that I still had a job to do, but it was impossible to give it the focus it required when all I could think about were my two sons in plastic boxes with a hundred tubes and devices that beeped. Work was sympathetic to my cause—with an *. As long as I was able to keep delivering something they could air, the get-well gifts kept comin'.

The boys' hearts finally healed, and they came home to a house with other hearts in distress. Brooke and I dove headfirst into an untenable domestic scenario before I had a fighting chance to make the one with D manageable. It wasn't fair to D and the girls, and it wasn't fair to B and the boys. (Forget about me, I'd been bounced outta the fair equation a couple sitcoms ago.)

In both relationships there was never a grace period to just sit back and enjoy the groovy reality of being married. It felt like a fukken montage in a movie where a chubby bridesmaid catches the tossed bouquet, and it's a smash-cut to a wailing newborn and a masked doctor announcing, "It's a boy!" It all went back to what I learned too late with my first wife, Donna: Trust the friendship that brought you together and the other stuff will follow. After awhile there was no friendship either of us could turn to or rely upon, it was just labels and roles.

I'd like to say that B and I did our best, but when I think back on some of the shit decisions we made inside that heavy-metal lullaby, we both know there was some extra room for improvement. She was more enamored with the idea of becoming a mom than actually being one. And that's fine—there are scores of new parents who make it all up as they go. That works for folks who wanna keep going and don't instead wander off into darker parts of the jungle without a map. For my part, I answered the bell to every fight D's lawyers picked with me, when in hindsight I should have let most of their drivel go straight to voicemail. Those unending conflicts created the stress that led to the rage and resentment, which traveled the full-circle route back to the cookie jar—filled with dope.

I needed pills again and recklessly shared them with B. I thought she could handle them like I could. I was wrong by two Saturns and a Uranus.

Even though I'd gobbled a pharmacy of Norco over the years, I still hadn't had a drink or hit the pipe since I'd left Promises in '98. Eleven years went up in actual smoke when both drugs found their way back into my home. That's code for "were brought there by someone not named me." I'm an adult and still had freedom of choice, but that gets murky when that freedom is hijacked.

The final straw was Christmas in Aspen. Santa loaded my stocking on that trip with coal as black as Vader's cape. I was losing more favor at work as the home life was veering toward a coma. B's affection was the only thing any of us boys wanted from her. It was made clear that she could barely manage two outta three. Not what I'd signed up for, and the rot from that delineation infected everything. The ship was sinking, and going down with it was not an option. It might have been a rash move, but the luxury of time was not on my side in a house completely engulfed in angst. I flipped the script and sent *my* large dood to serve the single-use paperwork—to Brooke.

It was messy, painful, and pricey. Again, as I stated with the details of the other divorce (a couple pages ago), it's in really poor taste to stoop down into any of that muck. The relationship I have today with D is solid, and the one with B is sustainable. Our North Star goal is a children-first directive, but since I don't control the weather, I can't always count on a clear view of Polaris through overcast skies.

The split from B left me numb, both in spirit and from the amount of booze and dope I showered my brain with to quell the debilitating frustrations. It was the flashpoint that left me unable to show up and execute my job with any focused consistency, and as a result *Two and a Half* came to a screeching halt with eight episodes still on the production schedule.

I went dark and made myself unreachable. The powers that be tolerated that for a couple days, but with so much riding on the show, they knew it was time to roll out their biggest gun.

I mentioned a theme earlier that dealt with the confluence of *fate versus luck*. How the simple result of a coin toss can forever alter the direction of our lives. A perfect example of that mystical intersection was when Les Full-MoonVes, the president of the network, showed up at my house.

Les was there to send me to rehab on the Warner jet, and in eight years, it was the first time the company bird had been offered. If I had surrendered and allowed myself (as Dad says) "to be ruled by him," I would have gotten the help I needed and gone back to work twenty-eight days later (just like Sandy Bullock in that goofy rehab movie. I love her, but that thing? C'mon.).

Like the dumbest guy in the history of all things stupid, I told him I was gonna pass on the lovely jet offer and get clean at home instead. Les is a good dood, fukken gangster at heart, and the look on his face when he heard my plan was a sadness that had nothing to do with commerce.

He left defeated and unconvinced, I renamed my house Sober Valley Lodge, and quit everything the following day. Here comes the shocker: It didn't go as planned. What I chose not to quit was the testosterone cream that I was slathering on in mind-altering gobs like a fukken Pond's commercial. After all, it was "legal." I'd been using it to get my body back into shape, not knowing that at the same time, I was being shape-shifted.

That drug is known to metabolize into the identical psych profile an anabolic steroid will produce. Anyone who bore witness to the raging demon I melded with—like a remake of *Altered States*—will hopefully glean some clarity for what my state of mind was up against. Not making excuses or asking for a pass, just putting it out there as a detail that may have been confused with a laundry list of other potential suspects. I've heard great things about that drug when used responsibly, but let's keep it real—*drugs* and *responsible* are two words I never made a habit of cramming into the same sentence.

CHAPTER 46

March 2011

Sober Valley Lodge, aka SVL, aka my house.

A few days before I sat down with Andrea Canning for the infamous *20/20* interview, I was upstairs at the Lodge watching *Baseball Tonight* with my old pal Tony T. The season was still a few weeks away, and like I'd done so often during times of woe, I turned to baseball as my port-of-solace to ride out the storm. More specifically, we were watching a highlight package devoted to a pitcher from the San Francisco Giants named Brian Wilson. His world-class talent caught my eye—his eccentric vibes kept that eye glued with curiosity. Can't fully explain it but I knew in that moment I had to speak with that man, and asked Tony if he could track him down. Keep in mind, this was someone I had never been in the same room with or spoken to at any point in my existence. It was Confucius who said, "Never give a sword to a man who can't dance." (I'm not sure exactly how that applied to what was coming, but I'm absolutely certain that it did.)

The next day I was hanging out with a few friends in my backyard when Tony walked up to me with his shitty Android extended, telling me, "B Dub is on the phone, wants to say hey."

It was another cosmic bend in the road, somehow taking place on the *identical* patch of synthetic lawn where Full-MoonVes offered the rehab Medevac. (They'll dig up that spot a century from now and find a nose ring from King Tut.)

Brian was instantly likable. Our conversation never made it to baseball. Thirty seconds into the call, BW was explaining how guys like us were different in that we have "tiger blood" running through our veins—veins held together with "Adonis DNA," a substrate so unique it was never programmed to "lose" because "guys like us" are always "__." (I don't need to write that seven-letter word. You can already hear me saying it, with that specific inflection and rhythm from atop Mount Bedlam.) That's how it went down. I was so jacked on the Krazy Kreem, those phrases went into my brain and stayed on a loop just below the surface. They were patient with one eye on the door, waiting for the right customer to show up, be seated, and casually ask about the specials. *"Well Ms. Canning, for starters..."*

(Andrea is really kool and didn't deserve all that madness our interview spilled forth. Considering what my Krazy Kreem did for her star, I doubt the whole thing really left that much of a welt.)

The day after the interview aired, the world I awoke to wasn't the same one I had just wished good night six hours earlier. The internet was already flooded with rap songs and folk ballads about me. Marches and rallies in my honor were on the move. The energy felt global, and even though "technically" I was still under CBS contract, rescuing my job didn't really jibe with the revolution I had accidentally started. Like I'd flipped some switch everyone was wired to, I struck a nerve with the masses far and wide as they congregated to await my next command. The surge took on a life of its own, bulldozing common sense in phases.

The first phase of my social media takeover was by far the most intense, touching down in places I never dreamed I'd initiate such a visceral bond. At its base level, people were unintentionally celebrating my demise with a carnivàle splendor, not fully grasping how far down Kurtz's razor I had slid. The symbology of that is quite tragic, and if I had in fact become his snail, then where was Captain Willard "to come take away the pain"? (He was overseas with Emilio, promoting a film.)

Phase two looked nothing like its pathfinder and rolled in with an agenda of boundless greed. Every crackpot merchandise ploy under the sun had descended on my Sober Lodge like a fleet of locusts—from the obvious energy drinks and vitamin rip-offs to the head of Lionsgate Studios pitching a live reality show. I remember feeling like I was in the famous scene from *Airplane!* where everyone in the aisle has a different weapon to use on the panicked passenger.

My house was a chaos factory, and just when I thought the bottom of the goon-barrel had been scraped clean, No. 88 would step right up *deli-style* with another harebrained product they wanted me to slap my name on. Mark was the gatekeeper for SVL's *Sheeni-con*, and I really wished he had purchased a much stronger lock. Maybe something that didn't need a key and looked more like a comfy chair and a patient ear. In the years that followed, I've combed through the mental health manual, and I still can't find the chapter on "vile exploitation" as a treatment protocol. At the end of the day, I do have to own the fact that it does take two to tango. Even though in that situation it actually felt more like two thousand.

Then the machete thing happened at the Live Nation headquarters.

That corporate genius-bar thought it to be a great idea that I turn the whole mess into a one-man show and take it on the road. I mean, you're fukken kidding me, right? Actually charge people to come watch me yell at my own failures like a homeless banshee for two hours? I could not believe what I was hearing. They weren't just building a diarrhea blimp, they wanted to fly it above a bunch of people and explode that fucker. *(Sorry about that! Here's a Handi Wipe, see ya at the merch counter.)*

With that imagery top o' mind, the only story from that pathetic "torpedo tour" I see as having any real merit occurred on the eve of opening night in Detroit, Michigan. The home to Lions and Tigers and blood—oh my.

April 2011: The Tour. I arrived in the Motor City to a horde of spirited fans outside the hotel. The catchphrase-chants were endless and the photo ops more so. Like koi fish with crumbled bread in the water, I fed them all and saved nothing for myself. I finally made it upstairs to my quarters, a sour suite with vending machines as room service. (It was good to know there was a 2 a.m. Zagnut on standby if I needed one.) My diet leading up to the trip had been all over the place, and I noticed I was taking in more food than I was giving back. It was most likely a combination of all the stress and the crazy hours I was keeping, in addition to the testosterone cream I was still applying by the tube. It did its job as promised with the two girls I brought on the trip but was playing unfriendly games with my regular bathroom cycle. The trade-off between the two seemed fair at first—but after the third day, all fairness could go fuck itself when it came to a *two*, that mattered way too much.

A couple hours later as the clock hit midnight, I was finally greeted with that lower-gut pain we all recognize as the first sign of oncoming freedom. I had been taking OTC laxatives for the past three nights, ignoring dosage guidelines that were about to exact revenge. My road babes ("the Goddesses"—dumbest label ever) were in the next room doing their shower rituals. I knew I had a window of roughly thirty minutes to release the hounds. I went in that bathroom, stuffed a towel into the bottom of the door, ran the sink faucet, fired up a Marlboro Red, and brought something into the world I thought for sure would have to be claimed as a dependent.

"Detroit: you're welcome!"

Feeling like a teenager again, I Gladed every cubic inch of the poisoned air. (Note to self: mix in some fiber and drink more water.) A simple flush was the only thing standing between a quick shower and a long night with the gals. I pushed down on the chrome handle—and the toilet walked off the job. Nothing was descending, the water was creeping upward with a hollow *hiss* to the edge of the bowl. I looked immediately for a nearby plunger that didn't exist—any tool that might help was something I'd have to build.

I raced to the closet for a wire coat hanger, only to discover my limited options were all made of wood. I broke that fucker in half over my knee and came away with two matching jagged wooden stakes. There was less than a quarter inch of space before the water crested its ridge, and with a mighty two-handed downward thrust into the heart of the Michigan Vampire, I went full Jim Morrison and broke on through to the other side. The toilet came alive and did what it does best, pulling the beast back down to the shadowy pits of Sewernifus. Score one for Team Sheen. (Sort of.)

I don't think there exists a better story to epitomize that miserable tour than the one I just shared. I hadn't even made it to the first date on the schedule and somehow found myself in an Ahab fight to the death with my own Moby-Turd. Freud woulda set aside an entire month to process that one. I only needed a day.

The following night at the Fox Theater, I was booed off stage before the intermission.

Fire up the blimp: one down, and twenty cities to go.

CHAPTER 47

June 2011. I hadn't had a single drink or a drug in the six weeks leading up to the tour, and continued that white-knuckle grind for the entire month on the road. When the show limped its way to last curtain and released me from my own clutches to finally return home, the Sober Valley Lodge was a wrap. Save for hardcore Sheenicans Natty Nape, Rexx, and Shady, I'd miss no one else. I unloaded the rest of the clown car I'd been barnstorming with, and began to enlist a new and improved crew. The madam roles evolved, as I tapped into a circuit of adult performers who all did privates away from their day jobs. To watch a skin flick and have one of the gals *in* that flick show up the same night, left me stoked to be me again for the entire summer. I'm the first to admit that it did push the limits of excess; guess I was making up for some lost time.

It worked out in such a way that I was able to form a core group that no longer required the middlewoman pit stop to organize the visits. Most of the time the girls would pack a bag for a few days and then stay long enough to have to do some laundry. (Even though clothes were always viewed as an optional detail with that roster of assassins.) There were a few moments poolside in my backyard when it dawned on me that the last time I'd seen such a level of sunbathing perfection was at the Playboy Mansion. (The only person missing was Mr. October.) On more than a few occasions, one of those stunning young ladies was a brunette who went by the name Capri.

If she sounds familiar, she and I made headlines during *Men*, for a big kerfuffle at the Plaza Hotel in Manhattan. As I stated earlier, the bottom of the page is seldom where the story ends. Capri and I also spent a week together—*after* the Plaza—in a Scottish castle on the shores of Loch Ness, taking a boat out at night and hoping for an encounter. She was tons of fun and as sharp as she is gorgeous; I still think of her often and fondly—I'd like to believe it's mutual.

The unforgettable summer of '11 was a perfect capture of time that could never be duplicated. It came on the heels of an impossible situation that needed to be scrubbed from my soul, and I chose the most reliable cleansers I had at my disposal to activate that purge: women and dope. What I didn't take into account was how quickly one side of that equation would reveal a shortfall, and I think it's obvious which side it wasn't. I needed a new dope man, and a force of nature rolled in to bridge that divide. He introduced himself as Marco, but halfway through our first shared bottle of Silver, I told him he looked a lot more like a Phil Hinze Jr. (I guess Ralph was already taken.)

His cover story was that we met at a car wash, my cover story was that I won him in a raffle. We didn't need fukken stories; that dood was DoorDash before it existed and had the best dope in town. We got to know each other quite well with drugs as our centerpiece, but as the summer continued in a haze of peerless debauch, he was no longer just the dope man; he was the *man* man. It didn't take long for the two of us to develop the most compressed shorthand when the dope-kitty was running low. My simple text of "gotta have it" would be instantly met with one word shot back my way at Hadron velocity: "coming."

A guy smokes that much crack and mixes up with that many ladies of, let's just say, licentious persuasion, the interactions can get a bit incendiary at times. Before those sparks could grow into flames, Phil H became my go-to fire extinguisher. He wasn't a bully and the ladies really liked having him around. I liked having him around too, as the girls weren't the only ones who needed the occasional "dousing."

A story that he and I still laugh about had to do with the aforementioned centerpiece. His supplier was south of the border and as we all know, those fukken guys don't play. (Met a few of 'em, we drank like we meant it, good times.) I'm not sure what the catalyst was, but I wound up on *the* most colossal run of all runs that saw me blast through almost two kilos in under three weeks. (I've always said: You can either be committed or *be* committed.)

Toward the end of that third week, the party hadn't ever really stopped, and when I reached out again for the yayo, Sir Phil of H said we needed to talk. His tone over the phone wasn't anything I'd heard previously, and it had my cracky-senses tingling. He was at the house twenty minutes later to inform me that I was officially being cut off by the cartel, and this "one time," the Sinaloans weren't gonna take it personally.

Take it personally, what the heck did that mean? Phil looked me right in the eyes and very evenly explained, "My guys are shutting you down because they're convinced that you're dealing. They've never seen this much dope go to one guy who *wasn't* dealing, and they're giving you a pass—because you're my guy."

I couldn't believe what I was hearing and neither could Phil. The unbreakable rule when doing business with those outfits: Any and all dope-dealing had to be preapproved and sanctioned by the shot callers. Those who went rogue to skirt that rule usually wound up hanging from a city bridge, choking on a cock-and-balls sandwich. *Very* far from the image I had in mind for my "end of summer/back to school" shindig.

Because of that new wrinkle, Phil told me that one of two things had to happen: either chase down a new dealer, or cut my pipe dreams in half. (Hinze was really kool, but that second part made him sound like he'd gone mad.) It's a difficult feeling to describe—on one hand it was a badge of honor that landed me in the crack Hall of Fame. On the other, I'd lost their trust and that was super no bueno. As high as I was, I still had the wherewithal to understand that it was business, and not a popularity contest. In a move to avoid the bridge-sandwich, and keep the Sheenius Express at full steam, I went with the go-fuck-yourself option and told Phil we were gonna do both—half from down south, the missing half from a new guy. Phil loved a challenge, he mulled it for a full second—then broke into that big crazy smile, wrapped me up into a giant hug, and screamed "I love you" into my hair.

And so we did just that. And on it went—*and the tree was happy.*

Woulda been nice to close out *eleven* with a kool movie as a positive note to an otherwise devastating year, career-wise. Such was not the case. The film I wound up getting talked into was a forgettable vanity project for its writer-director. Eleven needed a much groovier send-off, and I couldn't think of anything more fitting than a trip with a few friends to Colombia, the homeland of my favorite collaborator.

It had been eight months since my tumultuous departure from the show. I tried to distance myself from those two and a half men on that fake beach in Malibu, but they weren't gonna let that happen.

About a day into the trip the weather got gnarly and I was stuck in the middle of it, driving in an old jeep with my security guys to a much, much older church. Eddie B and Gabe were in the jeep behind me and I'm sure they too were feeling like we'd wandered into a remake of Friedkin's *Sorcerer*. The bellhop at the hotel I was getting my dope from recommended we see the ancient landmark. (Gotta love it when the dope man brings culture into the fold.)

The time-worn sacred structure sat atop a mountain, its peak hidden by the gray clouds dumping their tears into the mud of our journey. The perilous snake of road seemed barely wide enough for two mopeds to pass each other. I remember wondering how many people before us perished on that very trail during their pilgrimage to salvation. (Those are the kinds of ponder stipends ya get from growing up with Martin Sheen, the Pope of Malibu.)

Against all third-world transportational odds, we finally made it to the very soggy summit of Mount *Peligro*. The driver gave me an umbrella that I *penguined* open with a smooth push as I stepped outside the jeep. The rain had shifted sideways, forcing me to use the umbrella like the bulletproof James Bond version. Doing so exposed my face, and that was all *man with the donkey* needed. In a split second from fifty feet away, he recognized me like an old pal from his childhood. As soon as we made eye contact, my arcane watcher called out in an accent as thick as the downpour, "Hey man—the new guy sucks!"

If my jaw wasn't attached it would still be on the ground in that hallowed courtyard. We traded a slow-motion thumbs-up as I sloshed past my new favorite person and his trusty burro, into the shelter of the sacred abbey. Knowing exactly who he'd been referring to made the moment that much more surreal. In frikkin' Colombia—on a tip from the local dope man, at the oldest church on the continent, in a monsoon at the top of a mountain—*guy in mud with donkey* stood in solidarity rejecting the guy who replaced me on *Two and a Half Men*.

If that scene was in a movie, the screen would be pelted with bonbons and shoes. The illogical probability of our encounter doesn't exist in any realm I have the ability to access. I'll leave the quantum math to the experts—sometimes it rains, and sometimes you get stuck in that rain with people you'd never otherwise meet. (I spent the drive back to the hotel curious if the donkey shared the same opinion as its owner.) I'm not saying the hell I brought upon myself to arrive at that moment was worth it, because it most certainly was not. However, I will be telling *that* story more often than the one about Rose falling off Charlie Harper's deck during a network run-through.

CHAPTER 48

I wasn't ready to go back to work. Brown Dave wanted to take me somewhere far away to eat pineapple and jog on the fukken beach. Sounded awesome and we should have, but I knew I was in no shape to embrace it. After two bites and fifty yards, I'da been smoking puka shells with the locals. I hadn't yet confronted any of the central themes or nagging issues that had tanked my juju, and the last place any of that could achieve providence was on a sitcom telling junior-high dick jokes again.

The show in question was *Anger Management*. I didn't love the idea (but I did love the showrunner Bruce Helford), and the main reason I did it was to let those guys across town know that I was hirable again. Doing anything to prove a point is not the kind of motivation that builds team spirit. Might have been enough to get through a pilot, but after that—a pilot needs a plane and a whole squadron to fly with. Really hard to do with that many bullet holes in my wings.

By saying yes to *Anger*, I bit off a chunk I could barely fit through the door. It was yet another set of circumstances where the job couldn't spur the same drive in me that the extracurriculars could, and did.

The first six months went fairly smooth—but soon after, I took a page out of '11 and called it '13. The crew of thirteen was lean, focused, and on a mission. If '11 thought all socks had been knocked off, we were gonna find whatever they'd missed. Pulled up to the knee or otherwise, our plan was to knock a little harder.

Back in '98, I was at an NA meeting listening to a speaker take us through his insane experiences with the pipe. I could obviously relate to what he was throwin' down, but the redundant buzz phrase he kept repeating like a cheap slogan did leave me in curious limbo, "*You smoke enough crack, anything's possible,*" and yet he never got around to explaining what types of "anything" he was implying. He'd tell another crazy story that dropped us off at the same *anything*, and when he finally wrapped it up, I concluded that all of his anythings were just a big bag of nothings. (Pick a planet, *any* planet, you know the drill by now.)

Years later during my version of "smoke enough crack," that big bag of nothings was finally lugged into my bedroom and rummaged through with gusto. Take your pick, *Mr. Winning*, because just like the man said way back when, anything *was* suddenly possible. The mind veers into uncharted terrain on that drug: places not dissimilar to where the girls I was with had just spent the majority of their workday. Stands to reason that at some point with that much temptation abound, "one side of the menu" wasn't gonna satisfy this patron.

The unique details in the stories the girls shared could not be found anywhere on my side of that laminated manifest. I always fancied myself as someone who was open to new things, and at the time, believed no conclusions could be properly drawn without the crackiest of data.

Roundabout way to explain that I finally said *fuck it*, and flipped it over to see what all the fuss was about. Holy shit, man; they had to close down the whole restaurant for a very private party. When I poured bacchanalian exhilaration on top of Bananas Foster and hit purée on the Eros blender, the "other side of the menu" was catering the event.

Out of respect to the people involved, that's as far down this path as we're going. Has nothing to do with shame and everything to do with respecting the privacy of others. (And of course I'm referring to everyone involved as the consenting adults that they all absolutely were.) In fact lemme take the pressure off and answer a few questions so I don't get hit with them later on any fancy talk shows.

Was some of it fun? You betcha.

Was the "other side" in play without crack? Never.

Were those the times that led to the extortion you had to pay? Those times and others.

Is there a sense of relief to finally being honest about these experiences? A big one.

Are you busy later? We'll talk after the show.

As wild as some of those nights were, whatever came outta that blender rarely carried through to the mornings afterward. I'd come downstairs to the kitchen and find the gals all hanging out doing breakfast things, with fun girl-banter and their sexy ponytails skyward. Not gonna try to paint it like Rockwell might've, but the "snapshot version" didn't scream chaos, and most of the time, set the table with normalcy. Bottom line was that it never had a chance to become unacceptable, because the women already knew that it wasn't.

It was, however, a double-edged sword. When the ceiling is billowed with that much crack smoke, the absence of character judgment can very easily blur its way into poor judgment. We were playing with the type of fire that could've easily changed course and burned it all to the ground—with '13 plus one trapped inside. That fire I speak of was not the same one that freed all that base—it was the torches the villagers marched with to lure the monster from its cave. So much attention was dedicated to making sure the private parties *remained* private, my red-rimmed eyes didn't stay where they belonged—and I got careless.

Then something else fell outta that big bag of nothing.

"Alright Johnny, what is the next item up for bid on The Sheen Ain't Right?"

"Well Bob, courtesy of Sinaloa and Wicked Pictures, it's his entire bloodstream.*"*

The headaches were not from this world. Stabbing, nonstop clusters of white fire the dry heaves made hotter. Combined with delirious night sweats that redefined "waterbed," I thought for sure my days were numbered in single digits. I'd been in that state for fifty hours, doing everything I could to avoid the hospital. I had convinced myself if I did go, the malady they'd uncover would be that of grave consequence: brain cancer, spinal meningitis, a dying liver. They tapped my spine as soon as I arrived, and that was an experience I woulda been fine never owning.

When they finally got to the bottom of it, and informed me I'd joined the luckless ranks of the hivvers—I didn't say a word. I found a place way out beyond anything that wanted to be looked at, and sent a stare that wouldn't arrive for a hundred years.

I went through those five stages they talk about, and stumbled onto a sixth. As shocking and depressing as my new status was, number six was a feeling I wasn't expecting: relief.

The relief of knowing an entire discipline of high-tech medicine was at my disposal to drive that bastard into submission. To counterattack the invaders, the doctors loaded their expertise into what seemed like every IV bag in the city. The pricey meds couldn't kill that fucker, but they could keep it from killing my spirit.

Mom was with me the entire time at the hospital, as was my dear pal Steph M. They were both amazing to say the very least, and as much as they applauded the brave face I insisted on wearing, they had even more love for the one it kept replacing. As the days crept forward, the haze began to lift. The taste in my mouth no longer had the tang of something on the other side of the light. When Hemingway drew up his essential list of achievements to become a man, somewhere between planting a tree and having a son, he forgot to include staring down death. (Unless that's what he meant with the bullfight, and, if so, "I got that beat," too.)

It wasn't until day five that I had my first outing, when Steph took me up to Sunset Boulevard for a cheeseburger and a smoke. To reconnect with those three basic needs—comfort food, nicotine, and friendship—brought the first rays of normal, and with that, some actual hope. The sun felt brighter as I caught my reflection in the car window next to me, and that's when I saw myself finally smile. Leaving the burger joint heading back to Cedars, we passed my favorite '90s club, On the Rox. As I time-traveled back inside her thrilling cocoon with Bing, Heidi, and my twentysomething self, he was smiling too—but the one in the car was more peaceful.

I think about it once a day for twenty seconds because I have to, that's the time it takes to eat the poison that tames the evil stowaway.

Dr. Huizenga says in the long run it'll probably knock a few years off my lifespan. I'll take it; 93 percent of something is better than . . . (we all know the rest).

I have no interest in telling "my side" of the stories that galvanized the decision to sit with Matt Lauer on the *Today* show and confess *hivv* to the world. Regardless of how much those specious ninnies took from me, they forgot to leave with the one thing they claimed I handed over. *None* of 'em start their day with a trip to the medicine cabinet like I do, and if that doesn't tell the stories I won't, then nothing else will. Never kick a man when he's down; he just might be taking a nap on top of a hidden volcano or a gold mine.

He'll let you know when he wakes up.

CHAPTER 49

In the weeks after the Lauer sit-down, a befouling similar to the aftermath of the *20/20* interview was again let loose in the Sober Valley. While not nearly as packed buffoon-wise, there still oozed an identical vulturous energy from my house. Same tricks, different clowns, and a whole new twist on the idiom "out for blood." I was pissed and saw it as a complete waste of time, but if I didn't tolerate several meetings with a few hucksters and their various medicinal frauds—I wouldn't know what exactly I was telling to fuck off.

The highlight for me was a dood from a jungle village in the Republic of the Congo. He said it was the one place on earth where a miraculous root could be found, and wanted me to go there with him to set up camp for a month. It got better: His good buddy the witch doctor would also be there—and in order to be cured, all I had to do was avoid the deadly snakes and eat that root for thirty days. (Wasn't trying to be difficult, but I did have a few questions.) The first and most obvious one being, *Why the hell didn't he just bring the magic root with him on the trip?* Run a home trial, and if his phantasmic voodoo made a difference, *then* we discuss travel plans.

My second question should have been the first: If Doctor Root-Cure was so confident about his Congolese miracle, why wasn't he a billionaire with a Nobel Prize for medicine? I told the man I appreciated the consideration, but was gonna "roll the dice" with the hard science the doctors down the street were selling. He understood and we finished our meeting with about thirty selfies. If nothing else, I'd have a few new fans back in his rural, green mamba hamlet.

The initial public response to my disclosure ushered in a wave of renewed awareness and research, that was unlike anything the HIV community had witnessed in decades. They referred to it as the "Charlie Sheen effect" and it was the first time I saw the glass in my unfortunate situation as being half full. (Until, as it went, I saw the other very empty half.) With little effort to conceal the plot, that community did their best to hijack my vulnerability and nominate me for poster-child status. I went along with some of it, and ultimately wound up in the crosshairs of Dr. Oz and his televangelic medical circus.

I hated being on his show but I did owe that man a solid. When Bob and Max were discharged from the hospital, Oz was in the neighborhood and made a house call to check on their tiny tickers. When it came to all matters of the heart (save for romance), his thumbs-up was a cosign second to none. The yellow-brick-doctor was only with them for ten minutes and I wound up in four episodes of his show. Maybe Turkish even-Steven is a bit different and if so, I guess we both won. (But he for sure got way more Steves.)

The longer I loitered in their halls the more they started seeing me as a full-time guinea pig for the cause. I made it clear that I was merely there to shine a light, not become their prodigal sun. I wasn't turning my back on the movement, I was promoting common sense and practicality—both ideals supported by the stalwart antiviral pills I had in my front pocket. The nonprofits I dealt with didn't see it that way, and deemed most of the previous research as outdated and fruitless. I get it—there is no cure as of yet, but that cannot discount the fact that so many can now enjoy their own "cheeseburger and a smoke" bridge to normalcy.

I took all the ribbon pins off my jackets, thanked everyone for their support, and waited for a display of gratitude that never came. Once they realized I wasn't gonna be their *guy*, it was like someone threw a switch that disengaged with a meaty clank. No problem; I had a life before the invader got me, and permanent stowaway be damned, was gonna continue to have one moving forward. (At least that's what I told everyone.)

Forward wasn't where it used to be, and instead of a reliable heading that always brought me to a place, it became a haze I drifted through like a visitor in my own story. I didn't feel connected to my surroundings and just assumed it was a form of delayed shock or residual trauma. One previous contributor I could rule out as a catalyst was the fukken pipe. (Not a misprint, you read that correctly.) Right after the interview with Lauer, I went cold turkey off that vile shite and haven't picked it back up since.

The booze had other plans. Inside that dreamwalk, trying to stay focused and productive with some type of a daily routine, I got hit with a bout of depression that wouldn't let go. I'd been running on pure adrenaline for so long and when the bottom finally gave way, I plunged about as deep as anyone could fall. The reality of what I'd have to live with for the remainder of my days became a relentless, taunting chorus of voices. (Voices, I should point out, that were all mine—so it wasn't one of those deals.) Regardless of how recognizable that gallery sounded, the many me's shredded their target, and I was sent scrambling for the only tool I had left in my bag. That half-full glass I spoke of? It was as fully empty as I was, and we both needed to be filled up to the tippy top.

Some tools cut metal, others slosh—I stayed really hammered for the next two years.

CHAPTER 50

Leaving that LA hospital with my newly minted high-five status (hi-V), there were certain X factors the doctors couldn't warn me about. One of those unknowns that gouged the deepest was how the air seemed to bend when I'd walk into a store or a restaurant—or any place for that matter. It reminded me of a speeding flock of birds, when they instantaneously change direction with a telepathy we'll never understand. Some glances sympathetic, others dripped a venom their side-eyed thought bubbles couldn't contain. I tried to be patient with a hope it would correct itself, but that *other cheek* approach only invited the next blow to land with a greater impact. It was so mean and childish I decided to give LA the one-finger it deserved, and set my sights due south on a friendlier sunrise.

I love Mexico, always have. Might have something to do with the piece of myself I left stranded there in my fourth year on the planet. That scared kid in that small kitchen yearning for the comfort of something that didn't yet exist. Wish I could say my connection to that region was a recycled pilgrimage to rescue him and close that circle. I'm not gonna do that because it's graspy and convenient. Even if I had "magically" found him and the other kool things happened, there's not a chance I'd remember any of it—I was in Mexico to drink, and that place was always kind enough to let me.

From the moment I stepped off the plane, no one down there treated me like those three letters were sizzled into my forehead. Top to bottom they couldn't give a shit about any of it, and it was the absence of that very shit I sought to pursue and bask in with great frequency. I'd rally the troops and get a big villa with a bunch of rooms and set up shop in a nice hotel. There was no sightseeing, there were no activities planned; it was booze for breakfast and laughter all day long. We had our own brochure and a timeline that didn't involve clocks. The sunburn and midday naps, the food, Nerf football on the beach and more "naps," was all we asked the day to provide. As long as the sunset promised a similar tomorrow, our *schedule* would float with us down the lazy river.

I took a few fabulous trips there with a voluptuous gal I really dug named Amanda. She was a registered nurse who thankfully didn't travel with the getup or a bag filled with Nubain gear. She did travel with her training—and was great to have around with the amount of boiled agave I was guzzling. Laughter can only cure so much, and that young lady kept Humpty's yolk in his fukken skull most of the time. By leaps and bounds, tequila sits unchallenged in its own class as a dauntless panacea. It gets inside and finds who you think you're trying to be, then stops asking questions and takes you the rest of the way. Don't believe any of that zero-hangover crap, and, if anyone is still clinging to that myth, it's a guarantee we never drank together in Mexico.

Tony T was a mainstay on those itineraries, and whatever my able nurse couldn't handle, T was always there to step in and do his best to fix. I knew the risks and was willing to trade a few liver functions for whatever chicken soup my soul was in search of. Whether I found it or not, the quest was where the variables took flight. The smartest people with the best intentions can't always think of everything. Albeit, when up against a tequila-brain that *could*, my friends found out the hard way—they had no choice but to reinvent every solution I foiled.

It was our last day at the Mexican compound, and I awoke on an urgent mission to greet that final morning with the gulps my compass needed for proper alignment. As I moved through the living room, I noticed an off in my balance and a lead in my legs, both of which I attributed to the cave of drunken slumber last night's me was still exploring.

I hit the kitchen, found the Patron Silver, pulled a glass from a shelf—and saw the first tremor in my right hand. It was moving on its own in a way I'd never experienced before and it had my full attention. I stared at my paw like a kid on July 4 waiting for his brain to register the two blown-off fingers from a bootleg M-80.

I took a deep breath that stayed shallow, grabbed the bottle, and attempted a simple action I'd done effortlessly in the past, one million times. Out of nowhere, that same hand unleashed its violent second wave of quiver, and my ability to aim the spout jittered into failure. The shake was so bad, half of the clear liquid was splashing all over the counter. I was gripped in the panic of a brain-quake with no table to hide under. I felt like my old buddy Nic Cage at the bank trying to sign that check, but his shakes nabbed an Oscar while mine were lucky to peel a banana.

I shut down crazy-hand by pressing it firmly into the cold and expensive Four Seasons granite countertop. As the chilly rock brought my inner Richter back to its stable center, I could feel the hovering specter of the Saint John's AA cafeteria toasting my pathetic condition with a hundred flutes of mango juice. Punta Mita meet Vegas, just don't plan on leaving anytime soon.

A man who traveled with me and handled security very calmly took over and finished the simple task of pouring that elusive drink; getting it to my mouth without shattering my teeth was the second leg of the impossible challenge. Like a pearl-diver, I had to breathe my way into preparation for the fat tumbler to be lifted and chugged in one motion. When I finally sent it down the hole like a mortar, it took about seventy-five seconds to reach the smart parts behind my eyes. The shaking finally slithered back to its nest, with enough of my flesh to feed its evil children for a month.

I got right again and handled every stage of the second gut-dump without spilling a single drop. (Hey Nic, you fukken nailed it my man.) The math was simple: The booze killed the shakes, and without any onboard, the *dauntless* elixir had free rein to keep me feeble and turn my shining agave castle into an ankle monitor with seagull shit.

I was back in a kitchen in Mexico, not knowing what day it was, wanting very much to go home—terrified I wouldn't be able to get there.

Toward the end of that same day (with another DT-saga approaching) the good nurse had seen enough and stepped in to take the fukken reins. She told security to call my buddy Bob, who owned a health resort in Arizona, and together they made arrangements to get my soggy ass checked in that night. "Muh-Manda" (as I'd call her when drunk) also brought Dr. H up to speed, so he could prescribe the booze-meds I'd need to start taking as soon as we touched down in the desert. It was a flurry of chaotic activity that involved eight people, a private jet, two countries, one plastered drunk, a pissed-off sexy nurse, and probably a chicken—as a traditional exclamation point on the whole mess.

I went there to escape the judgment of LA and almost died in a prison of my own Mexican freedom.

I had one goal when I arrived in Arizona, and that was to leave Bob's oasis with the restored ability to pour my liquids with precision. I refused to get swept up in the group's ominous scare tactics and minimized my situation as just being a loud backfire with a lot of smoke. By day four, the shakes were gone—along with my head, which was already back in LA shopping for a nice scotch to replace the faulty tequila spark plugs. Thirty hours later, the rest of me was flying there to complete the ensemble and get dressed up again.

The Arizona detour was merely a pause to get my trigger finger back, so I could stockpile the next cluster of blurry memories. The price I paid for my riots of self-will was Muh-Manda. She told me I had a choice: her or the bottle. Terrific gal but she lost in a landslide. I hope she found whatever happiness she was looking for and a Humpty who needed a little less glue.

CHAPTER 51

To fully understand a crucial aspect of my relationship to the bottle, I gotta roll it back a few frames to a converted garage at the top of Big Rock in the summer of '98. Group therapy at Promises to be exact, and in there I was with a mix of folks you'd never see huddled together in any other setting. If someone walked into that garage, they'd take one look around and assume twelve drifters found the same map to nowhere. The staff preached that you weren't supposed to judge your fellow strugglers, but they couldn't muzzle our thoughts and most of mine wore a black cloak and banged a gavel. I took special aim at the career boozers—without any haunting tales of crack, H, or meth, I didn't buy that they'd been fully burned down to the studs.

Booze—that one mind-altering drug you can just walk in and buy in front of a cop, and your dealer is only unavailable for the five hours between 2 a.m. and seven. (Also, he never runs out of product.) Boohoo Mr. CEO, you had too many rum and Cokes at the Christmas party, peed on Santa, and the board sent you to the pricey garage. You too, regal lady in flowing silks and Harry-Dubya ice, that story about drunk-driving your Bentley into the neighbor's topiary made me feel all the pathos of an earthworm. How dare they show up in that spit-shined flimflam chamber and claim to be veterans of Downey's unspeakable trenches? I tuned out most of their whining and set in stone that we had nothing in common.

When I put down the pipe and swore a vow to the bottle, I had an unshakable plan that would show "Edward and Sylvia" how it was gonna be done *MaSheen* style. Santa would stay dry and the boxwood-hedge giraffe wouldn't have to run for its still-life. I'd do everything those two forgot how to manage and tame the bottled spirits like a cobra charmer in the streets of Jaipur. I knew if my bespoke approach painted inside the lines and the floors stayed clean, I'd have a friend for life to help me navigate the potholes and landmines the future had in store.

What I didn't take into account was how any true friend in this life had already been with me for most of the journey. Pledging that type of blind allegiance was either gonna get me another Brown Dave, or a really pissed-off cobra.

Rare was any moment in 2017 when my hand wasn't wrapped tightly around the neck of a bottle. I began to wonder where the booze ended and I began, and more importantly, which of us was being more fiercely consumed. I used to believe that the tie went to the runner, and found out the hard way that it all depends on what you're running from.

My house, sometime that fall, and if I said it was a Tuesday it wouldn't have been different from a Saturday; when the wheels were off, the day's name was just letters. My pal Gabe was there that night along with Slash's ex-wife Perla, who lived right up the street. A few years after *The Arrival*, Gabe became my full-time makeup artist for the fourteen years I spent on television. (I think I'm the godfather to a couple of kids, but I'd have to check—we were pretty hammered when he asked.) We'd been tossing 'em back for several hours, when P rolled in to grace us with her Cuban charm. Perla's from that same egg carton, and she and I had known each other as far back as Malibu Lake. She rescued me one night from a rehab in Ventura County, right after I'd scored a clean oh-zee from a fellow patient I assumed was cleaner. (It tasted like the yayo White Dave used to call "Disco" as a reference to the ether-washed quality from the '80s.) Perla and I made fine use of that Z over a weekend that probably saw Wednesday. On Thursday she didn't drive me back to the rehab; as stated—only letters.

Just as Perla arrived, Gabe and I had taken every hot sauce from my fridge to concoct a series of unique shooters we were knocking back with passion and gag. (She was too polite to criticize, and too smart to partake.) Mighta made more sense if the baseline was tequila, but we'd already inhaled all the Silver and were deep into the cheap scotch. Gabe and I weren't only redesigning the hot toddy, we were haphazardly desecrating it for future generations. I was three or four *Sheen-specials* deep, when my stomach had to leave the party and clear a path to chunder the perps.

Upstairs in the bar off my bedroom, I rushed to the balcony and sent the first ejection into the night air. The landscape lighting caught the mist at the perfect angle, with a crimson tint I blamed on Tapatío, or on some other guy named Frank. Purges three and four had a much different hue; and the look on Gabe's face was a testament to my suspicions. Perla saw it too, and the three of us were parked in that strange place that floats between dire and denial. No one wanted to voice the obvious and it still sounded like someone else when I finally choked out the words, "my blood; fuck."

The mama-bear in Perla sprang forward as she quickly led me to the bathroom to begin some type of water cleanse. I've never been to Cuba, and had no idea if she was calling on a tradition from her youth that had helped her rum-soaked granddad. However it came to be, the tap-gallon of H_2O Perla flushed me with rendered the final output colorless. P wrapped me in a calming hug before closing the door behind her and leaving me alone in the "water closet." I was exhausted and deeply shaken, but grateful.

I peered into the mirror and past myself, drifting through a kaleidoscope of memories that felt like a time machine. The red ring around the tops of my teeth took me all the way back to Paris in '92. Different sink, same blood, and way more than should have been on the outside.

On a weekend off from *Musketeers* in Vienna, I'd flown by myself to the French Open, met a dood named Pascal, and drank the night away at the fancy club he managed. (He was a pro and at 3 a.m. switched to water; I was a pro too and at 5 a.m. switched to Percocet.) Pascal came to my room the next morning, with a plan for us to watch Capriati take on a determined Mary Pierce. He could already hear me from the hallway, my echoed retching from somewhere in the depths of my baroque suite at the *George Cinq*.

The gleaming white porcelain sink I was hunched over, flooded with a scarlet pour from the bottom of my food pouch. *Too red to be real* was all I could think as those words whipped through my vision. Pascal rushed into that Parisian bathroom and slammed the brakes like he'd impaled an invisible wall. When a guy's expecting a toilet with mushroom soup, and instead gets a sink from Ed Gein, the plot needs a rewrite.

Decades and continents apart, Pascal wore the same incredulous mask my future friends tried to hide behind on that bar balcony at the Hammered Valley Lodge. He was my first Gabe and Perla; we just didn't know it yet.

A group of friends, separated by a quarter-century, who witnessed my body rejecting my lifestyle—an unsightly aftermath that usually requires a gun or a knife to paint such a picture. With the bottle as my brush and red the only choice on my palette, my body's message to those friends was the color of war.

CHAPTER 52

One of the advantages that booze had over the crack pipe (and there weren't many) was my ability to stay moderately sociable while still inside the ten-to-fifteen-drink barrier. A guideline as it were, my friends used to jokingly refer to as my version of the *legal limit*. Anything past that was usually when *other-me* would make his rumbustious presence known.

He was the guy who'd climb inside the aquarium in my living room and then jump in the pool with a samurai sword. The same fukken lunatic who threw parties he'd be asked to leave. (Just reporting the kind of shit I'd be told the following morning.) I could handle the fun recaps, but what really started to get old was apologizing for things I couldn't remember doing. Actions that were impossible to defend and being at the mercy of the retelling from others became more frustrating every time I crossed the 20-drink yard line. Other-me at home was one thing but taking that guy on the road required a lot more padding.

As much stock as I place on punctuality, I hold an equal measure of pride for how I feel about attendance. If I said I'd be somewhere I would always show up, and when it came to family gatherings, I didn't let my "legal limit" stand in the way.

Booze has a way of compressing days into hours, and shrinky-dinking a month down to a week. If you dump that blurry formula on top of my immediate and extended family with a bunch of kids runnin' around, it began to feel like there was a holiday get-together or a fukken birthday party every other day.

The events either took place at my folks' house, or just up the block from them at Emilio's. Generally speaking, because he still drank and could do so without fish tanks or Japanese swords, I had a lot more cover at E's crib with the bottle. He had a nice wine collection and would have a couple shots of the strong stuff and call it a night. The vibe at my parents' house was the exact opposite: no booze, no cover, no problem.

I'd have a couple shots before I left my place, maybe three or four on the drive in Dylan's limo (depending on the traffic), then one more *time-release* gulp right before I walked in *on time* to greet everyone. With a pocket and a mouth full of Altoids I still smelled like the outskirts of Tijuana, but I was there; maybe not emotionally but my "in the flesh" was undebatable. The next few hours with my family was when the challenges began. Much like the school supplies in high school, there exists a ceiling for how many believable phone calls in the parked limo one can get away with.

One night in particular, Dad followed me out there and the fireworks show we put on for Dylan was one I'm sure my trusty driver still thinks about.

When they'd monitor and stalk me on those nights and treat me like a child, I'd get so mad that I'd triple my intake and overshoot the mark. As if on cue, the curtains would part and "other-me" would take the stage for a performance no one bought a ticket to watch.

They deserved so much better, but those consequences are where the rubber met the road—the point of contact where I was willing to take the bad with the good and at times the horribly ugly. I knew deep down all that really mattered was *being* with them in the place where I grew up. The harm that I inflicted is a painful feeling to look back on; and yet somehow still be okay with the fact that I kept my word to *attend*.

As fucked up as it sounds, it was actually satisfying to give my parents the comfort of knowing (for those few short hours) that I wasn't toe-tagged in a morgue.

I hid for too long on that fukken pipe.

My boozy social "barrier" was mutable; my love for my parents is not.

CHAPTER 53

There's an overtold parable we've all heard about God trying to save a man from a deadly flood. He sends him everything he needs to be rescued, but the man chooses to ignore his every option, waiting instead for God to show up in person. The man ultimately dies from his own hubris and doesn't learn his lesson until he's standing at the Pearly Gates.

The more I heard it the more it resonated with nearly every aspect of my drinking. I saw the flood as the booze, and the boats and chopper as the people trying so hard to help me.

Up at the lake in the mid-'90s, I took a flawless-D pinkie-ring off my finger while drunk outta my mind in the bathroom and proposed to a porn star I was madly in lust with for three days. When I sobered up, and Steph told me what I'd done, I saddled her with the task of going to the girl's house with an apology, and strict orders to get the fukken ring back. Like a champ Steph did, but it still left me in a shame-pit and damn near ringless. Years later I proposed to *another* porn star, whom I met as a high-dollar call girl. I was so embalmed the second time, I invited all of my friends and family to a big engagement party for everyone to celebrate my porny future wife. Again, once just wasn't enough; I had to get thrown from that carnival ride a second time to confirm it as a rickety hazard. (My security guard had to deal with that one; her baggage was *way* too heavy for Steph to carry.) *God sent me a boat*, which I deemed unseaworthy.

During a stopover in Italy for a *Three Musketeers* wardrobe fitting, I was Mickey Finned by a crew of bandits and woke up the next morning in a strange house a hundred miles from Rome—with a flight that left that afternoon. Everything of value had been taken from me, and without one dollar or a single word of Italian to my name I had to hitchhike my way back. The driver spoke broken English and happened to be a big fan; three hours later I gave him 500 bucks when we reached the hotel. *God sent me a bigger boat.* I gave my seat to someone else.

The Italian Job scared the shit outta me. But it wasn't enough, it didn't *lock in*, I needed more proof.

On my birthday in '17, I Mickey Finned *myself* and blacked out in Iowa after a drinking contest with Wade Boggs (which they tell me I lost). I came to twelve hours later in a hotel room and had to call the front desk to find out that I was in fukken Dallas. There was an entire airport I have no memory of walking through, and a two-hour flight that exists nowhere in my mind. *God sent the helicopter.* It flew away without me.

I appreciated all the attempts from everyone who tried to help, but it was time for me to build my own boat. Water rises a lot faster than it does in the movies.

CHAPTER 54

I still get asked in the streets here and there if there's one moment I can point to as the *final straw* that broke my camel. It usually gets a laugh when I tell them it's really hard to choose one, with that many bales to pick through.

It was December 10, 2017, and by 9 a.m. I was on my third Macallan-spiked coffee. My phone rang and when I picked up, it was my daughter Sam asking what time we were leaving. *Shit*; her appointment that day had slipped my mind.

I've never mixed the cups with the wheel, so I called Tony T. to come bail me out of a situation he was all too familiar with. There's reliable and then there's that dood. My man was there in twenty-two minutes, and in very short order we were on the road with thirteen-year-old Sam in the back seat and the two adults up front. (Well, one adult for sure.)

Thanks to T, the trip was handled with a combination of precision and grace. On the drive back to my house, Sam was very quiet and I could see her back there from the two angles I had—the visor's vanity mirror as well as the side view on my right. I didn't need to be clairvoyant to know exactly what she was thinking.

Why is Dad not driving—again? Why isn't it just the two of us in the car like it used to be? When will that moment ever return? When will Dad ever return? I miss him.

I missed him too. There was only one thing that felt worse than betraying myself, and that was failing my children. In that car, on that day, with my best friend and a child I adore, I joined Sam in those mirrors and saw a guy who was desperate to finally come home for real. The details of that home were no longer scattered, and at long last I *did* have all the puzzle pieces to define it. I'm the one who left home, and yet somehow; it never left me. I knew exactly what had to be done. Like I've always said, life comes down to *doers* and *talkers*, and there was really nothing left for me to say—it was time to shut the fuck up and get busy doing. Sam wasn't my final straw; she was my first harvest.

CHAPTER 55

On December 11, I took two Valium and drank three beers. On December 12, I quit drinking for good.
Happy Birthday, Cassandra.

EPILOGUE

I'm doing pretty good these days. I made it home and stayed there. I wear a Timex and drive a Cadillac and still honor my credo of on-time as promised. Better news is that there's only "one" me who shows up, and I like to believe he's a guy most folks are happy to see. My new favorite word is no, and *like* has become just as valuable to me as love. Nobody has to raise my hand *for me* anymore, and that's a great thing—because I still have a lotta fukken questions.

I really like Cassandra and her husband Casey. Those two are quite the duo. They met as teenagers and have been together ever since. They had a baby girl named Luna and made me a frikkin' granddad at forty-eight, and Paula a grandmother at forty-nine. Overnight they took all of my kool and flushed it.

Now a Huffman, Cassandra and my son-in-law didn't stop at Luna and proceeded to bring twin girls Sara and Jade into our ever-expanding generational village. I mention those two perfect goofballs, because they were born a few weeks after I put down the bottle. Tony and Sam may have kick-started the whole shebang, but the Huffman twins put a timeline on it too cosmically poignant to ignore. Suffice it to say, the twins' next birthday celebration will be number eight—for all three of us.

The Huffman twins' calendar gift perfectly underscores what the past eight years have really been all about: family. If through her children I can give back to Cassandra some of the stuff that life snatched from both of us, I welcome those opportunities.

When it comes to the first *Sheen*s at birth, that beautiful quartet of Sam, Lola, Bob, and Max, my VACANCY sign hangs in the perpetual state of facing out. Regarding my parents and siblings, I'm fully aware that the *low-hanging* greatest gift Dad wanted on his fiftieth did take a minute to get here. I'm confident we all agree it was worth the wait.

There is no such thing as a one-size-fits-all. I ate their mangoes for a combined twenty-one years, until I finally decided to balance my own diet. There are no leaks in my boat, and the Miramar sill has a great fukken view.

ACKNOWLEDGMENTS

In all the books I've read over the years, I never quite understood why my favorite authors would express so much gratitude to their editors. I just assumed those folks would stroll in after it was all written, swap out a few semicolons, undo some over-*italicized* shit, and voila; nab a ton of credit. To honor a running theme; if the B. thing was off the mark by two Saturns and a Uranus—this "editorial" assumption of mine was *wide-right* by about fifty Jupiters. The editor in my case is Aimée Bell, and if she didn't "stroll in," you wouldn't be holding this book. Thank you A.B. More than I can ever express.

A few floors above Aimée in the executive branch sits Jen Bergstrom; the most *non*-executive I've ever had the pleasure of working with. On every occasion in this life when someone has been screaming at me over a phone, it's always been an unwelcomed drubbing. Jay Bee changed all of that with an excitement and an enthusiasm for me and this project that was delivered at *eleven*. No shit, there were times when she'd call and it felt like me and Phil Hinze celebrating a package from the southern border. Jen's cheerleading was an inspiration on many nights to vanquish fatigue and greet the sunrise with a badass finished chapter. Ka-pow: this is me screaming that love back at ya, Jen.

Rounding out the triptych-of-heroines is Betsy Berg. My earliest supporter with the project, and hands down the sole reason I was able to place my audition packet of sample-shite into the hands of the aforementioned lit/pub rock stars. You're an *authentican* Betz, and so is fukken Joel. My yelling through your phone was never on the groovy side of Jen-like, but hey, here the heck we are young lady.

I also need to send gratitude gift baskets to the front doors of Ian Kleinert and Jen Robinson, in dual recognition of your many selfless contributions to this—"Book of Teamwork."

Gonna list some names of people I know well, and a few I do not. Even though we've never met, their presence on my television throughout the entire process created a different type of support to get me through a calendar year of sleepless nights. The Renzz, Todd C, Jim Day, the lovely Jules S, a solid dood named Greg and the two awesome Robs (*let's check it out*).

Jeff B (RIP), B Cooper (RIP), the entire state of Tim Montana, Lisa Davis (too much to fit in parentheses), Pamula S (too much to fit in a book). Janelle, Kimberly, and Nicky (The Bathroom Club), Jeff Mann, Bob the fukken fish guy (just because), Mikey B (*UTEP!*), Linda and Marlene M, my Pavs crew of Annette, Nick, Alex, and Matt, and the queen of heartfelt arts and crafts, Connie Schoen.

Big honorable shout-outs extended to Janice A to Z Hare, Moira and Jon F, RJ O'Neill, The Isle of Dr. Morrow, Leobardo R, Dr. H-zing, Noli A McSteve, Joe Cosgrove (go Irish), Lance K, Jokton S, Darren P, Nicky C (NJ doesn't miss you), and Mathilda T (Sweden does miss you). Alysson S (the one that got away), Football Sunday Beth (the other one who got away), and last but not least, Freddie "Gibby" Freeman for his game-one walk-off and the koolest bat "drop" of all time—that level of greatness is inspiring and can often be contagious.

—Hey Mom, I hope this book left you somewhere close to as "mystified, hypnotized even," as you were in that front row, so many wonderful years ago—

x.

c